THE
BIBLE
ON FAMILIES AND
HOUSEHOLDS

THE
BIBLE
ON FAMILIES AND
HOUSEHOLDS

Scripture-Based Reflections on Family Dynamics

DONNA L. HUISJEN

credo
house publishers

TABLE OF CONTENTS

CHAPTER 3: THE LAST PATRIARCH—JACOB 42

CHAPTER 4: THE JOSEPH STORY 56

CHAPTER 5: MOSES AND THE EXODUS, PART 1 72

PREFACE

"The fact is, there is no foundation, no secure ground, upon which people may stand today if it isn't the family. If you don't have the support and love and caring and concern that you get from a family, you don't have much at all. Love is so supremely important. As our great poet Auden said, 'Love each other or perish.'"

—MITCH ALBORN

"I CAN'T THINK OF ANYTHING TO WRITE ABOUT EXCEPT FAMILIES," observes Anna Quindlen. "They are a metaphor for every other part of society." I don't take the issue quite this far, but I resonate with her sentiment and, like her, gravitate toward issues related to family living. In fact, I've always been drawn to family matters. As a child I took pride in our large family. I recall visiting the library as an adolescent and asking the librarian for family stories; almost all of the available choices fit that criterion, since family life is, with rare and sad exceptions, intrinsic to kid-dom.

Unmarried at the age of thirty, I opted for a nontraditional family through the separate adoptions, over the course of a decade, of three daughters, between the ages of three and nine at time of welcome. I have no particular credentials in terms of education on family dynamics, no advanced degrees or titles by which to claim expertise, though I do, like you, have some experience. I'm writing to reflect my lifelong passion for two topics that are closely related in my mind: God's Word and family relationships.

While I'm on the subject of lack of credentials, it seems pertinent to share that I'm still unmarried. Allow me to assure you, first, that the reflections in this book don't shy away from marital issues on that basis—any more than Jesus or Paul did. I am, however, on an intimate basis with God and his Word, in part based on years of experience as an editor in the Bible department of a large Christian publishing house, as well as on a decade of writing Bible-based material.

A large percentage of the reflections in this book (the material is divided into 22 chapters, each composed of a chronologically organized series of meditations) are based on the Bible's historical books (stories from Genesis through Esther and Matthew through Acts). But I haven't neglected the psalms, wisdom literature, prophetic writings, or New Testament epistles. Within each of these genres Scripture has a great deal to say about family living.

Nor have I passed over the lovely metaphors, drawn from Jesus' words and those of the inspired authors of the New Testament letters, on the family life of believers as sons and daughters of the Father, siblings of our Brother Jesus Christ, and brothers and sisters in fellowship within his kingdom. In the words of Neil T. Anderson, "Aloneness can lead to loneliness. God's preventative for loneliness is intimacy—meaningful, open, sharing relationships with one another. In Christ we have the capacity for the fulfilling sense of belonging which comes from intimate fellowship with God and with other believers."

It didn't take long in my perusal of the Old Testament to run into the first gruesome references to family (a deceased concubine cut into pieces, starving mothers eating their own children). Nor did it take much consideration to decide to give *all* accounts and references equal opportunity to speak to us—provided they have something relevant to contribute to our context. No, I haven't written about either of the above examples, or about children being offered to the idol Molech, pregnant mothers being ripped open, or the psalmist's anticipation of gratification at hurling an enemy's little ones against the rocks. But neither did I shy away from the hurtful and heinous simply because it was hurtful and heinous. I believe we can become so desensitized to the unspeakable realities in our own world that we need a periodic reminder of the extent of the inhumanity around us. In such cases I've addressed you, my audience, as socially responsible Christians, rather than necessarily as family members.

I make no attempt in this book to exhaustively study any family situation (indeed, the detail offered is in most instances far too sparse). My goal is rather to identify in each vignette or commentary a point of reference to our twenty-first-century family situations that seems to suggest itself.

As a writer and editor I'm well aware of the importance of a targeted audience, but in this case the source material has obliged me to cast a wider than usual net. All of us have family connections, no matter what our age, stage, or life circumstances, and I've tried not to make too many assumptions in that area. That said, some reflections will touch your personal life in a manner that others will not. My hope is that these meditations, as well as their "post-ponderings" (thought/action prompts), will point you in the direction of being more and more pleasing to God in the ordinary life of the home, as well as in its inevitable challenges.

In closing, I offer an observation by Marge Kennedy that will hopefully inspire and motivate: "In truth a family is what you make it. It is made strong, not by number of heads counted at the dinner table, but by the rituals you help family members create, by the memories you share, by the commitment of time, caring, and love you show to one another, and by the hopes for the future you have as individuals and as a unit." Blessings to you as you negotiate your daily round of family life and engage one with another!

DONNA L. HUISJEN

THE
BIBLE
ON FAMILIES AND
HOUSEHOLDS

CHAPTER 1

EARLY HUMAN HISTORY— ADAM THROUGH JOB

CHAPTER
INTRODUCTION

The history of the human family prior to the patriarchs is frustratingly sparse on detail—just the facts, as we would say, but facts so selective as to leave us longing for more. There are fascinating glimmers of interaction between family members, but the pictures are painted in broad brushstrokes with little to make the characters come alive for us as the real people they were.

It's the book of Job—though written much later—that animates this early picture for me. One of the most beautifully poetic books in all the Bible, rich in imagery, this gem features a very ancient individual in all of his humanity as a husband, father, friend, and God-fearer. Part of the book's allure is its detailed, philosophical and theological and yet almost stream-of-consciousness dialogue—precisely the touch to assure us that these individuals were, indeed, deep thinkers as sentient and complicatedly human as ourselves.

ADAM AND EVE: NOT GOOD TO BE ALONE

Read Genesis 2:18–25.
Someone has noted that the first recorded instance of God's claiming something to be less than good appears in this passage: "The LORD God said, 'It is not good for the man to be alone. I will make a helper suitable for him.'" *Not good* . . . despite God's intimate strolls with the man in the garden?! Now that's saying something about the importance of *human* family in the lives of people. The obvious reality is that not everybody has anybody. For those of us so fortunate as to belong to the family of God, the need for human contact can often be met in the forms of hospitality, caring, and friendship. But the situation for those who feel—or in many ways are—literally all alone can be tragic and dire.

I come from a sizable clan in terms of my family of origin and its many offshoots. But not having married, I still opted for motherhood. Jotting some notes I had intended for my preface to this book, I caught myself in a faux pas that made me cringe: "Unmarried at age thirty, I 'created' my own nontraditional family through three separate special-needs adoptions." What was wrong with this assessment? Well, listen again, this time to a comment to Abram from the childless Sarai: "The LORD has kept me from having children. Go, sleep with my slave; perhaps I can build a family through her" (16:2). I didn't create a family for myself any more than Sarai built one. It's God, and God alone, who places the lonely in families. And he does so because this is good for us, given our human needs. This is one of the ways in which his grace is most manifest in our lives . . . and one of the benefits we can so easily overlook.

I appreciate this observation from Jim Elliot: "No one warns young people to follow Adam's example. He waited till God saw his need. Then God made Adam sleep, prepared his mate, and brought her to him. We need more of this 'being asleep' in the will of God. Then we can receive what He brings us in His own time, if at all."

Post-ponderings: In what ways have you been willing to "sleep" in the will of God? There's nothing wrong with prayer, of course, but when and how have you preferred to help him out by running ahead?

A Fleeting Glimpse of Ideal Marriage: The Cord of Three Strands

"The husband or wife who has Christ as their life, comes to their spousal relationship already satisfied. They do not come continually looking to [be] made happy by another person's attention; they bring Christ's life to their spouse."
—FRANCIS FRANGIPANE

"Then the man and his wife heard the sound of the LORD God as he was walking in the garden in the cool of the day, and they hid from the Lord God among the trees of the garden. But the LORD God called to the man, 'Where are you?'"
(Genesis 3:8–9)

Read Genesis 1:26–27; 2:23–25; 3:7–9.
Encountering the damning words of the verses above suggests in contrast how fulfilling those ambles in the garden with God must have been for the first couple. Imagine those carefree strolls, punctuated by easy conversation in the evening shade. I picture the first man and woman arm in arm, even after so short an acquaintance knowing one another so intimately that they could move in graceful synch, laughing and appreciating and pausing together to wiggle their toes in the cool grass.

None of us has trouble picturing this, but we don't know quite what to do—at least in terms of the visual paradigm—with the threesome created by the God component. Genesis 2:24 (quoted by Paul in Ephesians 5:31) pictures marriage partners melding into one another to become one flesh. But an analogy from the Old Testament intertwines God into the mix (please try not to picture this sturdy "braid" in a sexual context, which is unfortunately easy to do): "If two lie down together, they will keep warm. But how can one keep warm alone? Though one may be overpowered, two can defend themselves. A cord of three strands is not quickly broken" (Ecclesiastes 4:11–12).

We don't know how temporary this ideal relationship was—how long this routine had been established before it was broken. But how jarring it must have been for this couple to emerge from innocence in so unsuspecting a manner. Happily, the analogy, and its underlying reality, still stand, albeit to a less than perfect degree (the shortfall, it goes without saying, is on our side!).

Post-ponderings: If you're married, how have you incorporated God into your union? How have you brought Christ's life to your spouse? If you're single, what part does the Lord play in your life?

ADAM AND EVE: THE BLAME GAME

> "Shame, blame, disrespect, betrayal, and the withholding of affection damage the roots from which love grows. Love can only survive these injuries if they are acknowledged, healed and rare."
> —BRENÉ BROWN

> *"The man said, 'The woman you put here with me—she gave me some fruit from the tree, and I ate it.'... The woman said, 'The serpent deceived me, and I ate.'"*
> *(Genesis 3:12–13)*

Read Genesis 3:1–13.
We've gotten slightly ahead of ourselves in alluding to that fall from grace. Time for a quick backtrack, which you've caught if you read the Genesis 3 portion for the preceding reflection—or, as I suspect, if this material was already more than familiar.

Isn't it interesting that the first time anyone exercised the sin option, the blame game immediately came into its own? There are two ways to play, either of which can involve family—as here—or a wider societal context. The first is mystification, utter bafflement: *"Wh-aaa-t? I haven't the foggiest idea what you're talking about."* With my three daughters this blatant and seemingly innocuous denial almost invariably took the form of the unison "Not me!" I kidded them that my fourth daughter, "Not Me, Not Me, Not Me," was either a particularly naughty kid or conveniently took the rap for anything and everything.

The second, and more hurtful, version involves finger pointing within the group, a form of scapegoating. Despite their love for each other, this husband and wife were more than willing to assign blame—Adam to his wife and Eve to the serpent, who was at least outside the family unit. Both had a point in terms of suggestion, but that's as far as it went.

How rarely do we encounter the more godlike option of accepting blame that is not one's own for the purpose of protecting or covering the guilty loved one! While this is not necessarily to be recommended, it can be refreshing to see it happen. And isn't that after all what God's salvation plan is about?

Post-ponderings: In what ways is the blame game prevalent in your family life? How can you discipline yourself to quit playing?

ADAM AND EVE: FALL AND FALLOUT

"Real life's nasty. It's cruel. It doesn't care about heroes and happy endings and the way things should be. In real life, bad things happen. People die. Fights are lost. Evil often wins. I just wanted to make that clear before I begin."
—DARREN SHAN

"So the LORD God banished [Adam] from the Garden of Eden to work the ground from which he had been taken. After he drove the man out, he placed on the east side of the Garden of Eden cherubim and a flaming sword flashing back and forth to guard the way to the tree of life." (Genesis 3:23–24)

Read Genesis 3:14–24.
We don't, of course, know what shape family life would have taken had the first couple's good start not been interrupted. I suspect life on the new earth will to some degree answer that question. But Jesus made clear to the Pharisees (Luke 20:34–36) that marriage won't be a part of the equation—clearly different from the "marital" experience of the first couple.

There are some things we do know. The first is the fallout from the fall. Human experience says it all too well, though these effects are to some degree alleviated for us who live by the Spirit. I'm not suggesting that our suffering is ameliorated—that may or may not be the case. But the presence in our lives of grace makes all the difference. The other point of knowledge is the importance God places on family life, not only for his divinely elected children but for the other humans he also loves. We have no need to know the "shape" of family life through eternity, but we can be assured of the best possible scenario.

Post-ponderings: Knowing there will be no disappointment on the new earth, how do you picture your ongoing family life? How important is it for you to recognize and pick up where you left off with your departed loved ones?

CAIN AND ABEL:
ENVY'S ULTIMATE OUTCOME

"When he heard his father call out for Abel and he saw his brother go forth, it made him feel like he was nothing. He couldn't even say that he felt like Cain anymore. One could not feel like Cain because it had no flavor. Cain was the absence of flavor. Cain was like saliva or a Wednesday."
—JONATHAN GOLDSTEIN

"By faith Abel brought God a better offering than Cain did. By faith he was commended as righteous, when God spoke well of his offerings. And by faith Abel still speaks, even though he is dead." (Hebrews 11:4)

Read Genesis 4:1–12.
Genesis doesn't clarify why God honored one brother's gift but not the other's, though the issue was undoubtedly not one of grain versus meat. But John addresses this issue in 1 John 3:12: "Do not be like Cain, who belonged to the evil one and murdered his brother. And why did he murder him? Because his own actions were evil and his brother's were righteous." Abel's better offering depended on his better perspective and behavior—indicative of the faith that continues to speak despite his foreshortened life span.

It's amazing what a little jealousy can do, even—and perhaps especially—within a family context. In fact, that seemingly innocuous seed of envy (ever notice that the tenth commandment prohibits a *feeling*, not an action?) underlies so many seemingly more egregious shortcomings.

James addresses this issue in strong words: "What causes fights and quarrels among you? Don't they come from your desires that battle within you? You desire but do not have, *so you kill*" (James 4:1–2, emphasis added). Whoa! Is there a step missing here? Yet my mind immediately reverts to other biblical brother combos: Joseph and his brothers, or how about the resentful "good son" in Jesus' parable of the lost son? We don't know the outcome of that one (it's a story, so there really isn't one), but we can imagine the worst. The out-of-the-limelight sibling can indeed feel like the absence of flavor, or value, or love-worthiness.

Post-ponderings: If you're a parent, what are you doing to prevent the envy weed from flourishing in your kids? If you're a son/daughter/sibling who's struggling with this issue, how can you most effectively confront the problem and engage with the other(s) involved?

"No Fair!"

"Life isn't fair. It's just fairer than death, that's all."
—WILLIAM GOODMAN

"Cain said to the LORD, 'My punishment is more than I can bear. Today you are driving me from the land, and I will be hidden from your presence; I will be a restless wanderer on the earth, and whoever finds me will kill me.'"
(Genesis 4:13–14)

Read Genesis 4:13–16.

"That's not *fair!*" How often doesn't that classic emerge from the lips of any kid . . . of any age? And can we believe our ears when Cain worries that some stranger (wherever this person might come from) might reach out and *kill* him? Were the irony less tragic, we'd be tempted to chuckle! Those behaviors we recognize as universal took hold already when the human race was young.

No, the sin situation with all its ramifications wasn't "fair" to Cain. Or to Abel . . . or to anyone else, alive then or since. But Cain's live outcome was decidedly fairer, or less unfair, than Abel's death. It was too late to rectify *that* situation, but that isn't always the case. Fairness can be so relative, and nursing a grudge comes easily to us. Less natural is the effort to step back far enough to glimpse the opposite perspective. This applies as much to spousal relationships, of course, as to those between parents/kids or siblings. What a difference it would make if we as family members would seek to deliberately cultivate this discipline.

Post-ponderings: What example of unfairness comes immediately to mind when you consider your family situation—either your family of origin or the one you now parent? Now try to view this situation from the opposite side. Do any insights suggest themselves?

SETH:
REPLACEMENT CHILD

"Making the decision to have a child—it is momentous. It is to decide forever to have your heart go walking around outside your body."
—ELIZABETH STONE

"Adam made love to his wife again, and she gave birth to a son and named him Seth, saying, 'God has granted me another child in place of Abel, since Cain killed him.'" (Genesis 4:25)

Read Genesis 4:17–26.
No, we don't know where those other people came from. But honing in on what we do know from the above verse, I wonder whether Seth might have been conceived as a replacement not only for the son lost through death but also for the one estranged on account of the murder.

Parents opt for additional children for all sorts of reasons, some of them pragmatic and targeted. I recall a situation some years ago that drew media attention over suggested ethical implications: a couple conceived in the hope of giving birth to a marrow donor for their leukemia-stricken only daughter.

I'm in no way suggesting that conceiving or adopting a replacement child following a loss is wrong or ill-advised. Much the opposite: this can be a "saving" grace for bereaved parents. A couple of concerns do occur to me, though: (1) the need to guard against unhealthy or unrealistic expectations of the new child, and (2) the inadvisability of "replacing" a child who isn't really gone but simply a disappointment.

Post-ponderings: What do you make of the provocative ending (italicized sentence below) to Genesis 4: "Seth also had a son, and he named him Enosh. *At that time people began to call on the name of the* LORD"?

NOAH AND HIS FAMILY: CHOSEN

"Family faces are magic mirrors. Looking at people who belong to us, we see the past, present, and future."
—GAIL LUMET BUCKLEY

"By faith Noah, when warned about things not yet seen, in holy fear built an ark to save his family. By his faith he condemned the world and became heir of the righteousness that is in keeping with faith." (Hebrews 11:7)

Read Genesis 7–8.
Your and my families haven't been chosen in the way Noah's was—or Adam and Eve's in an earlier start. But you (singular and plural) *have* been chosen. If that weren't the case, you probably wouldn't be reading this right now. In Peter's words, "you are a chosen people, a royal priesthood, a holy nation, God's special possession" (1 Peter 2:9). His reference is wide—to God's people communally—but its application fits just as well with the microcosm that's you and your family. And the analogy can be stretched long as well as wide. If you're privileged to come from a family of faith going back generationally, you understand something of the image in the Buckley quote.

God describes himself in Exodus 20:6 as "showing love to a thousand generations of those who love me and keep my commandments." When we gaze into the faces of family, from the squinty features of the newly minted infant to the expressions of those peopling old family albums, we go beyond identifying physical similarities. In those timeless images we may glimpse stances and mannerisms suggesting familiar character and personality traits. A quote from Dr. George Landberg, while lacking a spiritual component, speaks to me: "The linking of the generations, the historical lineage of the family, the sharing of love—gives purpose to life." Chances are our overriding impression when we allow our thoughts to stray backward and forward along this line will be of God's faithfulness *to us* over time rather than ours to him.

Noah and his family weren't truly alone; they carried within themselves the stream of that faithfulness, flowing unabated in both directions. They carried within themselves the inheritance of the righteous that is in keeping with faith. And so do you (in the singular and in the plural)!

Post-ponderings: Imagine for a moment that God has chosen *your* immediate family—the handful of you—for humanity's fresh start. We know from post-disembarkation history that Noah's family was hardly perfect. And neither is yours. Still, what qualities in *your* family might recommend it for such a role?

NOAH AND HIS SONS:
FACE SAVING IN THE FAMILY

"Modesty is invisibility . . . Never forget it. To be seen . . . is to be . . . penetrated."
—MARGARET ATWOOD

*"[Noah] became drunk and lay uncovered inside his tent. Ham, the father of Canaan,
saw his father naked and told his two brothers outside. But Shem and Japheth took
a garment and laid it across their shoulders; then they walked in backward and
covered their father's naked body. Their faces were turned the other way so that
they would not see their father naked." (Genesis 9:21–23)*

Read Genesis 9:18–27.

For purposes of this reflection, we won't consider Noah's perplexing curse
on Canaan, Ham's son, in response to Ham's disrespect. An *NIV Study
Bible* note explains that verses 25–27 target the author's Israelite audience,
who would have experienced firsthand the *Canaan*ite wickedness related
to Noah's curse.

This vignette won't pertain to your family interaction. But points of reference still suggest themselves. The first needs no articulation: the respect
of the younger generation, mandated by Scripture, must be unconditional.
(Obedience to parental demands that break civil law—not to mention God's
law—is another matter.)

A broader application involves all of us, at whatever age or stage or in
whatever family role. No one likes to be embarrassed, and kids in particular
can be acutely sensitive to perceived mockery or humiliation. The Atwood
quote seems uncomfortably explicit, but it can apply to the emotional as
well as to the physical. Being caught in a faux pas (lets use the example of
a little one using a big word out of context) can make us feel vulnerable—
penetrated, even. So mortified we long for invisibility. Whenever any of us
is willing to save face for any other, we do that other a tremendous favor.
Whatever we can do to present one another—even to themselves—in the
best possible light will be blessed and a blessing.

Post-ponderings: When in your family life has respect for someone else's
feelings caused you to stifle laughter at their blunder? When has someone
shown this courtesy to you?

JOB AND HIS FAMILY: GOD'S HEDGE

"He that raises a large family does, indeed, while he lives to observe them, stand a broader mark for sorrow; but then he stands a broader mark for pleasure too."
—BENJAMIN FRANKLIN

"'Does Job fear God for nothing?' Satan replied. 'Have you not put a hedge around him and his household and everything he has?'" (Job 1:9)

Read Job 1.
I've placed the Job reflections within this early sequence since the story is very ancient (though perhaps recorded during the early Israelite monarchy). Job is thought to have lived at around the time of the patriarchs; given that context I'm particularly struck by the level of sophistication of the book's arguments. Many readers avoid Job on the basis of its heavy subject matter, but I heartily recommend this exquisite book as the literary and spiritual masterpiece it is.

The principle is familiar: the more we have, the more we stand to lose. A case can, of course, be made for the opposite: the smaller our family, the more vulnerable we are to losing our "everyone" in a tragedy, or even a falling out. In Job's worst-case reality a thriving brood of ten—all seven sons and three daughters—was snuffed out in a building collapse during a celebration.

Job had to this point led a seemingly charmed existence. We see in him a model father and God-fearer, righteous in the eyes of God and people. I'm particularly struck by the lengths to which he would go to ensure that his children were right with God. This reality wasn't lost on Satan, who asked God rhetorically, "Why wouldn't this man fear you with that hedge of protection around him?" Why not indeed . . . ?

Post-ponderings: Think back to a time when God's safekeeping was evident in your family life. Were you struck by the assurance that this was no co-incidence? Then consider an occasion when God allowed suffering to penetrate your circle. Were you brought closer to him through that experience?

"Curse God and Die!"

"[Job's] wife said to him, 'Are you still maintaining your integrity? Curse God and die!' He replied, 'You are talking like a foolish woman. Shall we accept good from God, and not trouble?'" (Job 2:9–10)

Read Job 2:1–10.
Trouble doesn't have to be self-limiting. It doesn't need to diminish us or our perspective, to shrivel our souls or stunt our growth in grace. In fact, suffering can be the impetus for character development and enlargement. Such would be the outcome for Job, though it would take some time to unfold.

His wife's perspective was different. We hear little of her—which is the reason I didn't identify Job in the last reflection as a good husband—though I have no reason to doubt he was. I may be reading too much into one impression, but I picture her from this cameo functioning as a damper on this (or any?) situation, as the one ready to infuse the downer to prevent enthusiasm from getting out of hand.

Are you and your spouse complementary in terms of personality traits (complimentary is good too)? There's nothing wrong with checks and balances, but in this situation a positive and a negative aren't likely to produce a charge.

Post-ponderings: If as a couple one of you is clearly the optimist and the other the pessimist, try to identify some helpful counterbalancing that may be taking place. Then consider the negative ramifications for your marriage and family life. What can *you* do to promote a more smoothly functioning unit?

Job Rues His Birth: Hedged in by God?

"'What is mankind that you make so much of them, that you give them so much attention, that you examine them every morning and test them every moment? Will you not look away from me, or let me alone even for an instant?'" (Job 7:17–19)

Read Job 3.

There it is again—that hedge (see the reflection on Job 1). I'm struck by the contrast between Satan's use of the term (as protection) in chapter 1 and Job's allusion to the concept (as restriction) here. I'm reminded of David's words in Psalm 139:5: "You hem me in behind and before, and you lay your hand upon me." Sounds like a complaint reminiscent of Job's here. But listen on to the psalmist's surprising conclusion: "Such knowledge is too wonderful for me, too lofty for me to attain." So much has to do with our perspective on God's involvement in our lives and those of our families.

Who of us appreciates the claustrophobia of feeling hemmed in? Perhaps the issue has to do with rules originating from within the extended family, society, church or religious tradition, or God's Word. Even as independent adults, spouses can be rankled by the demands or expectations of their partner's family of origin. We can so easily feel judged when our decisions for our own family run counter to unwritten norms. Such issues become especially dicey when the husband's and wife's families are markedly different in their outlooks, values, or habits.

I find it helpful to remember, from the biblical side, that Jesus' law of love has freed New Covenant believers from the letter of the Old Testament law. Beyond that mandate to love, many of the specific expectations that may be foisted on us as parents are based on personal preference.

Post-ponderings: Do you find the knowledge of God's intimate involvement in your life cloying or comforting? On the whole, do you consider God's "hedge" around your marriage and family to be protective or restrictive?

OFFENSIVE IN ANGUISH
TO LOVED ONES

"What are you if the people who are supposed to love you can leave you like you're nothing?"
—ELIZABETH SCOTT

"My breath is offensive to my wife; I am loathsome to my own family. Even the little boys scorn me; when I appear, they ridicule me. All my intimate friends detest me; those I love have turned against me." (Job 19:17–19)

Read Job 19:13–29.

In Psalm 41:7–9 David echoes Job's sentiment here: "All my enemies whisper together against me; they imagine the worst for me, saying, 'A vile disease has afflicted him; he will never get up from the place where he lies.' Even my close friend, someone I trusted, one who shared my bread, has turned against me."

A camouflaging effect of modern medicine means that few of us will become so ill as to be repulsive to our loved ones; nor are we likely to find ourselves repulsed by the condition of those we love. But alienation and desertion can occur for reasons other than physical revulsion. Perhaps a member or extended member of our family has shamed or embarrassed us all, in some way tarnishing our good name in the church and/or community. Gregory Maguire suggests another, hypothetical "perhaps," one we—maybe particularly as Christians—don't like to consider: "Perhaps family itself, like beauty, is temporary, and no discredit need attach to impermanence."

It takes a strong family to continue to embrace its black sheep, misfits, loose cannons, or whatever other metaphor may fit. But isn't that precisely what God asks us to do when this hurting individual is a member of his larger family?

Post-ponderings: Who is it in your family who rankles you, perhaps simply on the basis of mannerisms or attitudes that rub you the wrong way? What would it take for you to apply with regard to this individual Paul's injunction in Romans 12:18, "If it is possible, as far as it depends on you, live at peace with _____"?

THE CHILDREN
OF THE DESTITUTE

"In destitution, even of feeling or purpose, a human being is more hauntingly human and vulnerable to kindnesses because there is a sense that things should be otherwise, and then the thought of what is wanting and what alleviation would be, and how the soul could be put at ease, restored. At home. But the soul finds its own home if it ever has a home at all."
—MARILYNNE ROBINSON

"'Like wild donkeys in the desert, the poor go about their labor of foraging food; the wasteland provides food for their children. . . . The fatherless child is snatched from the breast; the infant of the poor is seized for a debt.'" (Job 24:5, 9)

Read Job 24:1–12.
Such destitution is almost certainly foreign to our lives and those of our children. But we as believers can be acutely sensitive to the plight of the many in our world who may never experience the felicities we take for granted. Hurting on behalf of the hurting is intrinsic to who we are. It's the impetus for the Christ-like behavior our Lord expects from us.

A written documentary that rocked me to the core is Katherine Boo's 2012 *Behind the Beautiful Forevers: Life, Death and Hope in a Mumbai Undercity*. I found myself riveted by one memorable vignette of an unattached young boy from the slums near the Mumbai airport in India. Leaning over a high railing with the realization that he could easily plunge to his death, he recognizes with a start that, even though he probably matters to no one else, he matters to *himself!* As I learned in my earliest years from a childhood song, God sees the little sparrow fall! He is indeed Father to the fatherless—even to those fatherless who may have no knowledge of him.

Post-ponderings: What have you as a family done, or could you do—radical or otherwise—to alleviate the suffering of someone (or some *ones*), somewhere?

Nostalgia's Mockery:
The Good Old Days

"Time was passing like a hand waving from a train I wanted to be on. I hope you never have to think about anything as much as I think about you."
—JONATHAN SAFRAN FOER

"'Oh, for the days when I was in my prime, when God's intimate friendship blessed my house, when the Almighty was still with me and my children were around me.'"
(Job 29:4–5)

Read Job 29.
Nostalgia has its upsides, but the feeling is often bittersweet, if not sad. Depending upon where we sit on time's continuum, we're at any given moment most fully present in the future, the present, or the past, often in that order as time glides by. Job's transition from focus on the busy present to dwelling on the past was jarring in a way few of us will ever experience. His angst wasn't a matter of regret, as is so often the case for those who may over time have allowed opportunities to slip by. Job had been living well and fully. He had been engaged and vital. His misfortunes had truly happened *to* him.

We can only imagine that Job's situation was unique in human history in terms of its why—which is not to say we know this for certain. Our own misfortunes most likely have causes that are quite different. What we do know is that, whatever we may be called upon to suffer in this life, God's intention is for our good. How often don't we wish our past had been different, in turn having altered the disposition of our present and future? The blessed reality to which we can cling is that our long-term future will be glorious beyond imagination.

Post-ponderings: Hone in on a misfortune that has permanently altered the course of your own or your family's life. Is regret over a lost opportunity a factor, or was this event beyond your control? Are you able at this juncture to identify one or more positive outcomes? What difference does long-term hope make in terms of your outlook?

Happily Ever After?

"He also had seven sons and three daughters. The first daughter he named Jemimah, the second Keziah and the third Keren-Happuch. Nowhere in all the land were there found women as beautiful as Job's daughters, and their father granted them an inheritance along with their brothers." (Job 42:13–16)

Read Job 42:7–17.

I'll admit to being both pleasantly surprised and mildly mystified by this author's concentration in his closing on Job's three new daughters, as opposed to his seven new sons. Why the inclusion of their names and references to their beauty and inheritances so many centuries before the account of Zelophehad's heiresses in Numbers 27:1–11? The Bible is often sparse on detail, but its references to specific girls and women often take me aback. I suppose daddies have throughout history doted on their daughters.

This happily-ever-after ending—reminiscent for us of the stuff of fairytales—in itself comes as a surprise, not quite in keeping with the rambling, conversational nature of the book. Our lives don't often return to absolute resolution following a setback. But recovery can exceed our expectations, and even our original situation.

Post-ponderings: Identify a time in your family life when an unforeseen and seemingly negative challenge turned out to be a blessing. At what point did you realize this serendipity? Have you thanked the Lord for this course correction?

THE EARLY PATRIARCHS—
ABRAM THROUGH ISAAC

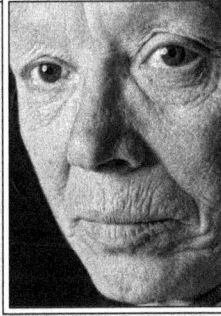

CHAPTER
INTRODUCTION

The Old Testament's historical books (Genesis through Esther, corresponding with chapters 1–13 in this book) are rich in details of family life in all of its iterations. Their extended stories of numerous unforgettable characters, most of them family members, make for riveting reading; the only drawback, unfortunately, is often their—or our—very familiarity.

Chapter 2 covers the first two of these stories, starting with the long life of Abram (we join him already as an old man, but there's a lot still to come) and taking us through the long life of Isaac, encompassing the early history of his twin sons, Esau and Jacob. "Father Abraham," the founder of the nation of Israel and hence, ultimately, of the Christian faith, is no random historical character for us; we have a vested interest in his story because it marks the beginning of our own. He's family in a way the early representatives of the human race covered in chapter 1 were not.

ABRAM AND SARAI:
VENTURING OUT IN BLIND FAITH

"Faith isn't the ability to believe long and far into the misty future. It's simply taking God at His word and taking the next step."
—JONI EARECKSON TADA

"By faith Abraham, when called to go to a place he would later receive as his inheritance, obeyed and went, even though he did not know where he was going. By faith he made his home in the promised land like a stranger in a foreign country." (Hebrews 11:8–9)

Read Genesis 12:1–9; Hebrews 11:8–12.

Why is it so many of us have come to think of finding God's will—or even *looking* for it—as some mysterious proposition? I was relieved some time ago to read that God's will for our lives is spelled out in his Word; it's right there in black and white. Why hadn't I thought of that? A related insight that has proved helpful to me is that there is often more than one possible path to take while still remaining securely within that will. So what about the issue of God calling us? I'm not referring to his call of salvation but to the Spirit's convicting or goading us in the direction of some new path. Even when we for some unidentifiable reason feel pulled in a given direction, we do well to search the Scripture, along with our hearts, for confirmation.

A pastor and his family considering a call from a congregation are not in a fundamentally different position from that of an "ordinary" couple or individual attempting to discern God's will with regard to a possible career change, relocation, educational opportunity, or family expansion. There are those situations when the Lord lays it upon our hearts to do something. But there are equally valid instances of his allowing *us* to formulate and go with an idea that doesn't in itself violate his revealed will. He may place or allow obstacles in our way, but even then he may be testing our resolve rather than deterring us.

No, you or I aren't a Noah, an Abram, or a Paul. Their parts in salvation history have passed. But God's callings on our individual lives, his nudges in the direction of his will for *us*, are vitally important. Will we follow along *by faith*? Will we, with our families, be willing to risk taking that next tenuous step?

Post-ponderings: What life changes are you considering? How can you determine the Lord's will?

Sarai:
The Used Spouse

"Selfishness is not living as one wishes to live, it is asking others to live as one wishes to live."
—OSCAR WILDE

"'I know what a beautiful woman you are. When the Egyptians see you, they will say, "This is his wife." Then they will kill me but will let you live. Say you are my sister, so that I will be treated well for your sake and my life will be spared because of you.'" (Genesis 12:11–13)

Read Genesis 12:10–20.
Have you noticed that Abram's two benefit statements both pertain to himself: (1) I will be treated well and (2) my life will be spared? In a back-handed sort of way the benefits to Abram reverted to Sarai, but which of the two bore the disgrace and felt the distress?

What Abram didn't foresee was the monetary benefit that would ac-crue to him after Pharaoh had his way with his wife. Interestingly, Pharaoh not only didn't murder Abram but sent him on his way, *along with* his pos-sessions, after a reproof for having allowed him to unknowingly violate Sarai. I doubt any of us as family members would use one another in so barefaced a manner. But a good end always falls short of justifying a bad means. And monetary success ought never to be weighed against emo-tional devastation.

Post-ponderings: When have you rationalized a questionable decision? Were there any casualties, whether or not you recognized them at the time? (Don't overlook the issue of modeling for your kids.)

ABRAM AND LOT:
BREATHING SPACE

"There is love in holding and there is love in letting go."
—ELIZABETH BERG

"So Lot chose for himself the whole plain of the Jordan and set out toward the east. The two men parted company." (Genesis 13:11)

Read Genesis 13.
Parting company at this juncture was very likely the path of wisdom. Rubbing shoulders on a daily basis had started to produce a grating friction that could be alleviated only by separation. The fact that Lot, given first dibs, chose the more fertile land could have rankled his uncle; if it did, Abram let it go, choosing not to let the situation escalate.

The skill of choosing our battles is essential to a smoothly running family life—as is that of inserting distance where it's needed. Potential skirmishes within a family are never far away, and sometimes it takes only breathing space to clear the air. This is especially true when conflict involves different generations—particularly in the case of parents and grown children. In this case Lot, upon invitation, chose his lot, and Uncle Abram graciously conceded. How detrimental it might have been had the outcome been otherwise!

Post-ponderings: Identify a situation in your family life when separation alleviated discord. Did you obtain the "right" amount of distance? Did you ultimately achieve understanding?

Sarai and Hagar:
Workaround and Turnabout

"At times, Sarah doubted God. She had trouble believing God would fulfill his promises, so she plunged ahead with her own solution."
—JACK ZAVADA

"'The Lord has kept me from having children. Go, sleep with my slave; perhaps I can build a family through her.'" (Genesis 16:2)

Read Genesis 16:1–6.
God's covenant with Abram in Genesis 15 was clear, though the Lord hadn't yet revealed that Sarai *herself* would bear a child. It's striking that Sarai attempted to control the situation in God's place (note the glaring *I* in the verse above). But when problems developed she proceeded to blame her compliant husband: "Then Sarai said to Abram, '*You* are responsible for the wrong I am suffering. I put my slave in your arms, and now that she knows she is pregnant, she despises me. May the Lord judge between *you and me.*' 'Your slave is in your hands,' Abram said. 'Do with her whatever you think best'" (emphasis added).

Sarai lacked the benefit of God's as yet unspoken words "I am the Lord your God, who teaches you what is best for you" (Isaiah 48:17). Notice that God doesn't say he *gives* us what is best. He wants to, but he doesn't always take the automatic or immediate approach. In this case Sarai lacked the discipline to wait on his impeccable timing.

Have you ever pursued something you believed to be good—or at least neutral—but found yourself thwarted at every turn? Sometimes the issue is one of timing. God's implied no may really be a not yet. But like Sarai we insist on helping him do it our way. God didn't allow me to do that with my second adoption (see the reflection on Genesis 2:18–25), for which I waited ten years. That isn't to say I didn't try to sidestep his will (I explored several unlikely and expensive adopt-quick schemes, which he graciously thwarted on my behalf). It was only when I let go of the reins that he gave me exactly the best I'd been seeking. It turned out to be a difficult best, and I needed every ounce of added maturity those ten years had afforded.

Post-ponderings: In what ways is God directing you at this juncture? Are you accepting his answers without reminding or prodding him along?

EXPECTANT MOM SANS EXPECTATION: "THE GOD WHO SEES ME"

"It wasn't that she was sad—sadness had very little to do with it, really, considering that most of the time, she felt close to nothing at all. Feeling required nerves, connections, sensory input. The only thing she felt was numb. And tired. Yes, she very frequently felt tired."
—NENIA CAMPBELL

"[Hagar] gave this name to the LORD who spoke to her: 'You are the God who sees me,' for she said, 'I have now seen the One who sees me.'" (Genesis 16:13)

Read Genesis 16:7–16.
I can only imagine that this vital young girl, obliged to idle her enthusiasm to function as a drone, might have made impulsive mistakes when presented with the unfamiliar prospect of options. If anyone had bothered to explain this seemingly serendipitous turn of events, this sudden passion for progeny on the part of an old man, she would have come to recognize that this for-one-practical-purpose husband expected *her* to deliver on a promise from a deity. As it was, this formerly unassuming young woman began all too quickly to presume upon a status that would never be hers. It didn't take long for her to recognize her mistake, but the damage had been done. We can imagine her helpless aloneness, compounded by pregnancy.

Imagine Hagar's shock at realizing not only that God was aware of her plight but that he was condescending to communicate with her! That his gaze was not aloof and cold but tender. That she, born into the constricting circumstance of slavery, was a person of consequence in his sight.

The writer of Psalm 10 declares in verse 14, "But you, God, see the trouble of the afflicted; you consider their grief and take it in hand. The victims commit themselves to you; you are the helper of the fatherless." And the opening verses of Psalm 123 depict reciprocal gazing into God's eyes: "I lift up my eyes to you, to you who sit enthroned in heaven. As the eyes of slaves look to the hand of their master, as the eyes of a female slave look to the hand of her mistress, so our eyes look to the LORD our God, till he shows us his mercy."

Our lives too can be fraught with trouble and complication. What a comfort to acknowledge that God's searching eyes envelop us and our situations, ensuring us that we're never alone, no matter how convoluted our circumstances may be from an earthly perspective.

Post-ponderings: Think back to an "unsolvable" or "lose/lose" situation in your marriage or family life. Did you come to recognize God's interest and investment? Have you taken the time to thank him for his intervention?

LOT AND HIS DAUGHTERS: DEVALUATION OF FAMILY

"You need to make time for your family no matter what happens in your life."
—MATTHEW QUICK

The men of Sodom "called to Lot, 'Where are the men who came to you tonight? Bring them out to us so that we can have sex with them.' Lot went outside to meet them and shut the door behind him and said, 'No, my friends. Don't do this wicked thing. Look, I have two daughters who have never slept with a man. Let me bring them out to you, and you can do what you like with them. But don't do anything to these men, for they have come under the protection of my roof.'" (Genesis 19:5–8)

Read Genesis 19:1–9.
This disturbing account is remarkably similar to that in Judges 19:22–24. Such devaluation of women in deference to male guests was horrendous, but no more heinous than the atrocities of our world. Whatever we as responsible Christians can do to combat such practices as sex trafficking can make a difference. Whether our involvement is hands-on or behind-the-scenes, we must make our voices heard—and trust God to take it from there!

There may be a touch point here in terms of ways in which we downplay the importance of family members in our attempts to impress others. Which matters more to us as parents, our family's public face or our children's well-being as they face a not always well-meaning world? Are we anxious to look good even if that means keeping close to home a problem our child is experiencing that could benefit from outside intervention or confrontation? Do we assume our family members will understand if they play second fiddle in terms of our relational responsibilities? It's well possible this isn't an issue in your family. But it doesn't hurt to remind ourselves of the importance of resisting any temptation to favor others above our own.

Post-ponderings: When did you assume that your kids, spouse, or extended family members would understand your lack of attention while you were juggling multiple commitments? Did you take the time to explain the circumstances? Did you attempt to make it up to them after your crunch time?

LOT'S WIFE: FINAL GAZE

"There's many a forward look in a backward glance."
—AUTHOR UNKNOWN

"Then the LORD rained down burning sulfur on Sodom and Gomorrah . . . But Lot's wife looked back, and she became a pillar of salt." (Genesis 19:24, 26)

Read Genesis 19:10–29.
There's nothing noncommittal about a gaze, as opposed to a glance; it connotes longing and, if it's backward, reluctance. Which isn't to say that a final, over-the-shoulder look is always wrong; at least, we can rationalize, we've made the decision to leave behind whatever temptation has been causing us trouble. In the case of Lot's wife this look wasn't one of curiosity or raw terror but of the dawning of regret and a futile yearning for what had so recently been her norm. There may have been ambivalence in her eyes, along with some resignation, but relief over the narrow escape may not have been in the mix. Lot's insistence that he run only as far as Zoar may indicate reservation on his part as well.

God didn't view this woman's gaze as innocuous. There are times when vacillation is intolerable from the divine perspective. We see this in the seemingly "minor" infractions of Achan (Joshua 7) and Ananias and Sapphira (Acts 5:1–11). Here in Genesis 19 God was making a significant statement about sin. This volcanic activity, if that's what it was, didn't match the flood in intensity or consequence, but the message was unequivocal.

God takes sin seriously, no less in our day than in the past. When we with the Spirit's help turn from temptation, our about-face needs to be all about meaning it. Hesitation has no place when it comes to obedience.

Post-ponderings: What temptation have you overcome in your marriage or family life? Were you decisive in your response?

Lot's Daughters: Culpable?

"I felt like an animal, and animals don't know sin, do they?"
—JESS C. SCOTT

"Lot and his two daughters left Zoar and settled in the mountains, for he was afraid to stay in Zoar. He and his two daughters lived in a cave. One day the older daughter said to the younger, 'Our father is old, and there is no man around here to give us children—as is the custom all over the earth. Let's get our father to drink wine and then sleep with him and preserve our family line through our father.'"
(Genesis 19:30–32)

Read Genesis 19:30–38.

The preservation of a family line is of little importance to us, even though we may desire and delight in children. Our lives and values are so immediate and "me" oriented that the meandering flow of generations doesn't pique our interest. But Lot's daughters sensed a cutting off point in terms of life and opportunity as they'd known it.

So many Old Testament stories are brutal or sordid—nearly unthinkable for us. And yet they frequently deal with families, functional and intact or otherwise. Lot's daughters felt cornered and desperate. As ancient women they understood themselves to have a prescribed role, a function that in early history was important in terms of the generation of whole people groups. Still today there are times when family circumstances force people to make compromises and concessions they would never otherwise consider. The agonizing choices surrounding illegal immigration come to mind. When people feel themselves cornered by limited options, they may see questionable actions as matters of necessity and impunity.

Our Lord expects us to combat injustice and advocate for the oppressed in whatever way we can. It's easy to become desensitized in our sanitized worlds. Could it be that some exposure to jarring Old Testament stories is God's intention for us—his goad to personal engagement and action?

Post-ponderings: What is your reaction to biblical accounts like this one? Are you inclined to pass them over as irrelevant? Have you paused to wonder why God chose to include them in his Word?

Abraham with Sarah and Abimelek: Slow Learner

> "It is not because the truth is too difficult to see that we make mistakes . . .
> We make mistakes because the easiest and most comfortable course for us is
> to seek insight where it accords with our emotions—especially selfish ones."
> —ALEKSANDR SOLZHENITSYN

> *"Then Abimelek called Abraham in and said, 'What have you done to us? How have
> I wronged you that you have brought such great guilt upon me and my kingdom?
> You have done things to me that should never be done. . . . What was your reason
> for doing this?'" (Genesis 20:9–10)*

Read Genesis 20.

This was the second time around for Abraham to use this ploy (see the reflection on Genesis 12:10–20). Was the patriarch driven by an irrational or even a legitimate fear of Abimelek and trying to protect his own neck, or was he concerned for the well-being of his (already pregnant?) wife? Was he attempting to intervene so God's promise of a son wouldn't be thwarted? Did he suffer from a blind spot when it came to this particular sin? To complicate our confusion, Abraham's actions in both stories seem to be out of character for him. God's intervention in the form of Abimelek's dream did prevent any harm being done to the mother of the promised son, but this hardly exonerated Abraham for his half-truth.

Perhaps our first takeaway, as we've considered before, is that a potentially good end never justifies a bad means. More importantly, our implicit trust in God should override any inclination to resort to questionable actions.

Post-ponderings: When in your marriage or family life have you rationalized a not-quite-right decision you felt was necessary to prevent a bad outcome? Did you leave this in the past and simply move on, or did you feel compelled at some point to come to terms with your choice?

ABRAHAM AND SARAH:
THE MANY FACES OF LAUGHTER

"At the height of laughter, the universe is flung into a kaleidoscope of new possibilities."
—JEAN HOUSTON

"Abraham fell facedown; he laughed and said to himself, 'Will a son be born to a man a hundred years old? Will Sarah bear a child at the age of ninety?'" (Genesis 17:17)

"'Why did Sarah laugh and say, "Will I really have a child, now that I am old?" Is anything too hard for the LORD?'" (Genesis 18:13–14)

"Sarah said, 'God has brought me laughter, and everyone who hears about this will laugh with me.'" (Genesis 21:6)

Read Genesis 17:15–22; 18:1–15; 21:1–7.
"What monstrous absurdities and paradoxes have resisted whole batteries of serious arguments, and then crumbled swiftly into dust before the ringing death-knell of a laugh!" reflects Agnes Repplier. Laughter is one of the more compelling—and complicated—reflections of emotion. From the sardonic to the exuberant, how many human feelings don't manifest themselves through this full-service release mechanism? And how often doesn't laughter, at its best, lubricate the machinery of family life? I particularly love one descriptor of the noble wife described in Proverbs: "she can laugh at the days to come" (31:25).

I've chosen to highlight not one but three Scripture references. The first two, involving first Abraham and later Sarah, are similar in nature. But what a welcome contrast in Sarah's bubbling response following the fulfillment of God's promise. Have you found yourself overcome by infectious laughter, perhaps joining in even when you didn't know the story? I'm drawn to Norman Cousins' assessment of this God-given stress reducer: "Laughter is a form of internal jogging. It moves your internal organs around. It enhances respiration. It is an igniter of great expectations." And to the advice of an unknown author: "Even if there is nothing to laugh about, laugh on credit."

Post-ponderings: What therapeutic role does laughter play in your marital/family relationships? What inside joke never fails to elicit a response? To approach this reflection from a different angle, with what "improbable" blessing has God thrilled you? Have you remembered to thank him, then, later, or lately?

ABRAHAM AND ISHMAEL:
THE INDECISIVE PARENT

"Indecision and delays are the parents of failure."
—GEORGE CANNING

"Sarah saw that the son whom Hagar the Egyptian had borne to Abraham was mocking, and she said to Abraham, 'Get rid of that slave woman and her son, for that woman's son will never share in the inheritance with my son Isaac.' The matter distressed Abraham greatly because it concerned his son." (Genesis 21:9–11)

Read Genesis 21:8–21.
Moving ahead in terms of biblical chronology, I'm reminded of Jacob's later inaction when it came to the conflict brewing between his ten older sons and the favored Joseph (37:11) and of David's similar reluctance to act (2 Samuel 13:39—15:12). There are times when decisiveness and timely intervention on the part of a parent are critical. This seems to have been a shared area of deficiency on the parts of some notable Old Testament men of God. Did these dads—if I may legitimately consider them together for purposes of this reflection—for whatever reason feel unentitled or unempowered when it came to dealing with their sons? Was Abraham cowed by Sarah's strong personality, as seems to have been the case with the pregnant Hagar's flight years earlier (see the reflection on Genesis 16:1–6)?

This story may have a more direct purchase on our lives than some of those we've considered. Do we as parents at times hesitate to intervene, particularly with our older sons and daughters, for fear of pushing a still more negative outcome? Because we're leery of losing popularity or status with them? Are we afraid they'll shut down and do what they want regardless of what we say? These stories may be eye-opening for those of us who consider this to be a uniquely modern problem. Evidently it's been around for as long as kids have been testing boundaries—e.g., for as long as kids have been around.

Post-ponderings: Think back to a time when you found yourself at a loss in dealing with a child-related situation. Did you opt for inaction, hoping the issue would blow over? What was the outcome?

ABRAHAM AND ISAAC:
FAITH IN ACTION

"I see enormous loves growing immense and finally crushing me."
—ANAÏS NIN

"By faith Abraham, when God tested him, offered Isaac as a sacrifice. He who had embraced the promises was about to sacrifice his one and only son, even though God had said to him, 'It is through Isaac that your offspring will be reckoned.' Abraham reasoned that God could even raise the dead, and so in a manner of speaking he did receive Isaac back from death." (Hebrews 11:17–19)

Read Genesis 22:1–19.

There's a sense in which "enormous loves" can indeed by crushing. That's because of the emotional risks we take to wholeheartedly love other humans. Love is vulnerability—the greater the love, the higher the level of exposure. God's promise of Isaac's birth and place in the covenant could have factored in to Abraham's awareness in either of two ways. For years I assumed the memory of that promise made God's request of Abraham feel like a double whammy. How must the patriarch have felt, I wondered, first accepting this miracle child and then facing his loss at God's command?

Upon encountering the explanation in the Hebrews quote, I interpreted Abraham's reaction differently, though I wasn't convinced he expected God to raise Isaac immediately. Here was a man who had learned well the lesson of patience. Abraham was, generations before Paul, a Romans 8:28 man, believing implicitly that "in all things God works for the good of those who love him, who have been called according to his purpose." Isn't that precisely what faith is all about—believing without seeing, without "getting it," without being able even to *visualize the possibility* of seeing? It's trusting . . . period! No matter what! No matter how! Without an inkling of the why.

Moving ahead in terms of chronology, I'm reminded of the story of Elisha and the Shunammite woman in 2 Kings 4:8–37. Let's listen in for a moment: "'Did I ask you for a son, my lord?' she said. 'Didn't I tell you, "Don't raise my hopes"?'" This is a classic picture of guarding emotions, a self-protective mechanism to which we all resort. Yet Abraham, despite his initial, incredulous laughter at God's unlikely promise, chose to fully embrace it.

Post-ponderings: What experience in your life stands out in terms of God's unexpected provision or solution?

Abraham and Ephron: Solidarity in Grief

"We're fascinated by the words—but where we meet is in the silence behind them."
—RAM DASS

"'Listen to me; I give you the field, and I give you the cave that is in it. I give it to you in the presence of my people. . . . [T]he land is worth four hundred shekels of silver, but what is that between you and me? Bury your dead.'" (Genesis 23:11, 14)

Read Genesis 23.

The universality of family grief comes out strongly in this vignette. This shared human connection transcends the differences among people. In times like this silence speaks resoundingly, and people-to-people communication happens as though by osmosis.

I write in May of 2014, shortly after the terrorist kidnapping of the three hundred schoolgirls in Nigeria and the sinking of the Japanese cruise ship filled with eager high school seniors anticipating a graduation that will never happen for them. These are only two of the atrocities and calamities rocking our world within an all too brief span of time. Take any span on the calendar for any year, and you'll have no trouble coming up with a similar list.

In these days of "viral" Facebook communication and global shrinking, the shared human experiences of grief and joy can quickly engulf the globe and overwhelm our psyches. Due in part to the continuous barrage of sensory and media input, we conclude that our world is becoming steadily worse. But could this flood of fellowship, this global people-to-people bonding, be a manifestation of God's ameliorating grace? Could we humans, loved alike by our Creator, be becoming more and more a global family?

Post-ponderings: What recent events have helped you understand and appreciate the universality of human experience and emotion?

Taking No Chances—
Could Isaac Foil the Plan?

"A ship is safe in harbor, but that's not what ships are for."
—WILLIAM G. T. SHEDD

"'Make sure you do not take my son back there,' Abraham said, 'The LORD, the God of heaven, who brought me out of my father's household and my native land and who spoke to me and promised me on oath, saying, "To your offspring I will give this land"—he will send his angel before you so that you can get a wife for my son from there.'" (Genesis 24:6–7)

Read Genesis 24:1–9.
"Vital lives are about action," reflects Joan Earickson. "You can't feel warmth unless you create it, can't feel delight until you play, can't know serendipity unless you risk." At first glance Abraham's reluctance to send his son with his servant strikes me as overly cautious. After all, God had made firm promises—and had proven himself by staying Abraham's hand upon the mountain. Was the patriarch afraid this son of the promise might foil God's plan by opting to defect?

A quote from two chapters (representing two decades) later suggests to me that Abraham's misgivings about Isaac might have been justified: "The LORD appeared to Isaac and said, 'Do not go down to Egypt; live in the land where I tell you to live. Stay in this land for a while, and I will be with you and will bless you'" (26:2–3). I may be reading too much into these verses, but they seem to imply that Isaac was impressionable. Little we read about this second patriarch identifies him as a determined individual. Yet Isaac—dare I call him the bland patriarch?—was God's choice, and God used him to further salvation's cause.

Post-ponderings: When have you hedged on allowing an adolescent to take responsibility based on fear they wouldn't be ready to handle the situation? When, on the other hand, have you trusted them and seen them come through with flying colors?

Rebekah:
Momentous Decision in a Moment

"To say that one waits a lifetime for his soulmate to come around is a paradox. People eventually get sick of waiting, take a chance of someone, and by the art of commitment become soulmates, which takes a lifetime to perfect."
—CHRISS JAMI

"Then [Rebekah's brother and mother] said, 'Let's call the young woman and ask her about it.' So they called Rebekah and asked her, 'Will you go with this man?' 'I will go,' she said." (Genesis 24:57)

Read Genesis 24:10–61.
Arranged marriages. Mail order brides. Anachronisms to us in the West, though these practices still prevail in some cultures—and have been normative through much of human history. Infatuation and romantic love may not always result, but many such marital pairings have withstood the test of time, in terms not simply of tolerance but of deep, learned love, mutual respect, shared responsibility and pleasure, and commitment.

I'm fondly reminded of the timid, back-and-forth and in-and-out verbal sparring between Tevye and Golde in *Fiddler on the Roof,* that beloved musical set in Tsarist Russia in 1905. Let's listen in on a segment: "I'm your wife." "I know. But do you love me?" "Do I love him? For twenty-five years I've lived with him, fought with him, starved with him. Twenty-five years my bed is his. If that's not love, what is?" "Then do you love me?" "I suppose I do." "And I suppose I love you too." "It doesn't change a thing. But even so, after twenty-five years it's nice to know."

Golde was utterly taken aback by Tevye's irrelevant question. Would it have been the same, I wonder, if Isaac had asked this of Rebekah a quarter century into their union (five years after the births of the twins)? I imagine the response would have been something like, "Now what does *that* have to do with anything, you sentimental fool?" Borrowing from Chriss Jami, could it be said of Isaac and Rebekah that they "by the art of commitment become soulmates, which [took] a lifetime to perfect"?

Post-ponderings: If you're married, what roles, respectively, have romance and commitment played in your marriage? At this point in your union, how would you describe your primary bond?

Isaac and Rebekah:
Mom Substitute?

"I know enough to know that no woman should ever marry a man who hated his mother."
—MARTHA GELLHORN

"Isaac brought [Rebekah] into the tent of his mother Sarah, and he married Rebekah. So she became his wife, and he loved her; and Isaac was comforted after his mother's death." (Genesis 24:67)

Read Genesis 24:62–67.
The skeptical Sarah hadn't expected to parent a son until the laughter bubbled up in her throat at Isaac's miracle birth. This was to be her sole chance at motherhood, and we can imagine her clinging tightly to this living, breathing boy wonder. There's nothing in the story to suggest that the mother/son relationship was anything but wholesome, but the above verse suggests that it was close. Isaac's reluctance to loosen the ties with his mother may have played in to his somewhat later marriage (but note the similar marital ages for his sons to be). And Rebekah's love provided the solace he needed.

For parents whose children come later in life, or for those who settle for a smaller family than they might have preferred or lose a son or daughter in childhood, the temptation to overprotect may be fierce. The outcome for a son may be an unreasonable standard for an eventual spouse, or it can be an emotionally crippling "Mama's boy" approach to adulthood. If Mom is still in the picture, such a son may sense the need for her permission to cherish and make a separate life with his spouse. This is, of course, conjecture in terms of the Sarah/Isaac/Rebecca situation; we aren't told enough to move beyond the might have been.

Post-ponderings: When in your experience have close ties between a mother and her son placed a strain on his marriage? Or when has the involvement of a mother-in-law threatened to cause a rift between husband and wife? If either experience registers with you personally, what have you done to ease the tension?

A HOUSE DIVIDED—
WHAT WENT SO WRONG?

"I would tell people some years later that I was raised an only child and so was my brother."
—HOMER HICKAM

"The babies jostled each other within [Rebekah], and she said, 'Why is this happening to me?'" (Genesis 25:22)

"The boys grew up, and Esau became a skillful hunter, a man of the open country, while Jacob was content to stay at home among the tents. Isaac, who had a taste for wild game, loved Esau, but Rebekah loved Jacob." (Genesis 25:27–28)

Read Genesis 25:19–34.

It's interesting that Isaac married at forty but that due to Rebekah's infertility the twins were born when he was sixty. By this point we can imagine both spouses having become entrenched in their ways. Their divergent personal and parenting styles most likely happened naturally, according to each individual family member's bents and preferences.

What went wrong in this family went beyond the weaknesses of its members: "Rebekah's children were conceived at the same time by our father Isaac. Yet, before the twins were born or had done anything good or bad—in order that God's purpose in election might stand: not by works but by him who calls—she was told, 'The older will serve the younger.' Just as it is written: 'Jacob I loved, but Esau I hated'" (Romans 9:10–13).

And yet we hold these parents accountable for the far-reaching consequences of their choices. "Always being treated differently from your other siblings isn't fair," declares an unknown author. Yet today's parents are often fixated on the varying needs and sensitivities of the upcoming generation. Tailoring an upbringing to each child's disposition, interests, aptitudes, and limitations has become a hallmark of sensitive parenting. I'm not suggesting this is problematic. We're among the first generations with the luxuries of leisure, resources, and insight for innovative, individualistic nurture. The trouble in the Isaac/Rebekah household came from one parent gravitating in terms of *preference*, not merely common interest, to one son and the other to the opposite. What could have been a close-knit family was split into two diametrically opposed—and opposing—factions.

Post-ponderings: If you were to align your family into natural affinity groups, whom would you assign to each, and on what basis?

APPEARANCES:
ULTIMATE FAMILY GOTCHA!

"The thing about chameleoning your way through life is that it gets to
where nothing is real."
—JOHN GREEN

*"Jacob said to Rebekah his mother, 'But my brother Esau is a hairy man while
I have smooth skin. What if my father touches me? I would appear to be
tricking him and would bring down a curse on myself rather than a blessing.'"*
(Genesis 27:11–12)

Read Genesis 27:1–40.
A reflection by Arthur Conan Doyle hits the nail on the head when it comes
to the dynamics of this dysfunctional family: "Some people's affability is
more deadly than the violence of coarser souls." The plodding and predict-
able Esau, while shortsighted and far from perfect, was hardly dangerous.
He lived unquestioningly in immediate reality, so unlike his conniving
brother to whom appearance and long-term security meant everything. It's
interesting that Jacob didn't identify his mother's devious proposal as advocating *real* deception. How ironic his concern that, should he be found out,
he would *appear* to be tricking his father and so call down an all too real
curse upon himself! The crux for him lay not in deception but in exposure.

Appearance plays an enormous role in our individual and family lives.
At times while in some public venue it occurs to me that all those "beautiful people" within my visual range have personal lives that include the
mundane, the unbeautiful, and even the tragic and unmentionable . . . and
unmentioned. Why is it so important to put our best face forward? Why is
it that façade trumps fact in terms of our public persona?

I recently encountered the suggestion that Rebekah's collusion with
her son represented a noble effort to prevent Isaac from foiling God's purpose through his insistence on blessing the wrong son. The Bible doesn't
delve into the motivation of mother or son, but I'm skeptical of that explanation. Truth is, you or I couldn't foil God's plan if we tried—and, knowing
our weaknesses, what a comfort that is!

Post-ponderings: Identify a time when appearance took precedence over
reality—and honesty—in your family interactions. Has there been resolution?

ESAU:
CONVICTED OF PARENTAL DISPLEASURE

"Seeking approval of others is a way to avoid how deeply we disapprove of ourselves."

—AUTHOR UNKNOWN

"When Esau was forty years old, he married Judith daughter of Beeri the Hittite, and also Basemath daughter of Elon the Hittite. They were a source of grief to Isaac and Rebekah." (Genesis 26:34–35)

Read Genesis 27:41—28:9.

Rebekah's remark to Isaac, to follow, takes me aback: "I'm disgusted with living because of these Hittite women. If Jacob takes a wife from among the women of this land, from Hittite women like these, my life will not be worth living." I recognize this statement as a ploy to get Isaac to condone Jacob's flight to Paddan Aram. Was her implied threat an added barb to ensure that agreement?

It was only after Esau heard the ostensible reason for his father's dispatching Jacob to the old home place that it dawned on him "how displeasing the Canaanite women were to his father Isaac." In a kneejerk reaction this clueless brother "went to Ishmael and married Mahalath, the sister of Nebaioth and daughter of Ishmael son of Abraham, in addition to the wives he already had."

Esau's earlier marriages grieved both his parents. Yet his belated reaction to their displeasure leads me to question whether they had bothered to share their concerns with him at the time of these marriages. It's obvious that Esau, never a great thinker or communicator, did care about his parents' opinion and longed for their approval. Knowing he'd been twice duped by his conniving brother did nothing to enhance his self-esteem. How sad that this ineffective response to their displeasure is the last we hear of Esau until the time of Jacob's return.

Post-ponderings: Have you or someone else been guilty of double standards in your family dealings? Has an action overlooked or accepted in one child been treated as non-negotiable for another? What feelings might this have generated in the children?

CHAPTER 3

THE LAST PATRIARCH—
JACOB

CHAPTER
INTRODUCTION

Ah, Jacob! He's that complicated character on the family tree we don't know quite what to do with. And yet God loved him—passionately and unconditionally. There's no hint of God's loving this flawed patriarch "in spite of" or "anyway." God the Father chose him, just as he chose Abel, and just as he has chosen each of us, without apology or explanation.

Second only in the Bible to David's in terms of the depth and breadth of coverage, Jacob's story is rich and varied; most of it told in the context of family relationships. Because humanity as we know it in our sin-marred world entails so much trial and error, and often such heavy doses of consequence, we relate to this blemished protagonist even if his personality has little in common with our own. We do see growth in his character: beyond the mellowing of age, Jacob comes to terms with God. Even at the end of his story (chapter 4) we may not feel drawn to this petulant dad, but we come close to understanding him as the most fleshed-out individual in biblical history so far.

Jacob Hedges His Bets

"Integrity is not a conditional word. It doesn't blow in the wind or change with the weather. It is your inner image of yourself, and if you look in there and see a man who won't cheat, then you know he never will."
—JOHN D. MACDONALD

"Then Jacob made a vow, saying, 'If God will be with me and will watch over me on this journey I am taking and will give me food to eat and clothes to wear so that I return safely to my father's household, then the Lord will be my God.'" (Genesis 28:20–22)

Read Genesis 28:10–22.
One word that has no place in a statement of commitment or intention is "if." Perhaps a provisional promise makes some sense when we're dealing with inconsistent human beings, but it's inexcusable with reference to God. Despite what appears to be a dawning of good intentions, Jacob had it backward in his ill-conceived vow. There'd been no restrictive clauses in God's pledge to him. God was neither providing himself an "out" nor making demands on Jacob. "I will not leave you," the Lord finishes, "until I have done what I have promised you." (The adverb "until" is a little confusing here, but it in no way implies a limit or end date.)

And yet God honored this flawed patriarch's conditional commitment. God understands us so well that he's willing to accept our provisional faith. How much better for you and me, though, to trust implicitly from a heart that would never consider compromising its integrity. And how much better for the children who follow us to see and model that kind of commitment. They aren't easily duped!

Post-ponderings: Hone in on a promise God has made to you. What have you pledged to him in return, either as part of an official vow (as in baptism or marriage) or in prayer? Do you consider your promise to be unconditional, or have you provided yourself a release clause?

JACOB AND LABAN:
THE CHEAT CHEATED

"Just because something isn't a lie does not mean that it isn't deceptive. A liar knows that he is a liar, but one who speaks mere portions of truth in order to deceive is a craftsman of destruction."
—CRISS JAMI

"When morning came, there was Leah!" (Genesis 29:25)

Read Genesis 29:1–30.
The Jami quote fits to a tee the paired instances of Abraham's partial disclosures to Pharaoh and Abimelek about his relationship with Sarah, his sister/wife (12:10–20; 20). Although the deceit trait comes out more noticeably in Jacob, it was already present in Abraham and is now evident in Laban as well.

Transitioning back into the Jacob story, the six words of the verse above pack a punch, coming like a fist to the face! With the barest economy of words the author registers what must have caused the groom profound shock and dismay following the newlyweds' night in the dark. For better or worse, Jacob was married. How reminiscent of the situation surrounding his receipt of Isaac's blessing! Both outcomes were unintended (from the perspective of the party who wasn't cheating) and irrevocable. There was to be no annulment.

Oh, Laban had an explanation, all right (though it technically passed muster, we're quick to agree that it was hardly *all right!*). The planned nuptials for the real prize were soon to follow—along with seven more years of hard labor. Jacob had it coming. And yet the blatant unfairness—for Jacob, Leah, and Rachel—hits us hard. *When morning came, there was Leah!*—the understated epitome of an unbelievably dirty trick!

Post-ponderings: Who in your opinion got the shortest end of the stick in this transaction? How would Laban's trickery affect each of the duped participants, respectively?

FERTILITY WARS: A FRENZIED NUMBERS GAME

"Jealousy is love in competition."
—TOBA BETA

"[Leah] said, 'Now at last my husband will become attached to me, because I have borne him three sons.'" (Genesis 29:34)

"[Rachel] became pregnant and gave birth to a son and said, 'God has taken away my disgrace.' She named him Joseph, and said, 'May the LORD add to me another son.'" (Genesis 30:23–24)

Read Genesis 29:31—30:24.

Vying for the love of a shared husband is prominent in the Old Testament accounts of polygamous marriages. In the case of these intractable sister wives—literally sisters this time!—the author sets the scene succinctly: "When the LORD saw that Leah was not loved, he enabled her to conceive." What a beautiful statement of God's concern for the underdog! Leah's initial response to this consolation prize is poignant: "It is because the LORD has seen my misery. Surely my husband will love me now." How readily we convince ourselves of that which we yearn to believe! Because Leah had no other options if this wish were to prove a fantasy, she held to it tenaciously through the births of six sons and a daughter.

Rachel's demand of Jacob following her sister's fourth delivery—"Give me children, or I'll die!"—is met with exasperation: "Am I in the place of God, who has kept you from having children?" Hardly a sensitive response! Her next move, followed almost immediately by a similar ploy from Leah, echoes Sarah before her, startling us with a sensation of déjà vu: "Here is Bilhah, my servant. Sleep with her so that she can bear children for me and *I too can build a family through her*" (emphasis added). And so began in earnest the frenetic numbers wars.

Genesis 30:24 is anticlimactic. *"Another* son?" we ask, incredulous. *So soon?* Like Hannah after her (1 Samuel 1), this adored wife would see herself as second class as long as the offspring count was in her rival's favor. Nothing the doting husbands could do in either case to confirm their special love would have offset the shame. Tragically, the envy on the part of the less loved but more fruitful other wife in each story was acute; in Leah's case the desperate bid was not merely for her husband's fidelity but for his favor.

Post-ponderings: We have no reason to believe these sisters had been in competition beforehand. When, if ever, in your experience have family members been set up in a no-win situation?

LABAN AND HIS DAUGHTERS: DETERIORATING RELATIONSHIPS

"I know for me the subject of how to be in a relationship is precious and complicated and challenging. It wouldn't be right to make it look too easy."
—HELEN HUNT

"Then Rachel and Leah replied, 'Do we still have any share in the inheritance of our father's estate? Does he not regard us as foreigners? Not only has he sold us, but he has used up what was paid for us. Surely all the wealth that God took away from our father belongs to us and our children. So do whatever God has told you.'"
(Genesis 31:14–16)

Read Genesis 31:1–18.

In one area these rival sisters stood as a united front: their pining for love and evidence of value from their calculating father. By this point any hope for a demonstration of his affection had been dashed; cynicism over their joint lot moved both in the direction of their less heartless mutual husband.

Laban didn't bother with pretense when it came to his lack of regard for his daughters. A quote from Luigi Pirandello suggests to me his none too subtle write-off: "I present myself to you in a form suitable to the relationship I wish to achieve with you." *Take is or leave it, daughters of mine!* I hear. *What you see is all you can expect to get.*

It wasn't that there had been flagrant abuse, but the truth was all too painfully in their faces nonetheless. "In matters of truth and justice," notes Albert Einstein, "there is no difference between large and small problems, for issues concerning the treatment of people are all the same." Unrequited love from a parent carries permanent repercussions. No matter how old she gets or how long the offending parent has been gone from the scene, this issue will stay with the individual for life.

Post-ponderings: No matter how healthy your relationship has been with one or both of your parents, chances are you carry some unresolved resentment. What would it take to confront the matter with a goal of leaving it behind? You can do this with or without your parent's involvement.

RACHEL:
THE CASE OF THE PILFERED GODS

"Security is a strange thing, a myth that the brain allows in exchange for a brief moment of peace."
—ALLESANDRA TORRE

"When Laban had gone to shear his sheep, Rachel stole her father's household gods. Moreover, Jacob deceived Laban the Aramean by not telling him he was running away." (Genesis 31:19–20)

Read Genesis 31:19–37.
Evidently that deception gene had been passed along not only to Jacob but also to his cousin/wife. By this point the compounded treachery was getting decidedly out of hand: "*Moreover*, Jacob deceived Laban" (emphasis added). The complicated web the actors were weaving was becoming hopelessly tangled.

Rachel, not yet free of her pagan background, wanted tangible gods for protection and security on the long, uncertain journey. "We all have security blankets in this world," observes Rob Thurman. "Some are just sharper than others." In fact, there was nothing soft about this whole affair.

It's possible Rachel had come to believe in Jacob's God by this point but wanted the household gods as backup. Yet we know that Jacob himself, still tied to his provisional vow (see the reflection on Genesis 28:10–22), was dangling that seemingly innocuous "if" before God's face, challenging him to come through and prove himself.

It's difficult for us to comprehend blatant idolatry, but it goes without saying that we do the same thing in our more sophisticated way, layering security blankets one over another in the hope of a failsafe. On another level, there's something ironic about Rachel's last-minute "gotcha!"—her symbolic act of defiance before leaving her father's household forever.

Post-ponderings: Pause to reflect on this passage within its context, considering the many levels of deceit, moving in different directions, that underlie the action. Are there instances in your family life when deception has multiplied in this way?

JACOB AND LABAN:
UNEASY TRYST AND BEGRUDGING TRUST

"Distrust is like a vicious fire that keeps going and going, even put out, it will reignite itself, devouring the good with the bad, and still feeding on empty."
—ANTHONY LICCIONE

"'This heap is a witness, and this pillar is a witness, that I will not go past this heap to your side to harm you and that you will not go past this heap and pillar to my side to harm me.'" (Genesis 31:52)

Read Genesis 31:38–55.
These men were pretty evenly matched. Two individuals so alike in their calculating, advantage-seeking natures could never have moved beyond an uneasy dance of foil and counterfoil. How could either trust the other when self-trust was such an iffy proposition? How ironic that both uncle/father-in-law and nephew/son-in-law seem to have understood the stakes and realized the necessity of a pact to which both would have to remain uncharacteristically true. From a mutually selfish standpoint, their security was at stake.

Author L. M. Montgomery warns, "Never be silent with persons you love and distrust . . . Silence betrays." An interesting and tragic combination, love and distrust. The degree to which that first element played in to the picture is unknown, though presumably not all the vibes were negative between the two men. At the very least there was grudging respect on both sides for the other's cunning.

A suspicious nature, coupled with a propensity toward deceit, makes it difficult to trust God. Just as it's hard for one who has never experienced father love to love the Father, so the person who has never been trustworthy will balk at the call to trust. Perhaps this instance served as a steppingstone in Jacob's life and experience, moving him in the direction of that truce with God that would finally come at Peniel (32:22–32).

Post-ponderings: Take the time to read or browse the Genesis 32 passage, immediately above (covered in the next reflection), keeping Jacob's wily ways and lifetime of experience in mind.

Jacob and Esau: Reunion

"Esau ran to meet Jacob and embraced him; he threw his arms around his neck and kissed him. And they wept." (Genesis 33:4)

Read Genesis 32:1—33:11.
We see no evidence on Esau's part of anything but ingenuousness, though this straight shooter was about to be duped again. The Bible doesn't fill in for us the background of the animosity between Esau's descendants, the Edomites, and their Israelite cousins, but this was evidently to be a belated backlash. No matter how forgiving the easy-going Esau may have been, his proud descendants would remember and resent his ill treatment at his brother's hand.

Isaac had predicted as much, informing Esau after Jacob's pilfering of the blessing, "You will live by the sword and you will serve your brother. But when you grow restless, you will throw his yoke from off your neck" (27:40). This restlessness was evidently not in Esau's nature, but his descendants were only too happy to run with it.

In this case reunion didn't imply union. There had never been union between these opposite fraternal twins, nor would there be. Jacob's desire for Esau's forgiveness had everything to do with the value he placed on his own skin, not with true repentance for the wrongs he had inflicted on his gullible twin. God would ultimately hold Edom responsible for her oppression of her relatives (check out the short book of Obadiah), but he would endure this thorn in Israel's side with patience for a long time first. Yet there's a part of us that understands where Edom was coming from.

Post-ponderings: When have you forgiven someone outwardly—maybe even convinced yourself you were truly letting go of bygones—but maintained some smoldering animosity or suspicion deep within?

JACOB WITH ESAU:
POINTLESS DECEIT

"So that day Esau started on his way back to Seir. Jacob, however, went to Sukkoth, where he built a place for himself." (Genesis 33:16–17)

Read Genesis 33:12–20.
Jacob hadn't the slightest intention of pitching camp within sight of his long-estranged twin. And not doing so was his prerogative. Perhaps he'd had enough of the cloying closeness of living on his father-in-law's property, their lives intertwined in so many unhealthy ways. He might also have had some lingering suspicion that it might not take much to set off Esau, who had once vowed to kill him (27:41–45).

Rebekah had known her placid first-born well enough to recognize that, despite what may have been a low flashpoint, Esau's anger would soon fizzle. Her counsel to Jacob at that time: "Stay with [my brother Laban] for a while until your brother's fury subsides. When your brother is no longer angry with you and *forgets what you did to him*, I'll send word for you to come back from there" (emphasis added). Rebekah died before that summons could take place. Now there was only Esau, and the chronically distrusting Jacob would never have felt comfortable in his vicinity. Could it even have occurred to him that Esau, unlike the canny Laban, would be an all too easy target to dupe again?

There was nothing wrong with Jacob's reasoning, and he could have opted for full disclosure about his misgivings. Habitual liars often fall into a trap of random, gratuitous lying, lying for no apparent or valid reason—deceiving just because they can. Jacob had made a major spiritual break-through at Peniel (32:22–32), but long-established patterns of behavior die hard.

Post-ponderings: We read in Genesis 35:27–28 that Jacob finally made it home to his father, Isaac, who lived to be 180 years old—after which Jacob and Esau buried him. Are there siblings or other relatives with whom you interact minimally? Are you mutually civil, while avoiding intimacy? Is this the best-case scenario under the circumstances?

HAMOR AND JACOB: ATTRACTIVE PROPOSITION?

"There is a very fine line between loving life and being greedy for it."
—MAYA ANGELOU

"Hamor said to them, 'My son Shechem has his heart set on your daughter. Please give her to him as his wife. Intermarry with us; give us your daughters and take our daughters for yourselves.'" (Genesis 34:8–9)

Read Genesis 34:1–12.

There's a frustrating unknown in the beginning of this ugly story: Was Hamor aware of the evil his son had perpetrated on Dinah? The manners of father and son are impeccable in their approach to Jacob. Is this an implicit denial that the incident has taken place? Or an attempt on Hamor's part to appease the overindulged prince . . . or shove the elephant under the rug? It's hard to distinguish the "good guys" from their counterparts (as we'll see soon enough, there were to be atrocities on both sides!).

I wonder whether Jacob might have been tempted by Hamor's proposition had he been unaware of the underlying circumstances. And while I'm at it—the wondering, that is—why did Jacob, *knowing as he did* of Dinah's defilement—wait for his sons to return from the field before acting? He'd never been the indecisive sort and was still a vigorous man. Might he actually have considered compromising his daughter's dignity and reputation to take advantage of an opportunity?

It seems clear that Jacob was acting—or deliberately failing to act—on his own. As we'll see in the next reflection, though, God was at work behind the scenes, ensuring that his people would escape dissolution into a pagan culture. This is one of many biblical examples of the Lord bringing good out of evil. But that in no way exonerates his own from responsibility for wrongdoing.

Post-ponderings: The beginning of this story necessitates some reading between the lines. About what details do you wonder?

SIMEON AND LEVI: AVENGING BROTHERS

"Some men simply refuse to appear insulted. But then, having felt the sting from the slap on their cheek, know just where to slip the knife, their smile never fading."
—ANDREW LEVKOFF

"Then Jacob said to Simeon and Levi, 'You have brought trouble on me by making me obnoxious to the Canaanites and Perizzites, the people living in this land. . . .' But they replied, 'Should he have treated our sister like a prostitute?'"
(Genesis 34:30–31)

Read Genesis 34:13–31.

The problem wasn't just that the brothers exacted revenge. It was the smooth-talking, underhanded manner in which they went about it. Their resorting to a sacred rite reserved for *identification of* God's covenant people in order to indispose these outsiders was abhorrent to God, and should have been to them. There can be no doubt that Hamor, Shechem, and the other Hivites were up to no good, but Jacob's sons, and particularly Dinah's brothers Simeon and Levi, proved to be no better.

Jacob's immediate concern had more to do with becoming repulsive to the locals than with any scruple about the revenge or its method. On the basis of their brutal deed, however, Simeon and Levi were to be excluded from his blessing prior to his death (49:5–7). In Jacob's words, "Cursed be their anger, so fierce, and their fury, so cruel!" Had the aged patriarch finally come to recognize the true significance and implications of this heinous deed?

Still in a wondering mode (see the last reflection), it's interesting to speculate how this incident might have turned out had Jacob handled it firmly but discreetly in his initial dealing with Hamor and his spoiled son ("the most honored of all his father's family").

Early biblical history portrays some unbelievable insensitivity on the part of fathers to their daughters. In this case and, much later, that of David's daughter Tamar (2 Samuel 13:1–19), it was brothers, not fathers, who did the avenging. To what might this anomaly be attributed? Were these young men proving themselves to be in some sense more righteous than their fathers?

Post-ponderings: Why do you suppose Dinah hadn't come home earlier from Shechem's house? If she were being held there against her will, how do you suspect Jacob found out what had happened?

HOUSECLEANING

"Times of transition are strenuous, but I love them. They are an opportunity to purge, rethink priorities, and be intentional about new habits. We can make our new normal any way we want."
—KRISTIN ARMSTRONG

"So Jacob said to his household and to all who were with him, 'Get rid of the foreign gods you have with you, and purify yourselves and change your clothes.' . . . So they gave Jacob all the foreign gods they had and the rings in their ears, and Jacob buried them under the oak at Shechem." (Genesis 35:2, 4)

Read Genesis 35:1–15.
Jacob and his complicated family have remained a work in progress—and the drama is hardly over. At this juncture God approaches the family head. The Lord directs Jacob to settle in Bethel—the very spot at which God had made promises to him a lifetime earlier in a dream—and build an altar there. "I will give you and your descendants the land on which you are lying. . . . I will bring you back to this land," God had pledged to the fleeing young man. "How awesome is this place!" the younger Jacob had exclaimed. "This is none other than the house of God; this is the gate of heaven" (28:17).

Jacob had at that time set up as a pillar the stone on which he had lain his head, pouring oil on it to memorialize the occasion. This was the same night he had made his provisional vow to God (see the reflection on Genesis 28:10–22). An evolving Jacob has now come full circle—back to the gate of heaven. This is to be his home, and God fittingly changes his name to Israel. Once again God makes promises, and this time Jacob believes. Gone are the hedging and hesitation, the restlessness and advantage seeking.

Resolution. A fresh start. A clean page. Not for Jacob only but for his extensive household. The nation of Israel will struggle with idolatry and other egregious sins from exodus to exile, just as the man Israel has struggled. But for now the clan is unified in its allegiance to God. Israel, the patriarch, has emerged a changed man. We see no evidence of deceit or ungodliness from this point on.

Post-ponderings: When have you experienced an identifiable turnaround in your personal or family life? What brought about the change, and how has it affected your life from that point on?

RACHEL: DEPARTURE

"When you have come to the edge of all light that you know and are about to drop off into the darkness of the unknown, FAITH is knowing one of two things will happen: There will be something solid to stand on or you will be taught to fly."
—PATRICK OVERTON

"As [Rachel] was having great difficulty in childbirth, the midwife said to her, 'Don't despair, for you have another son.' As she breathed her last—for she was dying—she named her son Ben-Oni. But his father named him Benjamin."
(Genesis 35:17–18)

Read Genesis 35:16–20.

In light of the household's spiritual revitalization, we can approach Rachel's demise with a lighter heart. Presumably she who had so recently stolen her father's household idols had committed her future, brief as it was to be, to the God of Israel. What greater comfort for any of us than to know our loved one has died in the Lord?

And what a beautiful irony—concluding the part of the salvation story focusing on the third patriarch—that this long-awaited son of Israel made his appearance in Ephrath—Bethlehem! The name selected by his mother, "son of my trouble," is overridden by her husband, and Jacob's twelfth son enters the world as "son of my right hand."

How often in life don't endings transition seamlessly into beginnings! Rachel's bittersweet passage coincided with the promise of new life. That's the way God has designed it. Particularly when there are growing children in a family, progressive graduations (endings of one kind or another) become indistinguishable from commencements.

It's the same way with our passage from earthly life into the final phase of eternity. Each of us, and every family, experiences loss as generations come and go, caught up in time's inexorable forward thrust. But for the individual making the transition, time and decay, disappointment and sorrow, come to an abrupt halt. In this case, how impeccable God's timing in light of the recommitment at the beginning of the chapter. And, from a spiritual standpoint, what an auspicious beginning for Benjamin.

Post-ponderings: Are you among the fortunate believers whose loved ones have died in the Lord? What difference does that make when you remember them?

CHAPTER 4

THE JOSEPH STORY

CHAPTER
INTRODUCTION

Joseph's story is riveting, although much of its adult aspect doesn't incorporate family engagement, the focus of this book. Standing between his great-grandfather Abraham and Moses, Joseph takes his place as the second great hero of the faith covered in the Pentateuch. Despite his early indiscretion—unwittingly antagonizing his envious older brothers—and in stark contrast to his father, Jacob, Joseph is a man of unwavering and impeccable integrity.

Yet the family portions of the narrative, focused on his relationships with his brothers and, to a lesser extent, his father, make for fascinating reading. The Joseph account sets the stage for Israel's exodus, though Joseph's own story ends with satisfying resolution for Israel's (Jacob's) expanding family.

JACOB AND HIS SONS: TOXIC FAVORITISM

"Disfavoured children tend to have lower self-esteem, which can either make them try harder or give up too easily, (and also makes them rageaholics who spend a lifetime 'collecting injustices,' a mode of primary thinking and interpreting)."
—JAN ANDERSON

"Israel [Jacob] loved Joseph more than any of his other sons, because he had been born to him in his old age, and he made an ornate robe for him. When his brothers saw that their father loved him more than any of them, they hated him." (Genesis 37:3–4)

Read Genesis 37:1–9.
Disfavored children. Rageaholics and injustice collectors . . . times ten. The outcome of this lethal family arrangement couldn't have been positive. It hadn't occurred to me to explain Jacob's favoritism of this son in terms of Joseph's arrival in his father's old age. (This would have been even truer of Benjamin, on whom Jacob also doted.) I've always attributed this preferential treatment to both these boys being Rachel's and suspect there is more than a little truth to this. Jacob couldn't help his feelings; the problem came with acting on them. That multi-colored coat must have acted on those unremarkable older brothers like a red flag dangled before a bull.

If we're honest with ourselves, we as parents may be drawn to one child more than another (think back to Jacob's own upbringing in a household divided into distinct parent/child factions). This happens for any number of reasons, from personalities to shared interests and abilities to physical characteristics to gender to birth order to . . . whatever. Continuously berating ourselves over our natural inclination does no good. As with any feelings, the way we conduct ourselves (our behavior) makes the difference. When we think of love as a verb, we equip ourselves to love the more difficult or less appealing child equally with any others.

Post-ponderings: If you're parenting more than one child, you already know with which you feel more comfortable or from whom you derive more pleasure. Assess how well you're doing at keeping your feelings private (except, of course, for your honest disclosure with your spouse—who already knows anyway!).

JACOB'S INACTION:
KEEPING IT IN MIND

"I couldn't decide whether to take a nap or not, so I did what I always do when thinking over a decision—I slept on it."
—JAROD KINTZ

"His brothers were jealous of him, but his father kept the matter in mind."
(Genesis 37:11)

Read Genesis 37:10–11.
This indecision—or deferral of a decision—is the same trait Jacob had manifested with Dinah's crisis or Abraham with the taunting Ishmael. Unfortunately, time was of the essence; keeping the matter in mind was hardly conducive to an expedient resolution. Circumstances in so volatile a situation have a way of avalanching out of control.

In all fairness to Jacob, his "keeping" (mulling over) the matter may have been tantamount to Mary's "pondering" (Luke 2:19) following the birth of her miracle son. There were profound spiritual implications in both cases (foreshadowing the direction in which salvation history was moving), and I don't want to discount them or misread the author's intent in Genesis 37:11. Still, Jacob's immediate and decisive intervention might have circumvented a crisis.

Life's continuous flux affords both "a time to be silent and a time to speak" (Ecclesiastes 3:7). There are many occasions for which a pregnant silence is exactly the right response. Unfortunately, this wasn't one of them.

Post-ponderings: The principle voiced by Solomon in Ecclesiastes 3 is particularly apropos to family interaction. Identify scenarios from your experience in which silence or speaking out, respectively, were appropriate.

JOSEPH AND HIS BROTHERS: BUMBLED REVENGE

"Family quarrels are bitter things. They don't go by any rules. They're not like aches or wounds; they're more like splits in the skin that won't heal because there's not enough material."
—F. SCOTT FITZGERALD

"Joseph went after his brothers and found them near Dothan. But they saw him in the distance, and before he reached them, they plotted to kill him." (Genesis 37:17–18)

Read Genesis 37:12–30.
Judah's remark near the end of the passage affords a glimmer of hope: "After all, he is our brother." When I hear these words I expect a dawning of sense, a trace of empathy. But *selling* this seventeen-year-old half-brother versus killing him? What kind of choice was that?

Truth is, a shared family lineage is no predictor, and certainly no guarantee, of a loving relationship. In fact, this kind of bond, whether based on blood, adoption, or marriage into an extended family, can instead be a catalyst for problems as clashing personalities with differing agendas and competing interests and goals resist melding to settle instead for the burning friction of forced togetherness.

Damage control falls after the fact to the oldest, Reuben. Author Whitney Otto refers to this brother's difficult position as the "brotherhood of the firstborn . . . the expectations that run too high: being the bridge between adults and children, one foot in either place and the accompanying hollow lonely feeling of being nowhere."

Post-ponderings: Judah was wavering between two wrongs, two lose-lose situations, as today's lingo would assess it. What did the brothers stand to gain either way? Certainly not clear consciences.

JACOB:
INCONSOLABLE DAD

"The worst type of crying wasn't the kind everyone could see—the wailing on street corners, the tearing at clothes. No, the worst kind happened when your soul wept and no matter what you did, there was no way to comfort it. A section withered and became a scar on the part of your soul that survived."
—KATIE MCGARRY

"Jacob tore his clothes, put on sackcloth and mourned for his son many days. All his sons and daughters came to comfort him, but he refused to be comforted." (Genesis 37:34–35)

Read Genesis 37:31–35.
I'm reminded of this story when I read the later account of David's mourning for Absalom (2 Samuel 19:1–4). No, the situations aren't parallel in terms either of the character of the lost sons or the duration of the public grief, but the effect on the survivors must have been equally devastating—a knife twisted into a raw wound.

It appears that a subconscious identity transfer may have taken place in the aging patriarch's heart following the loss of his beloved Rachel. There's no indication that Joseph was an exceptional child. And the question arises in my mind whether Benjamin, the expiring Rachel's final contribution to the family tree, may have suffered from stunted emotional growth related to his protected—and protracted—upbringing.

Grief is intensely personal, and it's handled differently by each individual. But unresolved grief can be a canker as a family struggles to move on. There's a degree of selfishness involved when grief is indulged beyond a reasonable point—particularly if children are involved. It occurs to me that this is especially true for us as people of the resurrection.

Post-ponderings: What losses has your family together experienced? How has each of you handled the grieving process? How have you helped each other through?

JUDAH AND TAMAR: DOUBLE STANDARD EXPOSED

"Since we live in a world that relies on women to be tidy in all ways, to be quiet and obedient and agreeable and available (but never aggressive), those of us who color outside of the lines get called sluts. And that word is meant to keep us in line."
—JACLYN FRIEDMAN

"Judah recognized [his cord and staff] and said, 'She is more righteous than I, since I wouldn't give her to my son Shelah.' And he did not sleep with her again." (Genesis 38:26)

Read Genesis 38.
The rules surrounding levirate marriage were constricting: "If brothers are living together and one of them dies without a son, his widow must not marry outside the family. Her husband's brother shall take her and marry her and fulfill the duty of a brother-in-law to her. The first son she bears shall carry on the name of the dead brother so that his name will not be blotted out from Israel" (Deuteronomy 25:5–6, but see also 7–10).

Why is this seemingly parenthetical incident included—almost intruded, it would seem—in salvation history? This close-up of Judah provides a stark contrast to the character of Joseph. And the birth of Perez, reminiscent of the "drama" surrounding Rebekah's pregnancy with Esau and Jacob, provides a link (including yet another insertion of Canaanite blood into the family line) in the genealogy of Jesus.

That double standard in the Genesis stories involving the treatment of men versus women comes again to the fore. And the picture in some ways hasn't changed. A touch point may once again apply to us more as members of society than of families. Does our culture expect a higher standard of morality in women than in men? Are we quicker to excuse the grieving widower for sexual indiscretion than the woman with whom he is involved? Do we assume the woman is less driven by passion, better able to control her impulses, and therefore more accountable?

Post-ponderings: Has sexual sin touched your family or your congregation directly? Short of excusing either party, has the response included an outpouring of Christian love and forgiveness?

JACOB'S MATURING SONS:
THE MALIGNANCY OF UNVOICED REMORSE

"The greatest day in your life and mine is when we take total responsibility for our attitudes. That's the day we truly grow up."
—JOHN C. MAXWELL

"Then they said to one another, 'Surely we are being punished because of our brother. We saw how distressed he was when he pleaded with us for his life, but we would not listen; that's why this distress has come on us.'" (Genesis 42:21)

Read Genesis 42:1–24.
Time has passed, with only the Judah/Tamar interlude to keep us up on activities on the home front. Joseph's own amazing story has proceeded, but we pick up the family thread here in chapter 42. It takes only a few verses to begin to ascertain the state of the relational dynamics, first between father and sons and later among the ten. Listen: "When Jacob learned that there was grain in Egypt, he said to his sons, *'Why do you just keep looking at each other?* . . . I have heard that there is grain in Egypt'" (emphasis added). We detect sarcasm in Jacob's tone, something comparable to "Why do you just stand there like ninnies?" Verse 21, above, allows us to listen in on the brothers' shared dismay. The tension is palpable and ongoing, a slow torture for the guilt-ridden sons. Something has to give, and soon.

But the noose only tightens as the chapter progresses. How ironic the brothers' cowed response to interrogation by this intimidating stranger: "Your servants are honest men." There's an element of truth in their declaration—picking up from the point of a particular deceit they have no hope of outliving. Remorse is real and operative in their lives; they've been reduced to miserable shells of what they could have been, first by the jealousy of offended youth and later by a deep-seated shame they can't slough off.

Post-ponderings: It's easy for us as humans to entrench ourselves so deeply in deceit that we face diminishing returns when we finally consider coming clean. When, if ever, has this been an issue for you?

JOSEPH'S BROTHERS: LATE-BLOOMING EMPATHY

"Next time you're faced with a choice, do the right thing. It hurts everyone less in the long run."
—WENDELIN VAN DRAANEN

"Their father Jacob said to them, 'You have deprived me of my children. Joseph is no more and Simeon is no more, and now you want to take Benjamin. Everything is against me!' Then Reuben said to his father, 'You may put both of my sons to death if I do not bring him back to you. Entrust him to my care, and I will bring him back.' But Jacob said, 'My son will not go down there with you; his brother is dead and he is the only one left. If harm comes to him on the journey you are taking, you will bring my gray head down to the grave in sorrow.'" (Genesis 42:36–38)

Read Genesis 42:25—43:14.

"You have deprived me . . ." Calloused though it sounds, this accusation had a basis in reality never dreamed by the aged patriarch. But Benjamin being "the *only* one left"? That must have been insufferable to the penitent, and now badly frightened, older brothers.

To their credit, the ten have never lost respect for their tactless sire. We read in this chapter of Reuben's shocking offer. A suggestion to a *grandfather*? How could this even be possible? And in the next chapter Judah, while stopping short of offering his life or that of his own sons, attempts to conciliate: "Send the boy [Benjamin was hardly a youth at this juncture!] along with me . . . I myself will guarantee his safety; you can hold me personally responsible for him. If I do not bring him back to you and set him here before you, I will bear the blame before you all my life.'"

Not that such blame bearing wasn't already operative in his life! The brothers had technically gotten away with their ruse, but they were continuing to pay dearly with every passing day.

Post-ponderings: When have you, or someone else in your family, attempted to offset or cancel out a wrong by "committing" rights? Was this effective?

JOSEPH AND HIS BROTHERS: THE ULTIMATE TEST

"It has been my experience that guilt can burst through the smallest breach and cover the landscape, and abide in it in pools and danknesses, just as native as water."
—MARILYNNE ROBINSON

"The cup was found in Benjamin's sack. At this, they tore their clothes. They then all loaded their donkeys and returned to the city. . . . Joseph said to them, 'What is this you have done?' . . . 'What can we say to my lord?' Judah replied . . . 'God has uncovered your servants' guilt.'" (Genesis 44:12–13, 15–16)

Read Genesis 43:15—44:34.

The pathos throbbing through this dramatic story is almost tangible. Joseph's final test may seem cruel, but it was necessary for him to read his brothers' character. And they come through with flying colors.

How the plea of the penitent Judah must have wrung Joseph's soul: "'Now then, please let your servant remain here as my lord's slave in place of the boy, and let the boy return with his brothers. How can I go back to my father if the boy is not with me? No! Do not let me see the misery that would come on my father.'" How eye-opening that a tortured Judah couldn't deal with the thought of inflicting additional anguish on his father. Gone entirely was any twinge of jealousy, replaced by a tenacious and even desperate determination to protect Jacob from further pain.

The scene is set for the pivotal moment to come in chapter 45. One of the principal players to this point has been guilt. The guilt-ridden individual can move in at least a couple of directions. On the one hand, undisclosed or unresolved guiltiness can shrivel people's souls and poison, not to mention imprison their personalities. On the other, it can lead to regret, followed by remorse and culminated by repentance—the trajectory taken by these ten brothers.

Post-ponderings: Recall a time when you've dealt with the effects of guilt. How did you handle it? How was the matter resolved?

JOSEPH AND HIS BROTHERS: GRACE UNVEILED

"Christianity is not primarily a moral code but a grace-laden mystery; it is not essentially a philosophy of love but a love affair; it is not keeping rules with clenched fists but receiving a gift with open hands."
—BRENNAN MANNING

"Joseph could no longer control himself before all his attendants, and he cried out, 'Have everyone leave my presence!' So there was no one with Joseph when he made himself known to his brothers. And he wept so loudly that the Egyptians heard him, and Pharaoh's household heard about it. Joseph said to his brothers, 'I am Joseph! Is my father still living?'" (Genesis 45:1–3)

Read Genesis 45:1–15.
These brothers have paid dearly for their impulsive mistake, but in their minds the axe has yet to drop, and they wait in wary discomfort. Joseph's unexpected revelation hits them like a brick, the initial shock inducing terror. A tinge of relief begins to prickle their skin as it dawns on them that this intimidating stranger speaks reassuringly. Still they remain dumbfounded, hardly able to process what they're hearing.

We see in this chapter the lead-in to a "happily-ever-after" close (at least for this generation and those immediately to follow). We've been dealing throughout the Joseph account with a necessary step in salvation history; still, we know God doesn't manipulate people to act in ways that are contrary to their natures. In this beautiful turnabout, we see natures retouched by his grace.

This story is, first and foremost, about grace. Grace, as expressed by C. S. Lewis in his classic *Surprised by Grace*, is always a surprise. Because it's amazing and undeserved—which is precisely what it's all about. There's a major disconnect between what the world knows and expects of life and the influx of unexpected grace into our experience. That's true whether this grace is manifested directly from God or comes via one of his representatives on Earth.

Post-ponderings: Think of an instance in your family life when grace has triumphed over circumstances that could have led to a quite different outcome. God's grace surely came into play, but did you detect "secondary" grace coming from one or more of the players?

Joseph and His Brothers: Admonition for the Journey

"It does take great maturity to understand that the opinion we are arguing for is merely the hypothesis we favor, necessarily imperfect, probably transitory, which only very limited minds can declare to be a certainty or a truth."
—MILAN KUNDERA

"Then he sent his brothers away, and as they were leaving he said to them, 'Don't quarrel on the way!'" (Genesis 45:24)

Read Genesis 45:16–24.
Why did Joseph feel a need to counsel his older brothers not to bicker on the way home? It seems unlikely at this stage that he was thrusting one last jab based on the arrogance of his earlier, dreamer days. Was this admonition based on his prior knowledge of their characters, his recollection of earlier days when they'd vied for their father's attention and approval? Or was he concerned about their differing reactions to the astounding turn of events? Perhaps worried that they'd rehash that pivotal event of so many years earlier, laying fresh blame or disagreeing as to how *now* to explain the blood-stained coat and explain away their concocted story? We don't know, but the inclusion of this detail is provocative.

"Discussion is an exchange of knowledge; argument an exchange of ignorance," observes Robert Quillen. Yet how easily we as family members resort to the latter, whether as spouses, with extended family members, or as parents with our children. It's probably safe to say that no one ever wins an argument. The individual with the stronger personality, superior ability to articulate, or higher authority will at some point shut down the weaker party, but the end result will likely be a glowering resentment.

Post-ponderings: Think back to a recent argument among family members, whether or not you were involved. What, if anything, was accomplished?

DENOUEMENT:
JACOB'S BLESSING REALIZED

"We must never tolerate an instant's unbelief as to the goodness of the Lord; whatever else may be questioned, this is absolutely certain, that Jehovah is good; His dispensations may vary, but His nature is always the same."
—CHARLES H. SPURGEON

"Jacob said to Joseph, 'God Almighty appeared to me at Luz in the land of Canaan, and there he blessed me and said to me, "I am going to make you fruitful and increase your numbers. I will make you a community of peoples, and I will give this land as an everlasting possession to your descendants after you."'" (Genesis 48:3–4)

Read Genesis 45:25—46:7.
Jacob, it would seem, fell short of the mark in every area of his family life—as a son, a brother, a nephew, a husband, a son-in-law, a father, a grandfather, . . . and, most importantly, a God-fearer. We wonder whether he may have replaced deceit with bitterness and caustic resignation only after he grew too old and disillusioned for shenanigans.

Yet it isn't up to us to judge either how well Jacob performed or what was on his heart, beyond what Scripture tells us. We can only observe that he was a flawed character deeply loved by the God who had twice made promises to him at Bethel (Genesis 28; 35) in instances bracketing his sojourn in Paddan Aram. This was the same God who now spoke to him in a vision en route to Egypt, reassuring the patriarch of his blessing and reiterating his promises.

What tremendous hope this can afford each of us! "Can God be counted on?" asks Ann Voskamp rhetorically. "Count your blessings and find out how many of his bridges have already held." You and I, each in our own way, are no better than Jacob. And yet God's goodness and faithfulness to us are unconditional—based on who *he* is, not on who we are.

Post-ponderings: When, if ever, have you doubted God's goodness?

PHARAOH WITH JACOB:
DIGNITY EMBODIED

"Never take a person's dignity: it is worth everything to them, and nothing to you."
—FRANK X. BARRON

"Pharaoh asked [Jacob], 'How old are you?' And Jacob said to Pharaoh, 'The years of my pilgrimage are a hundred and thirty. My years have been few and difficult, and they do not equal the years of the pilgrimage of my fathers.' Then Jacob blessed Pharaoh and went out from his presence." (Genesis 47:7–10)

Read Genesis 47:1–12.
The Egyptians despised shepherds, but Pharaoh dealt with Joseph's elderly father graciously and with the utmost dignity (and Jacob reciprocated in kind). The possibility exists that this particular pharaoh, not an Egyptian by birth but part of a line of conquering rulers from a Semitic (and therefore sheepherding) background, was embracing common ground between himself and the aging patriarch by offering him and his family the best land in Egypt on which to graze their flocks. At any rate, his attitudes and actions, both here and from the beginning of the story, before he knew Joseph, are beyond reproach.

Biblical history frequently portrays unbelieving rulers and leaders in an excellent light, from stories we've considered so far (think of Abraham with an earlier pharaoh and with Abimelek) to later accounts of Hiram, Nebuchadnezzar, Darius, Cyrus, and representatives of the Roman government in Paul's day. Such rulers unknowingly acted as God's instruments, yes. But all of us encounter exemplary people in our lives or communities—people who manifest the traits we associate with godliness . . . without being godly!

God has allowed a measure of residual goodness in unbelievers to make life tolerable for all in a sinful world. He has imprinted on each human heart a moral awareness, an innate ability to distinguish right from wrong, along with an inkling of the requirements of grace and civility needed for humans to get along.

Post-ponderings: When have you encountered incredible goodness in an individual, couple, or family who makes no profession of Christ? How have you accounted for this?

JOSEPH AND HIS BROTHERS: FINAL REASSURANCE

"At the end of the day, a loving family should find everything forgivable."
—MARK V. OLSEN

"Joseph said to [his brothers], 'Don't be afraid. Am I in the place of God? You intended to harm me, but God intended it for good to accomplish what is now being done, the saving of many lives.'" (Genesis 50:19–20)

Read Genesis 50:15–21.

The Olsen quote expresses a noble thought, but the addition of "should" to any verb makes for an iffy proposition. As with many Bible stories, the fulfillment of salvation history was at stake. God wasn't about to leave that "should" to chance, but for us to write off Joseph's grace as a foregone conclusion would be simplistic. Joseph, a human being who was in no way acting on autopilot, had a choice whether or not to forgive. As we all do.

Hindsight. Retrospect. Putting forth the effort to take an honest gaze in a backward direction can make a huge difference in our lives. How often doesn't the will of God bounce into focus for us only after the fact? I'm referring not only to situations and crossroads in life that call for a decision but also to those tragedies and setbacks that can derail us to the point of doubting God's good intentions for us.

We aren't told whether Joseph had any doubts during those trying early years in Egypt. What we do see here is that he had taken that long look backward and recognized the working of God's gracious hand. Still, understanding and forgiving are two different steps in reconciling ourselves to a new reality. It's possible for us to intuit and accept God's purpose in an evil we've suffered without forgiving the one who has hurt us. When that person is outside the family, we may opt to avoid or shun her, or our paths might simply not cross again. But when it's one of our own—as is so often the case—the situation gets a little more dicey.

Post-ponderings: From which family member are you withholding forgiveness? Even if the circumstances are "forgotten" and you're civil or loving to one another, what difference could your forgiveness make?

CHAPTER 5

MOSES AND THE EXODUS, PART 1

CHAPTER
INTRODUCTION

Moses' personal history is complex, involving three separate family alliances representing markedly different periods of his life. The family aspects of his story leave a trail of disconnected dots, with lots of unanswered questions. Since God deals with us on a need-to-know basis, we can only conjecture about those seemingly awkward transitions that characterize his fragmented life story.

Beyond the infancy story, we know nothing of Moses' first four decades. But the forty years with his sheepherding family in Midian, followed by his active reentry into the lives of his birth brother and sister, offer plenty of material for reflection on family interaction.

Humility Extraordinaire: Moses' Family of Birth

"Life is a long lesson in humility."
—J. M. BARRIE

"'Then "a new king, to whom Joseph meant nothing, came to power in Egypt." He dealt treacherously with our people and oppressed our ancestors by forcing them to throw out their newborn babies so that they would die. At that time Moses was born, and he was no ordinary child.'" (Acts 7:18–20)

Read Exodus 2:1–10.

Just what was it about the infant Moses that was beyond the ordinary? Most of us as parents would admit that, despite those disarmingly unique personalities evident from day one, extraordinary traits seldom manifest in life's initial months. We're told in verse 2 only that Moses was a fine child; what is perhaps clearer is that he wasn't born to ordinary parents.

Despite his mother's refusal to capitulate, we don't get the impression that she was presumptuous or insolent. The truth seems to have been quite the opposite. I find it interesting that Numbers 12:3 depicts Moses as "a very humble man, more humble than anyone else on the face of the earth." In view of his uniquely privileged upbringing I'm surprised by this affirmation. In search of an explanation my mind takes me back to those formative years prior to Moses' weaning (most likely at the age of three).

Try to imagine the urgency for these Israelite parents of instilling within their toddler a short course in Israelite history and character training, knowing how brief a time they would have to influence their son. The extraordinary humility that was to characterize Moses—along with a lifelong trait of incredible patience (that long lesson in humility)—could only have come from a humbly extraordinary, not to mention an extraordinarily humble, mom and dad, part of God's equipment for this anything but ordinary servant. The opposite of humility isn't pride. A humble attitude, far from being self-deprecating, is realistic. It's seeing ourselves as God sees us—and wants *us* to see us. A humble person recognizes her giftedness, praising God for it and using it in his service.

Post-ponderings: Pause to consider your sense of worth, without being afraid to acknowledge your strengths. Does your self-image come closest to being prideful, realistic (humble), or critical? Then acknowledge and appreciate your status in God's eyes as his cherished daughter or son. If in doubt, check out Zephaniah 3:17.

A NONTRADITIONAL ADOPTION:
MOSES AND THE PRINCESS

"Race, blood, lineage, and nationality don't matter; they're just the way that small minds keep score. All that matters about blood is that it's warm and that it beats through a loving heart."
—SCOTT SIMON

"When the child grew older, she took him to Pharaoh's daughter and he became her son. She named him Moses, saying, 'I drew him out of the water.'" (Exodus 2:10)

Read Exodus 2:1–10.
Beyond Spirit intervention (the crux of this story from a salvation standpoint), what motivated Pharaoh's daughter to take this slave child as her own—or her father to allow it? God doesn't force-fit circumstances to resolve a dilemma or move along a historical situation from point A to point B. Every incident in history involves people—each of whom God has endowed with a will. Even if they respond to stimuli in ways that appear counterintuitive, it's good for us to remember that people act for reasons.

I've long wondered what might have motivated this (still single?) princess, raised with only the best Egypt had to offer, to take into her heart a doomed foreign slave child found bobbing on the Nile in a reed basket. If the princess had been acting on a whim, her follow-through would have been short-lived.

The bigger puzzler is what could have induced Pharaoh to oblige his daughter's fancy to the point of allowing this foundling to be raised in palace luxury. Even under "normal" circumstances this question would baffle us, but Pharaoh was busy enforcing infanticide on the male children of this horde of Israelites whose strength and numbers seemed so threatening. That's the reason this baby bounced in the reed boat. The story itself doesn't provide answers; we need to accept that, despite the Word's spare detail, God reveals himself on a need-to-know basis.

Post-ponderings: What big question about God's Word bothers you the most? Are you willing to accept that mystery as God's prerogative?

MOSES' FAMILY OF MARRIAGE: TURNABOUT EMBRACED?

"I draw from my family and my friends and I feel like that small-town person. The achievements, the materialistic possessions have really become meaningless."
—SHERYL CROW

"By faith Moses, when he had grown up, refused to be known as the son of Pharaoh's daughter. He chose to be mistreated along with the people of God rather than to enjoy the fleeting pleasures of sin. He regarded disgrace for the sake of Christ as of greater value than the treasures of Egypt, because he was looking ahead to his reward." (Hebrews 11:24–26)

Read Exodus 2:11–25.
Moses' lifetime divides neatly into contrasting thirds, each approximately forty years in length. While verse 11 advises us only that Moses had grown up, Acts 7:23 clarifies that he was forty years old when he went out to visit the Israelites. Despite his privileged upbringing, he had not forgotten who he was. It's rare for an adult to recall a great deal prior to the age of five or six; it seems clear that information about Moses' beginnings hadn't been squelched during his developmental years.

It isn't surprising that Moses' own people distrusted him at this point. His flight to Midian—necessary in light of Pharaoh's death threat—was immediate, and he traveled as he was (we read that Reuel's daughters recognized him as an Egyptian). In God's providence he ended up at the home of a Midianite priest whose name means "friend of God."

Moses' adaptation to life as a family man and sheepherder in what must have seemed primitive surroundings is remarkable. Once again the author (whom the Bible elsewhere identifies as Moses himself) doesn't bother with explanation, evidently considering this beyond the scope of the narrative. Moses names his son Gershom, meaning "I have become a foreigner in a foreign land." This new life was to last another forty years (7:7).

Did Moses embrace this dramatic turnabout in his life and fortunes, or did he merely accept it? The culture shock must have been intense. We assume he was grateful to God for having yet again delivered him from imminent death, yet once again we're left to wonder.

Post-ponderings: What do you make of the interesting reference to Christ in the Hebrews quote, above? Is this another hindsight issue?

MOSES AND AARON:
SKILLS SET SUPPLEMENTED

"There was brotherhood between people who had fed from the same breast, a kinship that even time could not break."
—KHALED HOSSEINI

Aaron "'will speak to the people for you, and it will be as if he were your mouth and as if you were God to him.'" (Exodus 4:16)

Read Exodus 4:1–17; 6:28—7:5.
"Moses," declares Stephen in Acts 7:22, "was educated in all the wisdom of the Egyptians and was powerful in speech and action." Yet Moses himself seems to belie this: "I have never been eloquent, neither in the past nor since you have spoken to your servant. I am slow of speech and tongue." Moses' attitude seems to be more of self-deprecation than of humility, which at its best reflects a *realistic* self-assessment.

We can't explain this seeming incongruity. We do know that God appoints Moses' older birth brother, Aaron, to stand in the gap, first between the Lord and the Israelite people and later on between God and Pharaoh.

The point of connection for this reflection is the brothers' connection. How is it that Moses even knew Aaron to be his brother, and how, if at all, had the two maintained contact? It would appear that Pharaoh's daughter had been unaware of the family connection between her adopted son and his nursemaid all those years earlier. Aaron, on the other hand, would have been well aware of the identity of his younger brother, though most likely not of his whereabouts over the past forty years.

It seems evident that God orchestrated the brothers' reunion prior to assigning them key roles in the exodus. Their falling so easily into synch at the ages of eighty-three and eighty, with Aaron even taking on an older brother role by filling in for Moses' insecurity, is remarkable.

Post-ponderings: To what do you attribute the evidently seamless reuniting of these birth brothers after so many years of divergent life experiences?

THE PLAGUE OF THE FIRSTBORN:
THE UNTHINKABLE

"A woman has two smiles that an angel might envy, the smile that accepts a lover before words are uttered, and the smile that lights on the first born babe, and assures it of a mother's love."
—THOMAS C. HALIBURTON

"'Every firstborn son in Egypt will die, from the firstborn son of Pharaoh, who sits on the throne, to the firstborn son of the female slave, who is at her hand mill, and all the firstborn of the cattle as well. There will be loud wailing throughout Egypt— worse than there has ever been or ever will be again.'" (Exodus 11:5–6)

Read Exodus 11.
Once again—and not for the last time—we encounter a difficult family story, one that seems too gruesome to consider. There would be no point in dwelling on the horror. It's self-evident, and our imaginations can fill in whatever detail we might allow ourselves to envision. It may be that the nature of this final, decisive plague was a direct response from God to the infanticide of the previous pharaoh.

Again I target this reflection to believing citizens of a global family. Our world, as we know too well, is hardly immune to atrocities, not to mention those natural calamities we rightly attribute to "acts of God." In fact, disasters have become so rampant that it's often we ourselves who are in danger of becoming immune. Desensitized even to fratricide, xenophobia . . . , we're no longer touched by the incoming barrage of news.

How blessed we are when our own families are intact and well. But what of those other families around the globe who—while also under the umbrella of God's grace, as believers or even as unbelievers—haven't fared so well? We can only acknowledge that God's thoughts, and therefore his ways, are infinitely higher than our own (Isaiah 55:8) and that he will in the final analysis rectify *all* wrongs. What blessed assurance!

Post-ponderings: What recent tragedy has managed to penetrate the chink in your emotional armor? How have you responded?

JETHRO AND MOSES:
THE TESTIMONY OF A SON-IN-LAW

"In the Christian life, godly influence is never conscious of itself."
—OSWALD CHAMBERS

"Jethro was delighted to hear about all the good things the LORD had done for Israel in rescuing them from the hand of the Egyptians. He said, '. . . Now I know that the LORD is greater than all other gods.'" (Exodus 18:9–11)

Read Exodus 18:1–12.

Reuel (aka Jethro) a priest of Midian, evidently worshiped the true God; his name, as we recall, means "friend of God" (see reflection on Exodus 2:11–25). But he was evidently pluralistic in his approach—the norm of the day beyond Israel. A spiritually tuned-in individual, he responded enthusiastically to news of God's saving work among Moses' people, going so far as to acknowledge God's superiority in what he viewed as a pantheon of deities.

Backtracking to pick up the narrative thread, Moses had sent his wife and sons back to her father during the exodus journey. Currently the Israelites are encamped at Mount Sinai. The fact that the four pay him a visit indicates not only that they remain on amicable terms but that the throng hasn't been hard for these Midianites to locate. In all likelihood word of the Hebrews' slow passage and whereabouts had traveled widely throughout the region.

As many of us know from experience, the quiet, unobtrusive testimony of a believing spouse can have a powerful effect on his or her watching in-laws. I'm drawn to the phraseology at the end of this reading: "Aaron came with all the elders of Israel to eat a meal with Moses' father-in-law in the presence of God." This was more than an informal, friendly repast; it was communion at its finest, a meal shared *with* God. There can be little doubt the experience wasn't lost on Jethro.

Post-ponderings: Family mealtimes shared in company with God can have a profound impact on guests. Recall a time when this seems to have been the case with your family.

A FATHER-IN-LAW'S ADVICE: TIMELY AND TIMELESS

"A simple life is not seeing how little we can get by with—that's poverty—but how efficiently we can put first things first."
—VICTORIA MORAN

"Moses' father-in-law replied, 'What you are doing is not good. You and these people who come to you will only wear yourselves out. The work is too heavy for you; you cannot handle it alone.'" (Exodus 18:17–18)

Read Exodus 18:13–27.

It can be hard to dispel a feeling of guilt when we turn down a service "opportunity." *I could have extended myself a little further,* we might berate ourselves, but the truth is that we might not have done so effectively. Each of us has strengths—that's the way Christ ordered his Church. Not only are we wise to focus on our best gifts, we do others a service by making room for them to utilize their strengths for the welfare of the body.

There's also the matter of prioritizing our spouses and children. Doing our best to provide an adequate and comfortable living does our family an invaluable service, but the fine line between enough and too much can be illusive. Voluntary service in Christ's name is no different in this regard. Our unquestioned first calling is to God and his kingdom. But we can't respond efficaciously if we neglect the spiritual welfare of those we hold dear.

Saying no to involvement in or responsibility for some activity in the church may benefit the congregation by allowing someone fresh and available to try their wings in a way they might find deeply satisfying. A healthy congregation utilizes the gifts of as many members as possible without overloading or allowing any to monopolize.

None of us is indispensible in God's family, and we all need restoration and encouragement. Perhaps we're less expendable in our family roles. This isn't to say God won't see our family through if our presence is no longer possible. But if you're a parent, *you* are the only mom or dad your child(ren) know.

Post-ponderings: We read of Moses sending Jethro on his way, but we can probably assume Moses' wife and children stayed with him. Imagine what a difference their presence must have made.

A Culture of Honor

"There was no respect for youth when I was young, and now that I am old, there is no respect for age—I missed it coming and going."
—J. B. PRIESTLY

"Children, obey your parents in the Lord, for this is right." (Ephesians 6:1)

Read Exodus 20:1–21.
It seems as though the first part of Priestly's facetious observation has seen greater change than the latter. At least in the more affluent segments of society, there seems to be no lack of attention paid to the needs, desires, and inherent promise of kids. This is the same demographic in which the older generation is often enjoying a healthy and prosperous retirement, independent of their own children and often doting—with their grown kids—on that third generation. Possibly for the first time in history, honoring parents often has little to do with actively caring for them.

Children raised this way may learn to relate to their grandparents (and great-grandparents) and others of their generations primarily in terms of an expectation of indulgence. While they may love and respect them, they aren't attuned to their needs and might be surprised to find they aren't totally self-sufficient. The way *we* engage with our parents can make a big difference in how our children perceive and interact with them. Honor includes sensitivity, and sensitivity requires concern for *their* needs and weaknesses.

In our congregations too, awareness of the presence, gifts, desires, and needs of the elderly enhances a culture of honor and allows those in life's later passages to enrich the rest of us in the special ways that only they can.

Post-ponderings: What does honoring your parents, or those older members of your congregation or extended family, look like for you?

THE SABBATH:
HOUSEHOLD R & R

"Every minute we spend watching television, listening to secular radio, surfing the Net, playing video games, reading newspapers & magazines, strolling through the mall—and a thousand other activities which beckon us—the more barren we become spiritually . . . the problem is often more a matter of the amount of accumulated time people spend in these different pursuits than in the evil nature of the programming."
—STEVE GALLAGHER

"'Six days do your work, but on the seventh day do not work, so that your ox and your donkey may rest, and so that the slave born in your household and the foreigner living among you may be refreshed.'" (Exodus 23:12)

Read Exodus 23:10–13.
Rest and refreshment, while related, aren't precisely the same. A difference between our lives and those of previous generations is in the nature of both our work and our fatigue. Backbreaking physical labor has in many cases given way to mind-numbing mental and emotional stress. Either kind of exhaustion cries out for rest, but our bodies, minds, and spirits may require rejuvenation of an even more positive nature. We need on a regular basis to be recharged, recalibrated, rewound, restored.

Jesus' words in Mark 2:27 are pertinent here: "The Sabbath was made for man, not man for the Sabbath." Following in God's footsteps on our day of worship, *we're* the ones who need all those critical *r*'s. Most of us are well beyond the days of inflexible seventh-day rules; we as Christians seem to have done an about-face on that issue. And for the most part that's okay. The critical factor in following the fourth commandment is the spirit with which we approach the day. Of foremost importance is the worship due God's name, not only, but still especially, on this his day. Secondarily, we do well to remember that God has ordained this weekly reprieve for our refreshment. If we with our families find ourselves restored and better prepared—physically, spiritually, and emotionally—to launch into a new workweek based on the way we've spent our Sabbath, we're doing something right.

Post-ponderings: How is your family's Sabbath qualitatively different from the other six days?

AARON:
CAPITULATION TO PEER PRESSURE

"Of course, peer pressure has a strong positive component. It provides the social cohesion that allows the very development of communal affiliation. But peer power as an extrinsic force is a lot like radiation: a little goes a long way."
—CHARLES D. HAYES

"Our ancestors refused to obey [God through Moses]. Instead, they rejected him and in their hearts turned back to Egypt. . . . That was the time they made an idol in the form of a calf. They brought sacrifices to it and reveled in what their hands had made. But God turned away from them." (Acts 7:39, 41–42)

Read Exodus 32

As Charles D. Hayes notes, peer pressure isn't necessarily negative. A certain amount can provide a degree of tension that keeps us sharp and in touch. So long as we're attuned to reality and not groupthink, we're wise to incorporate others' points of view as we formulate our opinions and plan our courses of action.

This story is only one biblical example of groupthink at its worst. Consider the fickle crowds in Jerusalem during Jesus' Passion week. This kind of influence takes its most insidious form when a group is worked up by the passion of a few charismatic or simply opinionated individuals. People find security in numbers, "nesting" themselves within a vocal and self-assured majority, often regardless of the validity of their stance.

It's amazing how readily Aaron turned his back not only on his brother and co-leader but on the very God the two were jointly representing. His pathetic explanation—"I threw [the gold] in the fire, and out came this calf!" (can't you just hear his *Imagine that!?*)—exposes the danger of peer pressure run amuck.

Most of us have developed the sophistication to withstand such emotional onslaught. Our adolescents may not be there yet. Parents of young people do well to probe and gently challenge their developing outlooks. This is particularly critical in those areas that could lead them to walk away from family and church—if not literally, in terms of attitudes and values. Exposure to the art of thinking for themselves might prove not only eye-opening but mind- and spirit-expanding.

Post-ponderings: A fascinating passage not addressed here is Exodus 33, as well as, in greater detail regarding the conversation between Moses and God, Moses' recounting of the incident in Deuteronomy 9:13–29. What do you make of this alarming exchange between God and Moses?

BEWARE THE INFLUENCE
OF FOREIGN WIVES

"'Don't marry out of your Church, or you'll regret it all your life.' So all Roman Catholic priests and many Protestant ministers warn their flocks. But most young people in love believe that love will conquer everything—including church dogma, rituals and customs."
—*TIME MAGAZINE* ARTICLE JANUARY 31, 1949

"'Be careful not to make a treaty with those who live in the land . . . And when you choose some of their daughters as wives for your sons and those daughters prostitute themselves to their gods, they will lead your sons to do the same.'" (Exodus 34:15–16)

Read Exodus 34:1–28.

God was open to the inclusion of aliens in Israel's number; already in those early days belonging to his people Israel wasn't simply a matter of ethnicity. In Exodus 12:38 we're told that "many other people went up with" the Israelites. And Jesus' genealogy in Matthew 1:1–5 specifies by name three foreign women (Tamar, Rahab, and Ruth). The Lord didn't reject God-fearing individuals from any background. There was no ban on evangelism or conversion, to use familiar terminology. The problem was the very real danger of an Israelite being nudged away from God by a pagan spouse.

Centuries later the apostle Paul would condone converts in the early Church remaining married to their unbelieving spouses, possibly thereby bringing them to faith (see the reflection on 1 Corinthians 7:12–16). But in his second epistle to the same church he warns against marrying such a person after having declared allegiance to Christ (2 Corinthians 6:14).

Teens and young adults frequently befriend troubled members of the opposite sex in the hope of helping them overcome hurdles. While their intentions may be honorable, they're wise to leave this kind of assistance to someone of the same gender (providing sexual identity isn't an issue) as a matter of self-preservation. It's never worth jeopardizing one's own value system for influence that can insidiously change direction!

Post-ponderings: Nearly every Christian is familiar with a situation like the one described above. If this has happened in your immediate or extended family, what has been the outcome? Are you still in a wait and see mode?

Nadab and Abihu:
Unauthorized Fire

"We experience the grace of an infinite God, but grace is not infinite. God sets limits to His patience and forbearance. He warns us over and over again that someday the ax will fall and His judgment will be poured out."
—R. C. SPROUL

"Aaron's sons Nadab and Abihu took their censers, put fire in them and added incense; and they offered unauthorized fire before the LORD, contrary to his command. So fire came out from the presence of the LORD and consumed them, and they died before the LORD." (Leviticus 10:1–2)

Read Leviticus 10.
These terse opening verses of the chapter set the scene. Moses then cautions his brother about the honor due God from his priests and summons two relatives—evidently first cousins—to remove the bodies from the sacred ground. He goes on to instruct the bereft father and his two remaining sons, "Do not let your hair become unkempt and do not tear your clothes, or you will die and the LORD will be angry with the whole community."

This consequence seems harsh, but we need to recognize the severity of the infraction, as well as the timing of God's warning—at the very beginning of the priestly era. This is one of two instances in which God forbids mourning, although the reasons are quite different (see the reflection on Ezekiel 24:15–27).

God never asks us to refrain from expressing grief. But a reminder of the seriousness with which he takes sin may function for us as a healthy reality jolt. His perfect love—the attribute on which we naturally focus following Christ's death and resurrection—in no ways cancels out a side of him we don't as often see: his just and absolute wrath against sin. Yes, we're God's cherished children, and we're redeemed sinners. But a lackadaisical attitude toward sin, based on the presumption that we're covered by Christ's blood, is a dangerous attitude that parents can unconsciously transmit to kids.

Post-ponderings: Reflect for a moment on Paul's sobering words on this issue, the conclusion of a protracted argument: "What shall we say, then? Shall we go on sinning so that grace may increase? By no means! We are those who have died to sin; how can we live in it any longer?" (Romans 6:1–2).

CHAPTER 6

MOSES AND THE EXODUS, PART 2

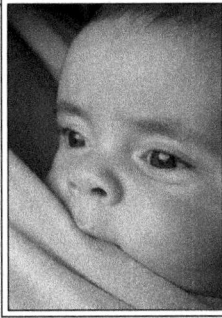

CHAPTER
INTRODUCTION

A continuation of chapter 5, chapter 6 focuses on the end of Moses' long life. While the reflections from Numbers are biographical in nature, the bulk of this chapter, covering Moses' discourses in Deuteronomy, covers the family theme from the perspective of a leader's words of wisdom to the Israelite families—and thereby to us.

MOSES AND HOBAB:
A FAITHFUL BROTHER-IN-LAW

"In some cases, a fellow who steps into a role as a brother-in-law becomes a member of the family so genuinely that he may be considered to be a blood relative and not just an in-law. The family welcomes him and enfolds him in the midst of a loving and supporting group of like minds and generous spirits."
—NOAH F.

"Now Moses said to Hobab son of Reuel [Jethro] the Midianite, Moses' father-in-law, 'We are setting out for the place about which the LORD said, "I will give it to you." Come with us and we will treat you well, for the LORD has promised good things to Israel. . . . You know where we should camp in the wilderness, and you can be our eyes.'" (Numbers 10:29, 31)

Read Numbers 10:29–34.

Moses appreciated family. Having left behind his adoptive mother, the Egyptian princess, when he was forty, he seems to have melded seamlessly with both his in-laws and his family of origin. This despite what must have been for him a jolting culture shock in both cases. Moses' wife's family stood behind him, visiting him there at Sinai with every intention of heading back to Midian when Israel undertook from there its first organized march.

Jethro, as we have seen, acted as a true father to his already eighty-year-old son-in-law, and Moses accepted his gracious advice and honored him with that special dinner in the presence of God (see the reflection on Exodus 18:13–27) before seeing him on his way. Jethro departed on the best of terms with his son-in-law, and his own son Hobab expected to do the same. Hobab's lifelong familiarity with the region—including its climate and potential dangers—ideally credentialed him to act as a scout or guide, and he acceded to Moses' request to accompany his sister's adopted people on their march. Moses had a way of perceiving and appreciating the value in others, and Hobab's vast experience no doubt stood the travelers in good stead.

At the same time Moses wasn't one to take advantage of someone's potential worth. "If you come with us," he pledged, "we will share with you whatever good things the LORD gives us" (Numbers 10:32). And they did: note Judges 4:11, 14–24; 5:24–27, which speak of Hobab's descendants. It's interesting that the husband of the well-known Jael of Judges 4 was Heber the Kenite, who "had left the other Kenites, the descendants of Hobab, Moses' brother-in-law, and pitched his tent by the great tree in Zaanannim near Kedesh."

Post-ponderings: To what degree do you honor and appreciate the family members on *both* sides of your marriage?

MOSES' CAREGIVER FATIGUE: ACCEPTING ALL AVAILABLE HELP

"Caregiving often calls us to lean into love we didn't know possible."
—TIA WALKER

"Moses was troubled. He asked the LORD, 'Why have you brought this trouble on your servant? What have I done to displease you that you put the burden of all these people on me? Did I conceive all these people? Did I give them birth? Why do you tell me to carry them in my arms, as a nurse carries an infant, to the land you promised on oath to their ancestors?'" (Numbers 11:10–12)

Read Numbers 11:10–34.
How poignant Moses' outpouring to his infinitely patient Father, related above. How vulnerable of him to open himself up to reveal his disillusionment, frustration, and exhaustion. His verbal barrage crescendos: "If this is how you are going to treat me, please go ahead and kill me—if I have found favor in your eyes—and do not let me face my own ruin." I don't know about you, but my prayers don't get anywhere near this audacious!

Far from taking insult, God moves into solution mode. The ability of the seventy to prophesy was a one-time event—precisely as was needed. But a potential scandal arose, and a self-important informant was all too ready to apprise Moses of the problem: "'Eldad and Medad [two elders not among the chosen seventy] are prophesying in the camp.' Joshua, son of Nun, who had been Moses' aide since youth, spoke up and said, 'Moses, my lord, *stop them!*'" (emphasis added). Moses in his humility lost no time in dousing *that* flame, chiding the overzealous Joshua, "Are you jealous for my sake? I wish that all the LORD's people were prophets and that the LORD would put his Spirit on them!"

To what degree has caregiver fatigue—whether of your aging parents, your demanding young children, a disabled spouse, or others who depend on you—reduced you to ineffectiveness or even near collapse? How willing are you to accept, from God and others, all the help you can get?

Post-ponderings: When has God met your need in a precise fashion—as in exactly what you needed at a given moment? Was his provision spiritual, or did it come through others? Did you accept the help and express your gratitude—both vertically and horizontally, if appropriate?

Miriam, Aaron, and Moses: Rivalry Erupts

"Our siblings. They resemble us just enough to make all their differences confusing, and no matter what we choose to make of this, we are cast in relation to them our whole lives long."
—SUSAN SCARF MERRELL

"Miriam and Aaron began to talk against Moses because of his Cushite wife, for he had married a Cushite. 'Has the LORD spoken only through Moses?' they asked. 'Hasn't he also spoken through us?' And the LORD heard this. (Now Moses was a very humble man, more humble than anyone else on the face of the earth.)" (Numbers 12:1–3)

Read Numbers 12.

It's hard to know what to make of Moses' marriage to a Cushite woman. The reference may be to his long-time Midianite (and most likely only) wife, Zipporah (note the juxtaposition of "Cushan" and "Midian" in Habakkuk 3:7). Aaron and Miriam were convinced for whatever reason that their indignation was righteous, but God didn't see it that way.

I'm intrigued that the parenthetical comment at the end of the verse above was inserted here. A contrast between Moses' humility and his siblings' self-pride is suggested. Their jealousy is evident—and inappropriate. Had they for whatever reason been spoiling for a fight, groping for a rationale to unleash some festering resentment?

In light of the decades during which these siblings had been separated, along with a lack of clarity regarding the timing and circumstances of their reunion, it's impossible to universalize their experience. Sibling relationships can be complicated for any number of reasons. Rivalry is most often resolved before adulthood, but when it does continue the issues need to be confronted and engaged if an ongoing relationship is mutually seen to be of value.

Post-ponderings: If you have adult siblings, what effort are you putting in to ensure healthy and enduring relationships?

AARON:
DEATH ON THE MOUNTAIN

"Sibling relationships . . . outlast marriages, survive the death of parents, resurface after quarrels that would sink any friendship. They flourish in a thousand incarnations of closeness and distance, warmth, loyalty and distrust."
—ERICA E. GOODE

"In the first month the whole Israelite community arrived at the Desert of Zin, and they stayed at Kadesh. There Miriam died and was buried." (Numbers 20:1)

"Moses did as the LORD commanded: They went up Mount Hor in the sight of the whole community. Moses removed Aaron's garments and put them on his son Eleazar. And Aaron died there on top of the mountain." (Numbers 20:27–28)

Read Numbers 20:1–13, 22–29.
What a difficult parting Aaron's death must have been for Moses, now bereft of the support of both siblings and facing the end of Israel's protracted journey with no pot of gold beyond the arc of his wanderings! The relationship among the three, interrupted for so many years between Moses' early childhood and middle adulthood, had remained intact through so many exigencies. I find it amazing, given the circumstances, that these connections had endured; this can be attributed to Spirit leading but also to determined and sustained investment on the parts of all three.

If you've faced the passing of a brother or sister, did you do so with regrets or a load of unfinished business, or were you able to let go with peace? Sibling bonds can grow with age. Perhaps it's only in our waning years that we invest the time to truly appreciate—and delight in!—what we may have taken for granted or been too busy to notice. It may be only then that we spend our time together in poignant reminiscing, often sprinkled with laughter, mutually reliving our shared past in a new light none of us has previously considered.

Post-ponderings: What positive memory of your shared childhood comes to mind? Would you consider reminding a sibling of the occasion, encouraging them to share their recollection of that experience?

ZELOPHEHAD'S DAUGHTERS: AMBIGUITY RESOLVED

> "Humankind is made up of two sexes, women and men. Is it possible for humankind to grow by the improvement of only one part while the other part is ignored? Is it possible that if half of a mass is tied to earth with chains that the other half can soar into skies?"
> —MUSTAFA KEMAL ATATÜRK

> "The daughters of Zelophehad . . . were Mahlah, Noah, Hoglah, Milkah and Tirzah. They came forward and stood before Moses, Eleazar the priest, the leaders and the whole assembly at the entrance to the tent of meeting and said, ' . . . Why should our father's name disappear from his clan because he had no son? Give us property among our father's relatives.'" (Number 27:1–2, 4)

Read Numbers 27:1–11; 36.
It's amazing to me not only that Scripture names these women (cf. the similar surprise in Job 42:14–15) but that this seemingly minor incident is recorded in Numbers 27 and revisited in chapter 36: "This is what the LORD commands for Zelophehad's daughters: They may marry anyone they please as long as they marry within their father's tribal clan. No inheritance in Israel is to pass from one tribe to another."

The incident itself wasn't the important thing; it was the precedent—in the same way certain well-know court cases in the United States have changed family law and hence the trajectory of society in some manner (so much so that the name of the case—Roe v. Wade, for example—stands as shorthand for the principle involved). In the case of Zelophehad's daughters God was implementing a permanent change not only in Israel's legal code but in her societal perspective on the worth and rights of women.

Our God is inclusive. We've seen this in his acceptance of foreigners into the constituency of his people. We see it in his repeated concern for the poor and oppressed, the widow and the orphan, the disabled and the blind. And we see it in the Father's gender "blindness" in terms of the intrinsic value of women and girls. God's infinite, unqualified love leaves no room for distinction in terms of valuation. And neither may our own.

Post-ponderings: Identify one criterion by which you tend to value or devalue people. Is it ability level? Weight or physical appearance? Social functioning? Class or echelon in society? How difficult is it for you to accept that God loves *all* people?

Held and Upheld:
In the Father's Arms

"'The Lord your God, who is going before you, will fight for you, as he did for you in Egypt, before your very eyes, and in the wilderness. There you saw how the Lord your God carried you, as a father carries his son, all the way you went until you reached this place.'" (Deuteronomy 1:30–31)

Read Deuteronomy 1:26–46.

A few years ago an advertisement appeared on one side of a double billboard near my home. It pictured a young girl wrinkling her nose in protest against the "pink stuff" on her family's Thanksgiving table. I don't recall what was being promoted, but she was cute and worth a chuckle.

Around Christmas, though, I was taken aback by a new ad, also featuring a little girl, on the adjoining billboard. This waif trudged along a windswept sidewalk, hand clasped in that of an otherwise unseen guardian. I remember precisely what was being endorsed—a homeless shelter in downtown Grand Rapids, Michigan.

This hapless youngster was in every way the foil of her unintended counterpart. The satiny dress gave way to a grimy coverall. Both faces were unhappy, but hers was dirty and pinched rather than peeved. She too was making an appeal: *"Please pick me up."*

What a solace to know God will gladly comply with our request to pick us up! In fact, we're already there in his arms. If you've never noticed the verse above, take a moment to let the words sink in. Wow! And he'll do the same for our kids, whatever their situation. Have we told them?

Post-ponderings: "Remember" or imagine the rhythm of being carried, step-by-step, in a parent's embrace. Feel the warmth and listen to the measured breathing. Then envision yourself in God's everlasting arms.

THE DIVINE MANDATE: PASS THE WORD ALONG

"Each day of our lives we make deposits in the memory banks of our children."
—CHARLES SWINDOLL

"These commandments that I give you today are to be on your hearts. Impress them on your children. Talk about them when you sit at home and when you walk along the road, when you lie down and when you get up." (Deuteronomy 6:6–7)

Read Deuteronomy 6; Psalm 78:1–8.
Most of us are familiar with ten words from Robert Fulghum: "All I really need to know . . . I learned in kindergarten." Margaret Thatcher, prime minister of the United Kingdom from 1979–90, made a similar observation: "It's passionately interesting for me that the things that I learned in a small town, in a very modest home, are just the things that I believe have won the election."

This principle applies particularly well to instilling spiritual values. Moses calls on parents to be intentional about the kind of teaching that will result in the learning these writers describe. Impressing our values on our kids won't happen by osmosis. And it won't happen at all if we try to fake it. It's vital for us to recognize that these standards must be sculpted into our hearts before the impression will "take" on theirs.

I thrill to David's exulting words at the conclusion of Psalm 22: "Posterity will serve him; future generations will be told about the Lord. They will proclaim his righteousness, declaring to a people yet unborn: He has done it!" My writer's eye focuses immediately, though, on that past tense "will be told." *Who*, I can't help but ask, *will do the telling?* That's neither an idle question nor a technicality. The answer is vital to that multigenerational string of telling on which the psalmist's premise depends. Lyrics from a song my congregation enjoys come immediately to mind: "How will they know unless we tell them so?" That lowly "we" makes all the difference when it comes to our kids!

Post-ponderings: To what degree do you feel comfortable leaving the telling to the professionals—the church or Christian school?

DURABLE SANDALS:
FOUR MAINTENANCE-FREE DECADES

"Letting go of our 'dependence on independence' and letting someone else take control goes against natural human instinct. We need to fight the urge to take over and just let God be God, because He can provide for us better than we can."

—CORALLIE BUCHANAN

"'For forty years you sustained [your people] in the wilderness; they lacked nothing, their clothes did not wear out nor did their feet become swollen.'" (Nehemiah 9:21)

Read Deuteronomy 8.

How much mental and emotional energy do we waste on needless worry, particularly if we're responsible for dependents? On the opposite end of the spectrum, how often do we think about, let alone thank God for, those potential problems that have somehow never materialized? For us as parents the possibilities are staggering.

While not all of us are vulnerability averse (there are plenty of hardy—some might say foolish—souls who find themselves unprepared and bewildered when challenges come), it seems fair to say that Christians tend toward the thoughtful side. Ironically, that often equates to more wary . . . which easily slides into less trusting. Perhaps it was to us responsible types that Jesus lovingly addressed his discourse on anxiety (Matthew 6:25–34). In direct contrast to the Nehemiah quote, above, listen to his gentle reminder: "Therefore I tell you, do not worry . . . about your body, what you will wear."

It's improbable the Father's providence in your case will manifest in terms of a forty-year guarantee on sandal leather. But if you're far enough along on the parenting spectrum, or beyond that stage, you can look back with surprise and gratitude on the hurdles he's seen you through or allowed you to avoid. So relax and let God be God—he's good at it, to voice the ultimate understatement. Which has everything to do with his goodness, period.

Post-ponderings: When have you worried needlessly about some issue related to your family's well-being? Looking back, how did this stress affect your functioning or effectiveness?

HISTORICAL MEMORY:
FROM GENERATION TO GENERATION

"Heirlooms we don't have in our family. But stories we've got."
—ROSE CHERIN

"In the future, when your son asks you, 'What is the meaning of the stipulations, decrees and laws the Lord our God has commanded you?' tell him: 'We were slaves of Pharaoh in Egypt, but the Lord brought us out of Egypt with a mighty hand.'"
(Deuteronomy 6:20–21)

Read Deuteronomy 11.
Humanity's compulsion to niche itself has recently hit upon a new zinger—hoarders. At the risk of oversimplification, a hoarder is often an individual who, distrusting memory and story, insists upon retaining visible reminders of the important or once important. I'm reminded of the young child who hasn't yet come to understand the permanence of anything or anyone that slips beyond her visual range. Reality for her needs to be tangible. One of the ideals and expectations of maturity is moving beyond that.

Nor is it only memory and story that represent invisible reality. In the case of the directive in the verses above, stipulations and laws can function the same way. At first glance this seems counterintuitive, but all laws are in place for historical reasons. They function as shorthand overriding the need to repeat negative experiential learning. *Trust me on this one!* is the implied premise.

God's discipline (and its retelling) is closely related. "Remember today," Moses instructed God's gathered people, "that your children were not the ones who saw and experienced the discipline of the Lord your God: his majesty, his mighty hand, his outstretched arm. . . . But it was your own eyes that saw all these great things the Lord has done.'" The sons of Korah reiterate the telling/retelling theme in Psalm 48:12–14: "Walk about Zion, go around her, count her towers, consider well her ramparts, view her citadels, that you may tell of them to the next generation. For this God is our God for ever and ever; he will be our guide even to the end."

What could be more important than passing along this knowing to those who follow along in our wake? Indeed, "stories we've got"—a veritable treasure trove in God's Word just waiting to be opened and shared. And the stories are enough for us: we of his extended family can travel light, with a spring in our step, knowing he's got it—and us—covered.

Post-ponderings: "I love to tell the story . . . ," as expressed in an old gospel song. What stories with spiritual import—either from your own experience or from the Bible—do you enjoy sharing?

Marriage Leave:
Progressive Social Policy

"The mark of a great man is one who knows when to set aside the important things in order to accomplish the vital ones."
—BRANDON SANDERSON

"If a man has recently married, he must not be sent to war or have any other duty laid on him. For one year he is to be free to stay at home and bring happiness to the wife he has married." (Deuteronomy 24:5)

Read Deuteronomy 21:10–14; 22:13–30; 24:1–5.
How often do we think in terms of the *privilege* of bringing happiness to those we love? Consciousness of the importance of family needs and corresponding social policy seem to be on the upswing in the West, although we in the United States find ourselves behind our European counterparts in finding a workable balance between our "lives" of work and of family engagement.

God's Word surprises us with factoids like the one above. The author of 1 Kings offers another: "King Solomon conscripted laborers from all Israel—thirty thousand men. He sent them off to Lebanon in shifts of ten thousand a month, so that they spent one month in Lebanon and two months at home" (5:13–14). Not too bad a split!

I can't help but notice that some biblical dads (like Samuel and David) whose lives incorporated a good deal of vocational or military travel experienced profound disappointment in their kids. (In the interest of a balanced "survey," the same was true for Aaron and Eli, both stay-at-home priests engaged 24/7 with their sons.) The consequences of time away from spouses and kids are well known in our hectic age. The situation can entail overcommitment or emotional distance due to preoccupation just as readily as business travel.

It does take a village to raise kids, as the saying goes, but increasingly the isolated "villagers" who interact with our youngsters are representing different villages, dealing with them with more specialization and less investment—not to mention the lack of a common voice, shared mutual interest in the child, a clear vision of the total child, or the ability to interact or debrief together. Involvement and commitment on the part of our churches can go a long way toward overriding these deficits. The family of God in its local iterations can mean more to our families than we might recognize.

Post-ponderings: If you're in an active parenting stage, make a mental list of those "villagers," beyond your extended family members, who constitute your primary support system. How many of them do you know through church or other Christian affiliation?

THE SECRET THINGS
AND THE THINGS REVEALED

"I leave God's secrets to himself. It is happy for me that God makes me of his court, and not of his council."

—JOSEPH HALL

"The secret things belong to the LORD our God, but the things revealed belong to us and to our children forever, that we may follow all the words of this law." (Deuteronomy 29:29)

Read Deuteronomy 29.

After searching unsuccessfully a few years ago for an item missing from my desktop, I asked my little granddaughter whether she knew where it was. Addie at that stage had a habit of confessing to sins committed by the dog, so I made sure my questions didn't come off as accusations. With a guilty, deer-in-the-headlights expression, though, she replied seriously, "It's a mystery." As it turns out, she wasn't responsible.

God has been selective in what he has chosen to reveal to us. And although we aren't wrong to speculate, we can go only so far in terms of delving into mysteries that have yet to be explained. God has already told us what we're capable of handling—certainly, at any rate, what we need to know. Jesus had this to say to his probing disciples: "About that day or hour [when heaven and earth will pass away] no one knows, not even the angels in heaven, nor the Son [in his human nature], but only the Father" (Mark 13:32).

One day, when we see God face-to-face, all will be clear. Until that time, let's cherish the revelation he has seen fit to share. Do our children know and understand—to the degree they are able—what he *has* revealed?

Post-Ponderings: About which not-yet-revealed spiritual issues are you most curious? Are you willing to trust God's heart for the time being?

THE GOD OF LIFE

"You can see God from anywhere if your mind is set to love and obey Him."
—AIDEN WILSON TOZER

"Now choose life, so that you and your children may live and that you may love the LORD your God, listen to his voice, and hold fast to him. For the LORD is your life."
(Deuteronomy 30:19–20)

Read Deuteronomy 30.
We can only conclude from these verses (if we were in doubt) that God is pro-life. We're quick with our buy-in on God loving and valuing life, but how often do we think of him as *being* our life?

God created us for his own pleasure and praise; as such, he's our sole reason for living. He also sustains us so that our every breath, our every involuntary heartbeat, is a gift. How sad that not all of us do love, listen to, and hold fast to God.

About that matter of choosing life, Moses wasn't talking about abortion, stem cell research, euthanasia, eugenics, or any other controversial contemporary term. There are, of course, countless ways in which we can choose life. But the emphasis in Deuteronomy is solidly on obedience/disobedience, associated, respectively, with life and death.

We're uncomfortable with that kind of black-and-white distinction. But our twenty-first-century perspective on the matter doesn't negate God's equations. No, we aren't saved by our good deeds. Yet as James points out in James 2:18, we have to question faith unaccompanied by obedience to God's overarching law of love.

Post-Ponderings: What kinds of life or death choices are you making, not just in terms of healthy and ethical living but of obedience to God?

CHAPTER 7

THE CONQUEST AND THE EARLY JUDGES ERA

CHAPTER

INTRODUCTION

A dilemma in attempting to write inclusively about biblical family dynamics is what to do with the horrendous Old Testament stories (and there are many!) that are not only "too hot to handle" but have no remote connection to twenty-first-century Western family reality. Some of these appear in Samuel and Kings but most are crowded, one upon another, near the end of Judges. These stories are helpful for the serious Bible reader in terms of demonstrating the spiraling anarchy, degradation, and dehumanization into which Israel had descended in this, its lowest period, but they are inappropriate for consideration in this book. I've elected to do no more than list some of these, below:

Gideon's son Abimelek (8:29—9:57)

Micah and His Mother (17–18)

A Levite and His Concubine (19:10—20:48)

Wives for the Benjamites (21)

RAHAB:
DEBATABLE CREDENTIALS?

"Only those who are truly aware of their sin can truly cherish grace."
—C. J. MAHONEY

"Was not even Rahab the prostitute considered righteous for what she did when she gave lodging to the spies and sent them off in a different direction?"
(James 2:25)

Read Joshua 2; 6:15–25.
We tend to categorize breaches of God's law in terms of how we perceive their seriousness. For whatever reason, sexual sin has a tendency to rank right up there with murder when it comes to our mental tally. It also occurs to me that the commandments that deal with our thoughts, as opposed to our "acting out" or practice, strike us as relatively innocuous. Yet Jesus made no such distinctions: on the matter of adultery, note Matthew 5:28; on murder, verses 21–22.

That sounds a little harsh, we might protest inwardly after reading Jesus' pronouncements. *After all, my thoughts are hard to control.* Still, Christ's expressed reality places each of us squarely in the sinner's box. When we ask forgiveness for our infractions of thought, word, and deed, we're acknowledging profound truth. Our attempts to ease Rahab off the hook based on her pagan background fall flat; the universality of God's moral law precludes such an argument. If no one sin is more egregious in God's eyes than any other, and if God forgives repentant sinners without qualification, James's point, above, deserves a second look.

"Joshua spared Rahab the prostitute, with her family and all who belonged to her, because she hid the men Joshua had sent as spies to Jericho—and she lives among the Israelites to this day." Rahab became one with, and one of, God's people—an ancestor of Jesus himself. Her sensitive heart and mind were redeemed by her life-changing encounters with God and his people.

Post-ponderings: Turn ahead in your Bible to John 8:1–11. How cautious are you when it comes to lobbing stones following a revelation of sexual sin within your family or church?

GOD'S STORYTELLERS

"'Thou shalt not' is soon forgotten, but 'Once upon a time' lasts forever."
—PHILIP PULLMAN

"Joshua set up at Gilgal the twelve stones [the Israelites] had taken out of the Jordan. He said to the Israelites, 'In the future when your descendants ask their parents, "What do these stones mean?" tell them, "Israel crossed the Jordan on dry ground."'" (Joshua 4:20–22)

Read Joshua 4.
We've covered this issue before, from a different angle (see the reflection on Deuteronomy 6; Psalm 78:1–8). I love reading—and listening. Although I can become engrossed in nonfiction, I'm first and foremost a sucker for a good story. When someone starts to tell one, whether it's a sermon illustration, a long-ago and far-away nostalgic recollection, or a humorous snippet or high-adventure account from the *Reader's Digest*, I consider it a treat.

"If a nation loses its storytellers," notes Peter Handke, "it loses its childhood." And if the church loses its childhood, it stands to lose something in the transition to its future. The Bible is one continuously unfolding salvation story, presented in a variety of genres. Within that larger context are included endless riveting short stories, together constituting a "gotcha!" that piques the interest of little ones and adults alike.

Ever wonder why the story of Paul's conversion, so pivotal to the church's infancy, is related three times in Acts (9:1–19; 22:2–21; 26:4–18)? Why did Luke bother to record Paul's first and second retellings word for word when he could have said something like "Paul related to the people in Jerusalem [or to King Agrippa] the story of his conversion experience on the road to Damascas"? In the words of Anne Watson, "Stories tell us of what we already knew and forgot, and remind us of what we haven't yet imagined." I'm not quite sure what she means by that last clause, but I do at least sense what she's getting at. It's one of those ponderables—like a good story.

Post-ponderings: What Bible story means the most to you? Why do you suppose it moves you as it does?

CALEB AND AKSAH:
ANOTHER DAUGHTER'S REQUEST

"Compared to other cultures of the [Old Testament] time, Jewish women enjoyed great liberty and esteem, and many women distinguished themselves as prophetesses and leaders in Jewish society. Women such as Deborah, Esther, Hannah, Huldah, Jochebed, Miriam, Noadiah, Rachel, Rebekeh, Rahab, Ruth and Sarah played important and decisive roles in Israel's history."
—AUTHOR UNSPECIFIED

"'Do me a special favor. Since you have given me land in the Negev, give me also springs of water.' So Caleb gave [Aksah] the upper and lower springs." (Judges 1:15)

Read Joshua 14:6–15; Judges 1:12–15.
Remember Caleb—the one Israelite spy who along with Joshua brought back a glowing minority report on the land of Canaan? Of the men alive at the time of the spy mission, only Joshua and Caleb made it, more than forty years later, to the Promised Land.

Joshua gave Caleb a portion of the allocation for the tribe of Judah, of which he in turn handed down a field to his daughter Aksah and her husband/cousin, Othniel (in the Joshua passage this parenthetical story is squeezed in to the itemized list of tribal allotments). For an earlier story similar in theme and spirit, check out the account of the negotiations of Zelophehad's daughters (see the reflection on Numbers 27:1–11; 36).

Biblical women had nowhere near the rights of men. But the stories of exceptions—and the inauguration of new precedents—in the Bible never cease to catch me off guard. Such ordinary stories by their very presence speak volumes, both about God's inclusivity and about his orientation. Aksah's request of her dad seems to have been reasonable and respectful (what good would the land have done her and her husband without access to water to enable life there?). And the fact that she felt sufficient entitlement to ask suggests a healthy father/daughter relationship.

Post-ponderings: What do you make of Aksah's urging her husband, Othniel, to ask Caleb for the field and then asking on her own accord for the springs of water?

MEMORIAL ALTAR EAST OF THE JORDAN

"The choices we make about the lives we live determine the kinds of legacies we leave."
—TAVIS SMILEY

This altar "'is to be a witness between us and you and the generations that follow, that we will worship the LORD at his sanctuary with our burnt offerings, sacrifices and fellowship offerings. Then in the future your descendants will not be able to say to ours, "You have no share in the LORD."'" (Joshua 22:27)

Read Joshua 22:10–34.
To Israel's credit, the handling of this potentially devastating misunderstanding was handled from both sides with tactful diplomacy. This uncharacteristic detente is a triumph, a biblical model our impulsive world would do well to follow!

Although the other Israelites' first-blush conclusion was understandable, the explanation for the altar offered by those tribes that had settled East of the Jordan provided the *aha!* moment: "We did it for fear that some day your descendants might say to ours, 'What do you have to do with the LORD, the God of Israel? The LORD has made the Jordan a boundary between us and you—you Reubenites and Gadites! You have no share in the LORD.' So your descendants might cause ours to stop fearing the LORD."

This minority group, along with their kinsmen, had inherited the Promised Land not from their ancestors but directly from God. But had they lacked the foresight to document that reality for the benefit of future generations, they would have been withdrawing from their children's trust fund.

History is notoriously forgetful. I'm reminded of a couple of postexilic stories in which unearthing a record of historical data made all the difference for the future of God's people (see Ezra 6:1–14; Esther 2:19–23; 6). When we as Christian spouses and parents and as members of Christ's Church maintain careful, organized records, historical misunderstandings even far down the road can be averted.

Post-ponderings: Are you and your spouse fully prepared in terms of legal documentation for the potential loss of either of you? Are your children secure? The issue applies, of course, both spiritually and financially.

"As for Me and My Household": Legislating Faith?

"This week we're finally getting back into a routine. So last night I laid down with Madison to pray. She went first—'God, I know we haven't prayed in a while . . .' Whoops! I love that she understands the importance of faith and that it plays a significant role in her life. It's a non-negotiable, a top priority for us."
—MICHAEL NICHOLS

"'If serving the LORD seems undesirable to you, then choose for yourselves this day whom you will serve . . . But as for me and my household, we will serve the LORD.'"
(Joshua 24:15)

Read Joshua 24:1–28.
Sadly, as we're reminded by today's exodus of young people from the church, it's impossible for us to legislate faith in our children. We can expect it; train them accordingly, through word and example; and pray for them faithfully, but it isn't up to us.

We can't mouth the final sentence of the verse above, in solidarity with Joshua, without changing some of the words. Some possibilities: *But as for me, I will serve the Lord. But as for me and my spouse, we will serve the Lord. But as for me (us), we will train our children to serve the Lord.* We can't include our kids in an assumed family faith package but can only plead with them to make a stand.

Yet we as parents have no business throwing in the towel. God will honor the promises he has made, promises contingent upon our raising our kids in his way. Our responsibility as godly parents is to claim those promises and rely on him to do his part. No amount of angst is needed to remind him to act. How, when, and even *if* he works in the hearts of our youth or grown children are matters hidden within his sovereignty. The outcomes and reasons will one day be clear. Our only viable course is to remain faith-filled and faithful, trusting implicitly in his unchanging faithfulness. (See also the reflection on Acts 2:14–41).

Post-ponderings: Does your family or extended family grieve over the spiritual disinterest of one or more precious children? Do you take the matter regularly to the Lord?

OTHNIEL, ISRAEL'S FIRST JUDGE: FAMILIAL FAITHFULNESS

"All five of us children decided to express thanks to our father and mother for one thing without consulting each other. Remarkably, all five of us thanked our mother for her prayers and all five of us thanked our father for his leadership of . . . family worship."
—AUTHOR UNKNOWN

"When [the Israelites] cried out to the LORD, he raised up for them a deliverer, Othniel son of Kenaz, Caleb's younger brother, who saved them." (Judges 3:9)

Read Judges 3:7–11.
Do you ever wonder why some families seem to be so successful, both within a given generation and in the generational lineup ahead and behind? Without doubt genetics plays a role, as do the attitudes, training, modeling, inspiration, and expectations of parents and other more senior members of the clan. Opportunity, context, and setting can be conducive to success, and younger members are often drawn to traditional family roles. Self-expectation, -confidence, and -discipline are also likely traits in a family of high achievers.

In the case of Caleb and his younger brother Kenaz, at least some of these factors were evidently at play. We've seen Caleb's daughter Aksah (the wife of her cousin Othniel) exhibit the foresight to recognize and act upon the couple's need for an additional component to their inheritance (see the reflection on Joshua 14:6–15; Judges 1:12–15). And now Othniel steps up to the plate as Israel's first God-appointed judge. Yet more than high achievement was going on in the lives of Caleb and Othniel. Theirs was not only an accomplished clan but a faithful one. When an extraordinary family like this channels its collective ability and energy toward the things of God, his kingdom is the ultimate winner.

Post-ponderings: What family do you know that seems to have more than its "share" of success stories? To what factors do you attribute this?

DEBORAH:
SOCIETAL MOM

"We've begun to raise daughters more like sons . . . but few have the courage to raise our sons more like our daughters."
—GLORIA STEINEM

"Villagers in Israel would not fight; they held back until I, Deborah, arose, until I arose, a mother in Israel." (Judges 5:7)

Read Judges 4–5.

What was there about the times of Deuteronomy, Joshua, and Judges that seems to have brought out the best in women? "Now Deborah, a prophet, the wife of Lappidoth, was leading Israel at that time. She held court under the Palm of Deborah between Ramah and Bethel in the hill country of Ephraim, and the Israelites went up to her to have their disputes decided." How had Deborah, this "mother in Israel," ascended to this role? Perhaps the times disallowed the luxury of following unspoken rules. Perhaps talent exhibited by either gender of necessity rose to the surface. It's possible too that in barbaric and unstable times Israel needed precisely what Deborah had to offer—the encouragement and softening of a decisive mother figure!

The narrative makes no disparaging comment about Barak's hesitancy, nor is there anything in the passage to suggest that he was less than a brave officer (interestingly, the author of Hebrews includes him in his chapter 11 faith hall of fame). Barak may well have been a wise strategist who saw the wisdom of accompaniment by a prophet leader. On the other hand, perhaps his reluctance offers a not unwelcome glimpse of a male soldier's feminine side. These two chapters suggest a curious cross-pollination in terms of gender roles and expectations. Does this strange account offer an early suggestion of gender equality?

Post-ponderings: If you're a mother, describe in a sentence or two the significant aspects of this role for you. If you're a son—or daughter—what are some important roles your mom has played in your life?

SISERA:
A MOTHER'S ANGST

"Your child is always your child, regardless of age. You feel their feelings,
share in their joys and hurt in their sorrows."
—NISHAN PANWAR

"'Through the window peered Sisera's mother; behind the lattice she cried out,
"Why is his chariot so long in coming? Why is the clatter of his chariots delayed?"'"
(Judges 5:28)

Read Judges 5:28–30.
We know that Deborah was married and a self-proclaimed "mother in Israel," but the Bible doesn't say she was literally a mother. It seems telling,
though, that she would poetically depict Sisera's death from the imagi-
nary perspective of his frantic mother. We can picture this distraught older
woman, every bodily sensor on high alert as she longs for her strained
senses to confirm the chariot's approach. Only another mother, it would
seem, would vicariously relate in this way to what might have been happening in that anguished heart.

It's almost comedic (in this case tragi-comic) the way in which the
imagined mom of the poem perpetuates her role as her vulnerable child's
(i.e., this Canaanite general's) protector and champion. Not all moms are
like that; many detach easily from grown and independent children, not
in terms of love but in terms of any desire to live vicariously through the
next generation or actively involve themselves in their daily lives. Parenting
styles vary to the same degree people do.

We Christians have something Sisera's mom, whatever she was like,
never had. Listen to David's words in Psalm 5:11: "Let all who take refuge in
you be glad; let them ever sing for joy. Spread your protection over them, that
those who love your name may rejoice in you." Whether your kids are five,
fifteen, or fifty, their security goes with them when they walk out your door.

Post-ponderings: On a scale of one to ten, rate yourself on this parenting issue, with ten being the most highly protective and one the most carefree and
trusting. How willing have you been to relinquish your kids to God's care?

GIDEON:
LEAST OF THE WEAKEST?

"God deliberately chooses weak, suffering and unlikely candidates to get His work done, so that in the end, the glory goes to God and not to the person."
—JONI EARECKSON TADA

"'Pardon me, my lord,' Gideon replied, 'but how can I save Israel? My clan is the weakest in Manasseh, and I am the least in my family.'" (Judges 6:15)

Read Judges 6–7.
"When the angel of the LORD appeared to Gideon, he said, 'The LORD is with you, mighty warrior.'" Sounds like an auspicious start, but the intimidated Gideon wasn't buying it. Where in this passage do we make the jump from cowering farmer to mighty warrior? Ironically, the skeptical Gideon doesn't question the angel's strange form of address but only God's ability to rescue his people, and later his own questionable credentials.

We see this thread throughout the Bible as God again and again calls unlikely, distrustful, and flawed characters to do his bidding. The reality is that God chooses and uses weaker vessels to showcase his own glory. But we also see evidence of characters growing to fit and fill the audacious purposes God has for them. Just look at Moses and Peter.

God alone sees our true potential. Whether he's calling you to something intimidating or comfortable, he has picked the right person for the job. This isn't to say our every undertaking for the Lord will be successful. Sometimes we attempt an avenue of service that just isn't "us." In such situations, instead of questioning God's judgment we're wise to ask whether that particular function was truly in line with his calling for us.

Post-ponderings: Might there be someone in your immediate or extended family who feels like the underdog, the disappointment—the last or the least? If so, how might you intercede to set the record straight?

"As Is the Man ...":
Jether's Reluctance

"Boyhood is the most complex and incomprehensible thing. Even when one has been through it, one does not understand what it was. A man can never quite understand a boy, even when he has been the boy."
—G. K. CHESTERTON

"Turning to Jether, his oldest son, [Gideon] said, 'Kill [the enemy kings]!' But Jether did not draw his sword, because he was only a boy and was afraid. . . . So Gideon stepped forward and killed them." (Judges 8:20–21)

Read Judges 8:1–21.
This frozen moment in time makes for riveting reading. The captured Midianite kings posed no threat, but the prospect of death at the hand of a boy violated their code of honor (quite likely Gideon's intention). Upon observing the boy's hesitation, they were quick to taunt the father: "Come, do it yourself. 'As is the man, so is his strength.'"

Jether, paralyzed by fear and revulsion at the unexpected request, might under different circumstances have shaken himself from his torpor and belatedly responded. Was this father right in taking over? Moving beyond the obvious fact that we would never ask a child to do something like this, the account is so spare on detail that it's impossible to determine motive. Was Gideon embarrassed by Jether's inaction before these kings he so wanted to degrade—so much so that he opted to save face as a last impression in their final seconds of life? Or did he recognize his mistake in expecting too much of his vulnerable young son? I somehow doubt the latter came into play.

Who, I wonder, was *really* humiliated in this scenario? Not these surly kings with their pitiful objection to the prospect of a disgraceful death. Not Gideon, for whom the boy's terror was hardly a personal discredit. It's probable that mortification over this moment remained with Jether all his life. He'd been called upon to do a man's job—and failed miserably! The obvious irony is the comparison between the Gideon of Judges 6–7—a grown man so cowed that he demanded three proofs from God before responding to *his* request—and this tormented, self-accusing, half-grown "man."

Post-ponderings: It can be difficult to know when to step in and take over for a reluctant child. When has this been a factor in your experience—either as the child or as the adult? Was the parent's decision the best one? Was the child able to save face?

Jephthah and His Brothers: Illegitimate Son / Mighty Warrior

"I believe that I understand gangs better than others. Because they're formed out of necessity. They're formed by people to keep from being suppressed."
—JACK BOWMAN

"Jephthah the Gileadite was a mighty warrior. His father was Gilead; his mother was a prostitute. Gilead's wife also bore him sons, and when they were grown up, they drove Jephthah away. . . . So Jephthah fled from his brothers and settled in the land of Tob, where a gang of scoundrels gathered around him and followed him." (Judges 11:1–3)

Read Judges 11:1–28.

Jephthah and his father's wife's sons shared a mutual parent. Beyond that there was nothing to identify them as brothers. The sons of Gilead's wife carried over to this hapless other son their disgust with their father for his union with a prostitute. Did Jephthah's proficiency with his spear stem in part from his boyhood need to make his way alone in the face of continual conflict? The description above fits remarkably well in today's context. Change the name to Craig and imagine fists instead of a spear, and this paragraph sounds contemporary enough. The gang component—that surrogate family—follows the script naturally.

This is yet another situation that addresses us not so much as parents or family members as concerned Christians embedded in a culture of evil. Not everyone around us is malevolent or immoral; God has allowed enough goodness in our world that many of us blithely live out our lives with no or few frightening encounters with reality's seamier side. We associate with our own and follow the rules of caution and common sense, responsibly building a hedge of security around ourselves and our families.

So what does our concern for the more intimidating variety of suffering people look like in practice? I'm not suggesting any particular response to the problems of troubled or abandoned youth or of gang violence. I'm merely asking the question. The answer is neither easy nor obvious.

Post-ponderings: How wide is your comfort zone when it comes to interacting with others in a diverse and at times terrifying world?

Jephthah and His Daughter: A Rash Impulse

"When you have brought up kids, there are memories you store directly in your tear ducts."
—ROBERT BRAULT

"From this comes the Israelite tradition that each year the young women of Israel go out for four days to commemorate the daughter of Jephthah the Gileadite."
(Judges 11:39–40)

Read Judges 11:29–40.
My image of this vibrant adolescent dancing out to meet her returning soldier daddy is both delightful and ominous (knowing the outcome in advance). The scene in my mind is in some sense a freeze frame; yet her nimble feet and laughing eyes connote vitality, not stillness. More haunting is my picture of the reality registering in Jephthah's eyes as he realizes the consequence of his rash vow.

As a preteen I found this story unbearable. It was years later that I learned with relief that although this girl never lost her virginity she was probably not condemned to death. But virginity and childlessness were devastating in her day. This can still be true; the difference for us is that there *are* other paths a young woman can take. Opting, or settling—a different proposition altogether—for the single life is at least socially acceptable.

If you're reading this as an unmarried woman, or if your daughter, sister, or friend is dealing with the disappointment of waiting for a married future she has always taken for granted, you may have some sense of the desolation Jephthah's daughter endured. Her period of mourning with her friends was very real; dashed hopes of love and family can feel very much like tangible losses.

Post-ponderings: In what way, if any, does the dilemma of this young woman hit home for you or your family? If this isn't applicable, what significant disappointment has impacted your life? How have you dealt with it?

Manoah and His Wife: A Plea for Guidance

"Whenever I held my newborn baby in my arms, I used to think that what I said and did to him could have an influence not only on him but on all whom he met, not only for a day or a month or a year, but for all eternity—a very challenging and exciting thought for a mother."
—ROSE KENNEDY

"'Pardon your servant, Lord. I beg you to let the man of God you sent to us come again to teach us how to bring up the boy who is to be born.'" (Judges 13:8)

Read Judges 13.

We don't bear children based on specific promises from the Lord—don't know their destinies from before God has implanted them in the womb. But along with Manoah and his wife we crave guidance for the parenting journey. Much of this is available from God's Word. Beyond that our children come to us, as believers, backed by God's covenant promises to sustain and encourage both them and us throughout the long nurturing process.

We learn from this chapter that "the Spirit of the LORD began to stir" in Samson at a certain point. Most of us are aware that this young man, despite having been raised under strict vows, would be anything but compliant. We need seemingly inexhaustible patience to glimpse any fruit either of his upbringing or of those early Spirit stirrings. In fact, the single righteous act about which we learn will come in Samson's dying moment.

And yet the writer of Hebrews includes this flawed individual, along with Gideon, Barak, and Jephthah, in his Hebrews 11 faith hall of fame. Like Manoah and his wife, we might wait a long time to see the fruit of God's promise in a child. And we know all too well that some moms and dads (the reasons hidden in God's sovereignty) ultimately experience profound disappointment. Still, our part as Christian parents is twofold: to request Spirit guidance from the outset and to pray and trust throughout the process of raising our children and beyond.

Post-ponderings: Do you feel entitled to indulge in audacious dreams for your kids, as Rose Kennedy did, and to pray audacious prayers for them?

WHEN PARENTS
WON'T LET GO

"First your parents, they give you your life, but then they try to give you their life."
—CHUCK PALAHNIUK

"When the man, with his concubine and his servant, got up to leave, his father-in-law, the woman's father, said, 'Now look, it's almost evening. Spend the night here; the day is nearly over. Stay and enjoy yourself.'" (Judges 19:9)

Read Judges 19:1–10.
This gruesome story, which spans the thirty verses of Judges 19, is one of the most appalling in the Bible. My intention had been to bypass it, perhaps only pointing out the similarity in the final two-thirds of the chapter to the incident in Sodom related in Genesis 19:1–9. But the opening ten verses tell an intriguing story in their own right. The word "unfaithful" (verse 2) has connotations that don't seem to be borne out, or at least aren't elaborated, in the chapter. We don't see the concubine running off with another man but instead skulking back to the security of her parents' home in Bethlehem. Might the more primitive lifestyle of a "remote area in the hill country of Ephraim" not have agreed with her? Might she simply have been young and overwhelmed and homesick?

The woman's husband comes to "persuade" her to return, and she appears willing enough. But her father insists upon incrementally prolonging the visit with strategically timed invitations to relax and enjoy some refreshment and conversation: *What's the hurry? Why, just look at the time. It's almost evening.* One gets the impression this family of birth—or at least the father and daughter—are mutually unwilling to cut the ties. The implications for our day need no elaboration. The pertinent principle appears already in Genesis 2:24: "That is why a man leaves his father and mother and is united to his wife, and they become one flesh."

Post-ponderings: The choreography of a couple's life beyond the wedding, in terms of the entrances and exits of the parents on both sides, requires balance and careful footwork. Has this been an issue in your family, particularly early on in a marriage?

CHAPTER 8

THE LATER JUDGES ERA— RUTH THROUGH SAMUEL

CHAPTER
INTRODUCTION

Despite the rough and anarchistic reputation of the judges period, the stories of Ruth and young Samuel, covered in this chapter, are beautiful and inspiring, peopled in large part by characters of integrity and sensitivity.

In terms of placement of the stories of Ruth and Samuel, respectively, within the judges era, note that "Jesse [Obed's son] had eight sons, and in Saul's time he was very old" (1 Samuel 17:12). Jesse must have been a contemporary or near contemporary of Samuel, meaning that the story of Ruth took place a couple of generations prior to that of Samuel, who provides the bridge between Israel's judgeship and early monarchy.

Naomi and Her Daughters-in-Law: "Go Back to Your Mother's Home"

"Human beings have always been an unfinished species, a story in the middle, a succession of families, tribes, and societies in transition to new awarenesses. . . . We're the only species that over and over again has deliberately transformed our surroundings in order to stretch our capacity for understanding and provoke new accomplishments. And our growing and enhanced understanding is our most valuable, and our most vulnerable, inheritance."
—TONY HISS

"Then Naomi said to her two daughters-in-law, 'Go back, each of you, to your mother's home. . . .' Then she kissed them goodbye and they wept aloud."
(Ruth 1:8–9)

Read Ruth 1:1–13.
Several years ago I had occasion to converse with a smartly dressed Bosnian sales associate. She was amazed at the number of American young people setting up independent housekeeping; in her country unmarried adults remain in their birth homes for a lifetime. Multigenerational households are common.

This is becoming increasingly true in the United States as well. "Blending" may include sons- or daughters-in-law (sometimes with kids from previous relationships), as well as family members from up to four generations. (My own household has included, repeatedly for months at a time, an ex-son-in-law, his girlfriend, her son, and my three grandchildren—at times four children under age four.) This phenomenon is cyclical in American culture, with an upsweep whenever the economy trends downward.

The word *family* is fluid in the current English vocabulary. It's a displaced term, seeking definition in the midst of flux and shakedown. If you're juggling the challenges of a multigenerational blended household, you can do no better than to remain close to your heavenly Father, your true patriarch and enabler. Your well-being is dearer to his heart than you can imagine.

Post Ponderings: Make your own or another intergenerational or otherwise blended family the focus of your prayer. Are you open to intergenerational dependency?

NAOMI AND RUTH: UNLIKELY ALLIANCE

"We have to be braver than we think we can be, because God is constantly calling us to be more than we are."
—MADELEINE L'ENGLE

"'Don't urge me to leave you or to turn back from you. Where you go I will go, and where you stay I will stay. Your people will be my people and your God my God.'"
(Ruth 1:16)

Read Ruth 1:14–18.
What was there about Naomi that so captivated her daughter-in-law? Surely not a sparkling personality or a sunny outlook. The two were united in a bond of shared suffering, but I suspect empathy for Ruth could just as well have come from Mom or Dad in Moab. And the probability of a fresh start for a vital young woman would have been far greater among her own people.

It's interesting that Ruth mentions God in her response to Naomi, above; the double reference is to "God," not "god." Evidently Naomi's God (a real and relational *person!*) played decisively into Ruth's determination to leave behind the familiar and comfortable to accompany her mother-in-law. Had Naomi's witness, notwithstanding her sometimes less than positive attitude, drawn this young woman?

Like Naomi, we have not only a God but also a people to recommend him to the world. And sometimes we do this most effectively—even if unintentionally—in our interactions with unbelieving family "members" through marriage or other association.

Post-ponderings: Who do you know personally who has been drawn to God by the testimony or lifestyle of his people?

NAOMI:
RUNNING ON EMPTY

"Women are the cup from which everyone drinks; Empowerment begins with Loving and Nurturing the self first—in order to quench the thirst of those who need us."
—MARIANNE GOLDWEBER

"'Call me Mara, because the Almighty has made my life very bitter. I went away full, but the LORD has brought me back empty.'" (Ruth 1:20)

Read Ruth 1:19–22.

The name Marah (bitter) has come up before in Old Testament history: a desert spring with acrid water earned itself that name when the disgruntled Israelites railed against Moses there (Exodus 15:23–24). A sour, resentful attitude strikes us as ungrateful and un-Christian. And it does nothing for the social status of the person giving in to it.

It's interesting that in neither of these accounts does God punish negativity or sulkiness. Jumping ahead to Ruth 4, Naomi will find her empty arms filled with a grandson who will become a forebear of Jesus. And in the exodus account God leads the Israelites on to a refreshing oasis. Is it possible that God is more gracious in this regard than we are? When we find ourselves frustrated by another's pessimism, we do well to pray for the ability both to withstand and to understand.

Life's fluctuating circumstances have a way of drawing from us impulsive reactions in lieu of considered responses. We can "blame" that on our emotions, but we're wise to remind ourselves that we're created in God's image to feel and express. The darker side of our feeling spectrum doesn't reflect God, but he in his infinite love expects, tolerates, and empathizes with our emotional highs and lows.

Post-ponderings: Identify another Bible story in which God responds to a "downer" attitude with understanding rather than censure. How open is the character in your chosen story in expressing his or her feelings to God?

VALUATION:
BOAZ'S GIFT OF DISCERNMENT

"His attentive treatment of her had nothing to do with the presumption that she was weak, and everything to do with the conviction that she was valuable."
—ANGELA N. BLOUNT

"Boaz replied, '. . . May the LORD repay you for what you have done. May you be richly rewarded by the LORD, the God of Israel, under whose wings you have come to take refuge.'" (Ruth 2:11–12)

Read Ruth 2.
Note the contrast between the behavior, attitudes, and godliness of the characters in this lyrical story and those depicted throughout most of Judges, which covers the same time period. There is some hint of the other reality in Naomi's warning that her daughter-in-law might be taken advantage of in a field other than that of Boaz. We aren't told during whose judgeship these events occurred, but the story does reassure us that God has not abandoned the faithful among his people. Bethlehem, the setting for the opening of the story of the Levite and his concubine in Judges 19:1–10, does seem to be an enclave of civility in the midst of an uncertain world.

Though well aware of Boaz's identity and status in the community, Naomi does not instruct Ruth at the outset to glean in his field. This righteous woman is not about to take advantage of the good graces of a relative or to orchestrate events in her own favor; she allows God to lead but is ready to confirm Ruth's auspicious—though random—choice when she sees evidence of blessing.

It's important that we see in this chapter more than the lead-in to a romance. Boaz was probably not a "catch" for Ruth in the way we might imagine. An older but still virile relative of Ruth's deceased father-in-law, he is a man of God who perceives and rewards virtue in this hardworking, loyal young woman.

The sensitivity to notice and reward the value in others is a gift too seldom recognized or exercised in a hectic, self-centered world. We take our cue for doing so from the person and nature of the God whose image we bear—the same God who ascribes infinite worth to every individual.

Post-ponderings: What difference does your faith make in terms of your valuation of others—both within and beyond your family?

RUTH:
REAPING FAVOR

"Once we recognize the fact that every individual is a treasury of hidden and unsuspected qualities, our lives become richer, our judgment better, and our world is more right. It is not love that is blind, it is only the unnoticed eye that cannot see the real qualities of people."
—CHARLES H. PERCY

"'The LORD bless you, my daughter,' [Boaz] replied. 'This kindness is greater than that which you showed earlier: You have not run after younger men, whether rich or poor.'" (Ruth 3:10)

Read Ruth 3.

Ruth's ritual enactment with Boaz seems brazen, but in the story's milieu this was the prescribed way for a woman to appeal to a relative's kinsman-redeemer obligation. Still, I can't imagine this young woman following through on her mother-in-law's instructions without trepidation.

Would Boaz be making a personal sacrifice in marrying Ruth? Or would the opposite be true? A case could be made for either or both, but we aren't apprised of the characters' feelings. It's evident that recognition of and appreciation for personal character transcends any other criteria—resulting in a love that supersedes other considerations.

Charles H. Percy makes an astute point about the touted blindness of love, but this discussion can take us in differing directions. An attraction based on the superficial can be shortsighted, visually impaired in terms of the ability to foresee painful realities to come. But an acuity of perception probing beneath the surface constitutes a deliberate blindness to the inconsequential and irrelevant. This is the eyes-wide-open quality of love that will stand and withstand, no matter what.

Post-ponderings: If you're married, in what sense would you describe your love as blind?

Boaz and Ruth:
Inviting Providence

"Concerning all acts of initiative (and creation), there is one elementary truth that ignorance of which kills countless ideas and splendid plans: that the moment one definitely commits oneself, then Providence moves too."
—WILLIAM HUTCHISON MURRAY

"'I have also acquired Ruth the Moabite, Mahlon's widow, as my wife, in order to maintain the name of the dead with his property, so that his name will not disappear from among the family or from the hometown. Today you are witnesses!'"
(Ruth 4:10)

Read Ruth 4:1–12.
In Boaz and Ruth two individuals of unusual character and integrity were able to see beyond their external differences to form a strong union. And that character "gene" would be passed along through Obed (see the next reflection) to Jesse and ultimately to David. Much as God would later select an unassuming young girl to bear his Son, so in this earlier time he hand-picked Ruth to bear Jesus' forebear.

It can be argued that this connection might never have developed had not Naomi, Ruth, and Boaz, each in turn, taken the initiative to invite Providence to step in. We've heard the catchy appeal from a Christian dating site that, contrary to our impulse to wait on God to reveal his will, he at times calls on us to take the next step. Simple as this may sound, it provides an intriguing take on the workings of the Spirit—one with the potential to stir in us the "aha!" moment, that epiphany that makes circumstances jump into focus. Might God be waiting for a good-faith gesture on our part to introduce something into our lives that is beyond wonderful? Might he long to see evidence of our commitment *before* opening that next door?

Post-ponderings: When have you taken a step of faith and *then* seen clear evidence of God's approval and confirmation?

NAOMI:
SATIATED AT LAST

"It is as grandmothers that our mothers come into the fullness of their grace."
—CHRISTOPHER MORLEY

"Then Naomi took the child in her arms and cared for him. The women living there said, 'Naomi has a son!'" (Ruth 4:16–17)

Read Ruth 4:13–22.
"May you live to see your children's children—peace be on Israel" (Psalm 128:6). And peace descended upon Naomi too as her arms tingled at the slight heft of this little one. No, Obed wasn't her birth grandson, but he was legally of Elimelek's line through the provision of Ruth's marriage to Naomi's kinsman-redeemer.

The empty/full theme with regard to Naomi is played out deftly in this beautifully constructed little book. The lilting words of the women of Bethlehem—formulaic though they may in part have been—echo in our ears: "Praise be to the LORD, who this day has not left you without a guardian-redeemer. May [Obed] become famous throughout Israel! He will renew your life and sustain you in your old age. For your daughter-in-law, who loves you and who is better to you than seven sons, has given him birth." What a lovely foil to the grotesque ending of the previous book.

Parenthetically, there's something to be said for those rituals of kindness and civility. Every society has them, and they facilitate the flow of human interaction. From some churches' liturgical "The Lord be with you" and its response "And also with you" to those polite exchanges we teach our kids, manners matter. In their own small way they soften our lives, daubing them with touches of grace.

Post-ponderings: When have you experienced a spiritual or emotional emptiness from which you emerged feeling full, satisfied, and gratified? To what do you attribute the change?

ELKANAH, HANNAH, AND PENINNAH: COMPENSATION DEBACLE

"Have they identified the gene that makes people pretend they're happy and that their life isn't a sham to compensate for broken dreams?"
—AUTHOR UNKNOWN

"To Hannah he gave a double portion because he loved her, and the LORD had closed her womb. . . . Her husband Elkanah would say to her, 'Hannah, why are you weeping? Why don't you eat? Why are you downhearted? Don't I mean more to you than ten sons?'" (1 Samuel 1:5, 8)

Read 1 Samuel 1:1–8.
The opening to 1 Samuel reminds me. I'm reminded by the desolate Hannah of the emptiness in Naomi. More striking, though, is the similarity of this family constellation to that of Jacob, Leah, and Rachel.

Elkanah's attempts to compensate Hannah for her childlessness unwittingly added fuel to Peninnah's jealous fire. His unapologetic preferential treatment of the obviously hurting Hannah, though well intentioned, only exacerbated the issue for the also hurting Peninnah, who longed above all else for evidence of her husband's love. I selected the above quote with Peninnah in mind. There seems to have been a whole lot of compensating going on! How sad that each of these dissatisfied women longed for precisely what the other had in plenty.

The hot box of polygamy aside, we may be compensating someone—one of our children, perhaps—for some disappointment, disability, or whatever. Our intention is to balance things out, to find a point of equilibrium in terms of contentment levels. But it seldom works that way; to begin with, we have no real idea of what's going on in each individual's heart of hearts. The successful, independent child may yearn for precisely the emotional "reward" the less competent sibling is reaping.

Post-ponderings: Have you given your children separate treatment they've perceived in some surprisingly way to be unequal or unfair?

Hannah and Eli:
The Art of Encouragement

"Instruction does much, but encouragement everything."
—JOHANN WOLFGANG VON GOETHE

"'Do not take your servant for a wicked woman; I have been praying here out of my great anguish and grief.'" (1 Samuel 1:16)

Read 1 Samuel 1:9–18.

It's interesting that Eli doesn't pry into the particulars of Hannah's anguish but simply voices a desire that God will grant her unnamed request. His restraint is laudable; surely his curiosity had been piqued. Eli's guarded approach appears to be precisely what Hannah needed.

There can be a fine line when engaged with a hurting person between probing beyond their comfort zone and working with the information they're willing to impart. It may be that acknowledging the emotion and offering encouragement based on a basic knowledge of the issues is enough. Our need to know may not be as extensive as we suppose.

Our impulse as modern Westerners is to rush immediately into solution mode when dealing with another's angst. We're uncomfortable with loose ends, wanting to tie them up quickly and send the "healed" person on their way, equipped with failsafe instructions for resolution. This applies as much to our dealings with family members as with friends, fellow church members, acquaintances, and strangers. We fail to perceive the felt need for empathy, not answers. As long as we point to the source of those answers—precisely where Hannah went in the first place—we're doing our part as Christ's representatives in a hurting world.

Post-ponderings: Would you characterize yourself as an encourager? Are you willing to adopt a less is more approach when wanting to extract detail about a problem or issue?

HANNAH AND SAMUEL: PENULTIMATE PARENTAL SACRIFICE

"Sacrifice alone, bare and unrelieved, is ghastly, unnatural, and dead; but self-sacrifice, illuminated by love, is warmth and life; it is the death of Christ, the life of God, and the blessedness and only proper life of man."
—FREDERICK W. ROBERTSON

"After [Samuel] was weaned, [Hannah] took the boy with her, young as he was . . . [T]hey brought the boy to Eli, and she said to him, 'Pardon me, my lord. As surely as you live, I am the woman who stood here beside you praying to the LORD. I prayed for this child, and the LORD has granted me what I asked of him. So now I give him to the LORD.'" (1 Samuel 1:24–28)

Read 1 Samuel 1:19–28.
Though less than the ultimate sacrifice of his only son Abraham was willing to make (Genesis 22:1–19), Hannah's offering was monumental. And it was voluntary. We don't read prior to her pregnancy of her making a vow—or, viewed in another light, a deal—with God. Her decision seems to have come after Samuel's birth in a radical demonstration of gratitude. Hannah's sacrifice preceded the advent of Jesus Christ by generations, yet it prepares us for the sacrifice of praise we owe the Lord of life.

It can be hard for us to shake natural feelings of entitlement to "our" kids, but the truth is that they belong to God; we're entrusted with the responsibility of raising them in his name. God's choosing us implies that we're credentialed for the job. Parental confidence isn't a given; many moms and dads struggle with feelings of inadequacy. In terms of his and our relationship to the children, God's ownership of and absolute investment in them can afford us unshakable comfort during the hard times.

Post-ponderings: How has your awareness of this three-way bond among you, God, and a child seen you through a specific parenting hurdle?

HOPHNI AND PHINEHAS: OUT-OF-CONTROL PRIESTLY SONS

"The God of the Old Testament is arguably the most unpleasant character in all fiction: jealous and proud of it; a petty, unjust, unforgiving control-freak; a vindictive, bloodthirsty ethnic cleanser; a misogynistic, homophobic, racist, infanticidal, genocidal, filicidal, pestilential, megalomaniacal, sadomasochistic, capriciously malevolent bully."

—RICHARD DAWKINS, OUTSPOKEN ATHEIST

"'No, my sons; the report I hear spreading among the LORD's people is not good. If one person sins against another, God may mediate for the offender; but if anyone sins against the Lord, who will intercede for them?' His sons, however, did not listen to their father's rebuke, for it was the LORD's will to put them to death."
(1 Samuel 2:24–25)

Read 1 Samuel 2:12–17, 22–25, 27–36.
As with similar Old Testament passages, we find verse 25 problematic, if not incomprehensible. Are we to conclude that God was working in conjunction with Eli's poor parenting—for which Eli would still be held responsible? We humans will never resolve this kind of dilemma. God's thoughts aren't simply higher than ours; they're on a wholly different plane to which we haven't been engineered to ascend (Isaiah 55:8–9). How easy for us to write God off because he "fails" to conform to our logical limits!

Have you noticed how often the Old Testament depicts godly fathers producing ungodly offspring—and vice versa? This is a theme that, ironically, will reappear with Samuel's grown sons (1 Samuel 7:15—8:5). As discussed in the last reflection, God's ownership of our kids can afford tremendous comfort, even when circumstances seem horribly wrong. There's a delicate balance between God orchestrating his big-picture plan and his investing in us to take responsibility for day-to-day parental decision making. As long as we're doing this, with the Spirit's guidance, to the best of our ability, we need not live with angst.

Post-ponderings: How would you respond—or have you responded—to a critic dismissing the "Old Testament God" as cruel or capricious in his dealings with humanity?

HANNAH:
GRACE ABOVE AND BEYOND

"However many blessings we expect from God, His infinite liberality will always exceed all our wishes and our thoughts."
—JOHN CALVIN

"The LORD was gracious to Hannah; she gave birth to three sons and two daughters." (1 Samuel 2:21)

Read 1 Samuel 2:18–21.
This delightful interlude, framed at both ends by the severe account of Eli and his sons, previews for us the "side" of God seen more consistently in the New Testament. The writer of Psalm 113 exults in verse 9 that the Lord "settles the childless woman in her home as a happy mother of children." And Paul enthuses in Ephesians 3:20, "Now to him who is able to do immeasurably more than all we ask or imagine, according to his power that is at work within us, to him be glory." How apropos to Hannah's unexpected serendipity!

The opening "But" of these four verses clues us in to the writer's desire to mitigate the harshness of the narrative with this understated contrast. It can feel natural for us to restrain our expectancy when it comes to blessing, to feel comfortable presenting our needs to the Father while suppressing expression of our wants. The truth is, though, that we serve a God who delights to provide not only our needs but also our desires, to lavish us with blessing beyond our expectation or request. This is the God of Zephaniah 3:17, the One who takes delight in us, rejoices over us with singing, and finds pleasure in surprising us with a surfeit of grace!

Post-ponderings: Does the paragraph above describe your modus operandi in approaching God? If so, do you see this as a conditioned response based on your upbringing or experience? How so?

SAMUEL:
THE DOCILE CHILD

"Fathers like to have children good-natured, well-behaved, and comfortable, but how to put them in that desirable condition is out of their philosophy."
—ERNESTINE ROSE

"Then Eli realized that the LORD was calling the boy. So Eli told Samuel, 'Go and lie down, and if he calls you, say, "Speak, LORD, for your servant is listening."'"
(1 Samuel 3:8–9)

Read 1 Samuel 3.

Eli's problem seems to have been passive parenting. As God expressed to young Samuel, "I told him that I would judge his family forever because of the sin he *knew about*; his sons blasphemed God, and he *failed to restrain them*" (emphasis added). We aren't told why Eli had allowed the situation to develop. Contributing factors may have been anything from the loss of the boys' mother to preoccupation with tabernacle duties, age, disillusionment, an indecisive nature, a felt lack of entitlement, physical limitations, or simple laziness.

Eli struggled with his own sons but was evidently more effective as a surrogate father to Samuel. We know from experience that some kids are by temperament more tractable than others; Samuel, it would appear, was observant and caring. It occurs to me that he may have taken upon himself the role of advocate for the old man, incapacitated as he was by near blindness and possible complications of obesity.

I picture Samuel as having to some extent "raised himself." Able to internalize discipline, he was likely counseled by his parents on their annual visits to be on his best behavior in the tabernacle environs. It's clear that the upbringing God provided prepared this prophet/judge for his decisive role in Israel's transition to a new phase of nationhood.

Post-ponderings: Would you characterize your children as compliant, challenging, or somewhere in between? Has your parenting style complemented their natures?

EARLY KINGSHIP—SAUL

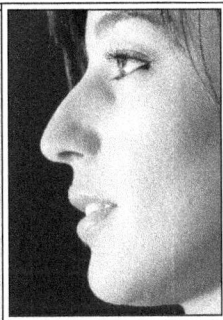

CHAPTER
INTRODUCTION

The complicated stories of Saul and David, Israel's first two kings, are intertwined almost from their beginnings, and together they have the distinction of being the most detailed and complete individual/family stories in the Bible, covering chapters 9–11 of this book. The family interactions are deep, running the gamut from noble to degenerate.

Chapter 9 details the saga of Israel's seriously flawed first king and its tragic effect on two young men of integrity who find themselves caught in the crossfire—Saul's own son Jonathan and Israel's future king, David. Because David's early story coincides with that of Saul, much of the material in this chapter focuses more on David than on Saul.

SAUL:
STIFLED MATURITY

"I am convinced that most people do not grow up . . . We marry and dare to have children and call that growing up. I think what we do is mostly grow old. We carry accumulation of years in our bodies, and on our faces, but generally our real selves, the children inside, are innocent and shy as magnolias."
—MAYA ANGELOU

Samuel said, "'To whom is all the desire of Israel turned, if not to you and your whole family line?' Saul answered, 'But am I not a Benjamite, from the smallest tribe of Israel, and is not my clan the least of all the clans of the tribe of Benjamin? Why do you say such a thing to me?'" (1 Samuel 9:20–21)

Read 1 Samuel 9–10.
Saul's lack of confidence reminds us of Gideon (Judges 6:15). Both men seem stunted in terms of maturity, clueless, engaged in the family business without question or innovation. As we know from familiarity with this ongoing story, although the physically towering Saul would rise to the occasion, his ascendency would be short-lived.

Saul's impressive stature showcases his social shortfalls: "So they inquired further of the LORD, 'Has the man come here yet?' And the LORD said, 'Yes, he has hidden himself among the supplies.' They ran and brought him out, and as he stood among the people he was a head taller than any of the others." Cowering in the baggage was hardly an optimal first impression for God's anointed! Against this backdrop I chuckle at a quote from Lev Vygotsky: "In play, a child always behaves beyond his average age, above his daily behavior. In play it is as though he were a head taller than himself."

Even under the harshest conditions, kids play. I wonder, facetiously: did Saul miss out as a kid on some imaginative play? God created us to be, like himself, inventive and ingenious. Regular time spent in leisure or recreation isn't a luxury, either for us as adults or for our kids. It helps prepare us for life's inevitable new roles and challenges.

Post-ponderings: How do you indulge your need to re-create through play? If you have young children or grandchildren, how does your playfulness benefit them?

SAUL AND JONATHAN: DEFICIENT PARENTING

"My dad had limitations. That's what my good-hearted mom always told us. He had limitations, but he meant no harm. It was kind of her to say, but he did do harm."
—GILLIAN FLYNN

"Jonathan said, 'My father has made trouble for the country. See how my eyes brightened when I tasted a little of this honey. How much better it would have been if the men had eaten today some of the plunder they took from their enemies.'" (1 Samuel 14:29–30)

Read 1 Samuel 14:24–48.
How unfortunate to be the offspring of a seriously deficient parent. We're all flawed, but it doesn't take kids long to realize that some flaws are terminal. Children in such a situation, recognizing the need for a functional adult in the household, are drawn, ready or not, to accept that role by default. I see it in my volunteer work with first-graders. These spunky quasi-adults exhibit signs of stress. Their observations about life and family are poignant and precocious. How tragi-common!

Jonathan was hardly a child. Yet it must have hurt to finally acknowledge Saul's failings. Some caring observers took the risk of intervening with the unpredictable Saul, uncertain of the outcome for themselves: "Should Jonathan die—he who has brought about this great deliverance in Israel? Never!"

David's words in Psalm 27:10 ring with pathos: "Though my father and mother forsake me, the LORD will receive me." Hopefully Jonathan could take comfort in the same assurance. And it can ring in our souls too, whether we find ourselves in the role of disappointed "child" or of interventionist. I strain to imagine what my perspective might be even today had I lacked excellent parents. How utterly devoid of encouragement are so many in our world today! And how fully equipped we are as God's children to step in to help!

Post-ponderings: Are you personally acquainted with a child who lacks responsible parenting? Do you have sufficient contact to function in a supportive role, even if it's unofficial and behind the scenes?

RATIONALIZATION AND LIMITED OBEDIENCE: SAUL'S DOWNWARD TRAJECTORY

"Partial obedience is not obedience at all; to single out easy things that do not oppose our lusts, which are not against our reputation, therein some will do more than they need; but our obedience must be universal to all God's commandments, and that because He commands it."
—RICHARD SIBBES

"Samuel said, 'Although you were once small in your own eyes, did you not become the head of the tribes of Israel?... Why did you not obey the LORD?'... 'But I did obey the LORD,' Saul said." (1 Samuel 15:17, 19–20)

Read 1 Samuel 15.
Saul indulged an unfortunate habit of partial or rationalized obedience and foolish choices. (Contrast this with Jonathan, his godly son.) Picking and choosing in the area of obedience is easier than we might recognize. Some obedience comes naturally to us; given our bents and inborn sensibilities, interests, and preferences, we might have no interest in addictive behaviors or cheating on our spouses. That wouldn't align with who we are. It would be out of character for us.

But other forms of disobedience—perhaps jealousy, hypercriticism, tale telling, or a lack of love—might suit our inclinations just fine. It's all too easy for moral, and even super moral people, to move through life complacently, oblivious to their failings in the more subjective, less measurable aspects of God's law. If we're parents, our kids are hardly fooled. They readily detect and identify hypocrisy, and that's one of the hardest labels for the Christian to overcome.

Post-ponderings: Which of God's commands do you find easiest or most natural to obey—the no brainers for you? Which are more difficult? What is there in your personality or character, or in the nature of the commandments themselves, that might explain this?

DAVID AND HIS FAMILY OF BIRTH: OVERLOOKED TAIL-ENDER

"If we are the younger, we may envy the older. If we are the older, we may feel that the younger is always being indulged. In other words, no matter what position we hold in family order of birth, we can prove beyond a doubt that we're being gypped."
—JUDITH VIORST

"[Samuel] asked Jesse, 'Are these all the sons you have?' 'There is still the youngest,' Jesse answered. 'He is tending the sheep.' Samuel said, 'Send for him; we will not sit down until he arrives.'" (1 Samuel 16:11)

Read 1 Samuel 16:1–11.

In some families the status of youngest connotes privilege and exemption from difficult challenges. Once the baby, always the baby. By way of example, Jacob's youngest son, Benjamin (still "the boy" well into his man years), was fiercely protected by his older siblings, particularly after Joseph's departure from the scene.

David's situation was quite opposite. As youngest, he was treated as an afterthought: the inheritor of hand-me-down, lowest-rung chores and the one of whom expectations were low to nonexistent. While this is atypical in our day of smaller families, it wasn't uncommon even a generation or two ago, when families tended to be large and upbringings regimented.

Even in the small family, it's inevitable that kids will play different roles and even experience different upbringings, depending in part on their birth-order status. And we can depend on it, human nature being what it is, that every child will grow up toting a unique bagful of resentments. Hopefully memory of perceived slights will diminish in retrospect with the broader perspective of age.

Post-ponderings: In what ways did you grow up convinced that you'd been gyped? Are these grievances still with you?

DAVID:
A BEAUTIFUL HEART

"God sees hearts as we see faces."
—GEORGE HERBERT

"'The LORD does not look at the things people look at. People look at the outward appearance, but the LORD looks at the heart.'" (1 Samuel 16:7)

Read 1 Samuel 16:7–13.
An anonymous saying has it that if we have a song of faith in our heart it will be "heard" by the look on our face. If that's true, our outward appearance reflects to others what God is already seeing/hearing in our heart. No, there's no automatic facelift involved here. But clear, sparkling eyes and lips turned more upward than downward will give a lift both to us and to all others with whom we come into contact.

A benediction found in Numbers twice mentions God's face: "The LORD make his face shine on you and be gracious to you; the LORD turn his face toward you and give you peace" (Numbers 6:25–26). And Exodus 34:29 relates what happened to Moses as the result of speaking to God face to face: "When Moses came down from Mount Sinai . . . he was not aware that his face was radiant because he had spoken with the LORD." In Moses' case, the luminosity was so extreme the people were afraid to look at him.

What about us as Christ's representatives? Is the wonder of having been with the Lord reflected in the clarity of our gaze and the brightness of our smile? And if we are indeed smiling, is our heart where our mouth is?

Post-ponderings: To what degree does your typical facial expression reflect to a watching world a God-centered heart condition?

DAVID AND HIS BROTHERS: THE GOLIATH INCIDENT

"Words don't have the power to hurt you, unless that person meant more to you than you were willing to confess."
—SHANNON L. ALDER

"When Eliab, David's oldest brother, heard him speaking with the men, he burned with anger at him and asked, 'Why have you come down here? And with whom did you leave those few sheep in the wilderness? I know how conceited you are and how wicked your heart is; you came down only to watch the battle.' 'Now what have I done?' said David. 'Can't I even speak?'" (1 Samuel 17:28–29)

Read 1 Samuel 17.
The verbal exchange between Eliab and David recorded in the above verses sounds almost comically typical of what we know of sibling interaction, right down to the frustrated "Can't I even *speak?*" The brothers were rankled, not to mention humiliated, at this afterthought brother's unexpected anointing. Beyond 1 Samuel 18:1–2 (see the quote for the next reflection) we don't read much about David's brothers following this story (but do see 22:1). Relationships may have remained less than cordial, but we can't assume this to have been the last word in sibling interface.

The success of one family member, particularly if it might be construed as being at the expense of another, can leave a bitter taste in the mouths of less visible siblings. If you're a brother or sister, in what incarnation of closeness or distance are your sibling relationships now, and why? Are you willing to take the initiative to foster a higher degree of understanding, acceptance, and mutual appreciation?

Post-ponderings: Reflect briefly on the intriguing similarities between this account and the story of Joseph being sent by his father to check on his brothers in the field (Genesis 37:12–36).

DAVID AND JONATHAN: CLOSER THAN BROTHERS

> "You know it's love when all you want is that person to be happy, even if you're not part of their happiness."
>
> —AUTHOR UNKNOWN

> *"After David had finished talking with Saul, Jonathan became one in spirit with David, and he loved him as himself. From that day Saul kept David with him and did not let him return home to his family." (1 Samuel 18:1–2)*

Read 1 Samuel 18:1–4.
Have you ever reflected on what Jonathan had at stake in his decision to protect and promote David? This was no ordinary friendship. Nor was Jonathan naïve about the inevitable. Listen to the beautiful affirmation five chapters later: "Saul's son Jonathan went to David at Horesh and helped him find strength in God. 'Don't be afraid,' he said. 'My father Saul will not lay a hand on you. You will be king over Israel, and I will be second to you. Even my father Saul knows this'" (23:16–17).

If we didn't know the story so well, this sacrificial friendship would come as a delightful surprise. Jonathan's alliance with David nudges us ahead to another serendipity, a sacrificial friendship marking the fulcrum point of history. This love too would entail the voluntary relinquishment of a throne. Jonathan's loving David "as himself" moves us to Jesus' directive to love our neighbor in this way (Mark 12:31). Could it even be possible, based on the examples of Jonathan and Jesus, to love a friend *better* than oneself?

In the words of Solomon, "One who has unreliable friends soon comes to ruin, but there is a friend who sticks closer than a brother" (Proverbs 18:24). What a privilege for each of us to claim that relationship with our Friend, Brother, Savior, and Lord!

Post-ponderings: What special human friendship has graced your life, either now or in the past? Aside from immediate family members, which person knows you best?

SAUL AND MICHAL: "OUTCOME ENGINEERS"

"You are a manipulator. I like to think of myself more as an outcome engineer."
—J. R. WARD

"When Saul realized that the LORD was with David and that his daughter Michal loved David, Saul became still more afraid of him, and he remained his enemy the rest of his days." (1 Samuel 18:28–29)

Read 1 Samuel 18:5—19:17.
A wily Saul had reneged on his promise to offer Michal's hand to the soldier who would slay the Philistine giant (17:25; though see 2 Samuel 3:14), and David declines Saul's offer of Merab. But a new opportunity presents itself: "Now Saul's daughter Michal was in love with David, and when they told Saul about it, he was pleased. 'I will give her to him,' he thought, 'so that she may be a snare to him and so that the hand of the Philistines may be against him.'"

A fascinating story, this, with all the stuff of a riveting fairytale. Michal, presented to David as a pawn, ends up protecting her husband from her father: "Michal let David down through a window, and he fled and escaped. Then Michal took an idol and laid it on the bed, covering it with a garment and putting some goats' hair at the head. When Saul sent the men to capture David, Michal said, 'He is ill.'"

Children who grow up manipulated can become masters of deceit. I chuckle at this quote from Flannery O'Connor: "Mrs. Hopewell had no bad qualities of her own but she was able to use other people's in such a constructive way that she never felt the lack." We learn at the end of chapter 25 that in David's absence Saul has given his daughter Michal to another man. Subjected to continued manipulation Michal would gain the sophistication to nurture negative qualities of her very own! (See the reflection on 2 Samuel 6.)

Post-ponderings: Who do you know who was in some way manipulated in childhood? If you are still acquainted with this person, are aftereffects apparent?

JONATHAN'S INCREDULITY: "IT ISN'T SO!"

"I guess love is the real suspension of disbelief."
—MELISSA BANK

"Saul's anger flared up at Jonathan and he said to him, 'You son of a perverse and rebellious woman! Don't I know that you have sided with the son of Jesse to your own shame and to the shame of the mother who bore you?'" (1 Samuel 20:30)

Read 1 Samuel 20.
Disparaging someone's mother can touch the rawest nerve; think of those formulaic slurs: "Your mama's a . . . " And a father's use of this ploy with his child is a low blow. Kids resist thinking the worst of either parent, and when one denigrates the other it can be hard to sort out loyalties. Sometimes the easiest solution is for the child to feel responsible for the presenting problem.

Kids tend to hold on to positive beliefs about bad parents, sometimes into adulthood. It took Jonathan a while to accept the extent of his father's animosity against his best friend: "*Why* should he be put to death? What has he *done?*" And we feel the anguish just prior to Jonathan's reluctant concession to reality: "But Saul hurled his spear at him to kill him. Then Jonathan knew that his father intended to kill David."

Jonathan's eyes were opened wide, and he would covertly support David from that point on. But open rebellion against, or estrangement from, his father we do not see. Was the adult Jonathan willing to retain some loyalty to his dad despite the suspension of his disbelief in the degree of Saul's depravity?

Post-ponderings: Recall a time when you found yourself deeply disappointed in a parent—or recognized that your child(ren) had legitimate reason to feel that way about you? How did you, or they, deal with the situation?

A Dad's Blinders:
"None of You Is Concerned about Me!"

"Mental illnesses have a resounding component of selfishness. Children are born selfish and it's a natural survival trait so what happens when children lose that God-given right and privilege? Fear, guilt, and shame take over the children's thoughts. Fear of things getting worse or losing the parent's love, guilt over having natural selfish feelings and needs of their own, and shame because your family is different."
—AUTHOR UNSPECIFIED

Saul said to his officials, "'Is that why you have all conspired against me? No one tells me when my son makes a covenant with the son of Jesse. None of you is concerned about me or tells me that my son has incited my servant to lie in wait for me, as he does today.'" (1 Samuel 22:8)

Read 1 Samuel 22:6–23.
What a tragic account—and all due to the paranoia, or narcissism, of a deeply disturbed ruler. Saul redirects his accusation of conspiracy, this time focusing on the unsuspecting priest Ahitub. The outcome, at the hands of the mercenary Doeg, is beyond appalling. Saul's words, above, hark back to the events of chapter 20, the story behind Jonathan urging David to flee for his life from his deranged father. It's amazing, two chapters later, that Saul attempts to channel the empathy in his own direction. Is this insanely jealous king the one in danger or the source of the danger? The pursued or the pursuer?

The children of a parent with mental illness may grow up in a private world that is unpredictable and irrational. If they have learned to conceal their humiliation to the point that no one outside the family notices or intervenes, the result can be devastating for their developing psyches. If you're acquainted with a family struggling with this kind of challenge, how might you respond to alleviate some of the trauma?

Post-ponderings: Is there a double standard between your family's, and/or your church's, responses to physical versus mental or emotional illness? Does an unspoken taboo exist in terms of acknowledging the latter?

ABIGAIL:
WIFE IN CLEANUP MODE

"The house does not rest upon the ground, but upon a woman."
—MEXICAN PROVERB

"'Please pay no attention, my lord, to that wicked man Nabal. He is just like his name—his name means Fool, and folly goes with him. And as for me, your servant, I did not see the men my lord sent.'" (1 Samuel 25:25)

Read 1 Samuel 25.

The story of Abigail seems for whatever reason to be a little known gem. This chapter characterizes wife and husband in a few to-the-point words: "She was an intelligent and beautiful woman, but her husband was surly and mean in his dealings."

"If you want to get across an idea," counsels Ralph Bunche, "wrap it up in person." This was Abigail's approach in engaging David following her husband's potentially costly gaffe. The point could be made that this remarkable woman was the ultimate diplomat, but I prefer to see her in a slightly softer light, as peacemaker extraordinaire. It seems to me that her story wouldn't have been included in the Bible if this were not the case. Abigail's decisive action averted what could have lived on in history as a serious blight on David's character. In terms of David's wives, we hear more about Michal and Bathsheba, both of whose stories include scandal. In contrast, Abigail takes her place in memory as the behind-the-scenes encourager and centering influence David needed to maintain balance.

Post-ponderings: Pause to consider the lovely imagery—a possibly idiomatic expression—in the italicized words to follow, spoken by Abigail to David: "*The life of my lord will be bound securely in the bundle of the living* by the LORD your God." What thoughts or feelings does this metaphor call up for you?

DAVID AND HIS ARMY AT ZIKLAG: A HUSBAND'S PROTECTOR ROLE

"She didn't need to understand the meaning of life; it was enough to find someone who did, and then fall asleep in his arms and sleep as a child sleeps, knowing
that someone stronger than you is protecting you from all evil and all danger."
—PAULO COELHO

*"When David and his men reached Ziklag, they found it destroyed by fire and their
wives and sons and daughters taken captive. So David and his men wept aloud
until they had no strength left to weep. David's two wives had been captured—
Ahinoam of Jezreel and Abigail, the widow of Nabal of Carmel." (1 Samuel 30:3–5)*

Read 1 Samuel 30.
David and his nomadic band of outlaws were essentially homeless, their
wives and children roving with them. Saul had already "taken back" David's
childless wife Michal, but the other two, Ahinoam and Abigail, were with
him (25:42–43).

We see in this story a touching and highly positive picture of David, not
only in his concern for the captured families but also in his kindness to the
men who had been too exhausted to pursue the raiding party and retrieve
the wives and children. This chapter sets both the scene and the tone for
the ending of 1 Samuel (Saul's suicide follows in the last chapter) and the
beginning of the second half of this divided book.

We see in this vignette a striking contrast between the outgoing king
and the soon-to-be incoming, as well as between David's own grief and his
decisive action. The combination of sensitive family man and take-charge
doer—David, as we know, was both a poet/musician and a warrior—strikes
us as the ideal mix for an effective husband and father.

Post-ponderings: If you're a husband, what positive contrasts characterize the different "sides" of you? If you're a wife, how would you answer this
question about your husband?

CHAPTER 10

EARLY KINGSHIP—DAVID, PART 1

CHAPTER
INTRODUCTION

David's complex relationships are an up-and-down proposition. A man of sensitivity and honor, his personality reflects a curious melding of poet and warrior. He suffers relational disappointments for which he is not responsible, but the tables turn five reflections from the end of this chapter when his unexplained decision not to accompany his army on its spring campaign leaves him off balance and subject to temptation.

While David's situation as king intersects much less with our own reality than, for instance, Jacob's more ordinary circumstances, we have much to learn from his very human interactions and indiscretions, particularly on the issue of parenting..

DAVID LAMENTS
A BROTHER

"We criticize males for 'only caring about one thing' and 'not being in touch with their emotions,' even while we judge them by their sexual achievements and emasculate them when they're too emotional or 'inappropriately' emotional according to masculinity's guidelines."
—AUTHOR UNSPECIFIED

"'I grieve for you, Jonathan my brother; you were very dear to me. Your love for me was wonderful, more wonderful than that of women.'" (2 Samuel 1:26)

Read 2 Samuel 1:17–27.
David's words in this verse aren't to be taken as the hint of a homosexual tendency. Western men face a taboo about expressing platonic affection for other men that isn't found in much of the rest of the world. Male friendships in North America often find expression in macho ways that might not be natural to some of those who adopt them. Back-slapping, hijinks, heavy drinking, and "manly" activities: all of these and other "coded" indications of attachment send a message that all is on the up and up, that men are just being men. Many do opt for a softer expression of rapport with male friends, of course; much depends on the cultural expectations of a man's personal circle and social stratum.

It's ironic that, while women in many ways still take—or feel they take—second place to men, the unwritten rules governing their behavior are much looser. There's a natural liberation in terms of expressing emotion and affection that has been their birthright. Little boys are being allowed greater leeway these days, but it doesn't take a long initiation into schooldays before they begin to lose ground in terms of gender constraints. As expressed in the reflection on 1 Samuel 30, David was in many ways a man of striking contrasts in beautiful equilibrium—a fitting model for modern Christian manhood.

Post-ponderings: Define the limit of your comfort level in terms of a man's platonic friendships.

JOAB AND ABNER: "BROTHERHOOD" AMBIGUITY AND AMBIVALENCE

"I will hurt you for this. I don't know how yet, but give me time. A day will come when you think yourself safe and happy, and suddenly your joy will turn to ashes in your mouth, and you'll know the debt is paid."
—GEORGE R. R. MARTIN

"All the people took note and were pleased; indeed, everything the king did pleased them. So on that day all the people there and all Israel knew that the king had no part in the murder of Abner son of Ner." (2 Samuel 3:36–37)

Read 2 Samuel 2; 3:6–39.
From the initial truce between Abner and Joab to Ish-Bosheth's accusation of Abner regarding Rizpah to David's demand for the return of Michal and the resulting grief of Paltiel, there's much discussion-worthy material here. I've chosen to bypass these earlier themes to focus on Joab's treachery.

The relationship between Abner and Joab, given their shared history, was ambivalent following the political realignment now casting them as opponents. Although Abner, in some sense spoiling for a showdown, had instigated the staged hand-to-hand skirmish that had turned so ugly, he still respected—and naively trusted—Joab. Listen to Abner's words to Asahel: "Stop chasing me! Why should I strike you down? How could I look your brother Joab in the face?" These commanders' entrenched military brotherhood couldn't easily be negated by shifting political circumstances.

Joab's duplicitous avenging of his birth brother's death was unconscionable. Brotherhood, as reflected in this sad account, can take on multifaceted and complex iterations. Human relationships, as we know so well, are seldom simple or straightforward.

Post-ponderings: Beyond the brotherhood and sisterhood of believers in Christ, who do you count as fulfilling these roles in your life? How healthy are your relationships with your birth or adoptive siblings?

POLITICAL EXPEDIENCY: MICHAL RETURNED

"Don't lock me in wedlock, I want marriage, an encounter."
—DENISE LEVERTOV

"David sent messengers to Ish-Bosheth [then king of the ten northern tribes] son of Saul, demanding, 'Give me my wife Michal, whom I betrothed to myself for the price of a hundred Philistine foreskins.' So Ish-Bosheth gave orders and had her taken away from her husband Paltiel son of Laish. Her husband, however, went with her, weeping behind her all the way to Bahurim. Then Abner said to him, 'Go back home!' So he went back." (2 Samuel 3:14–16)

Read 2 Samuel 3:1–16.
This short story is embedded in the passage covered in the last reflection. We aren't apprised here of Michal's feelings, though we may read between the lines. We know that she had at one point loved David, but based on Paltiel's grief we surmise that the more recent union had also been strong. Michal had evidently been played as a pawn one time too many, and we'll see clearly in the next reflection that she had changed. Although in some sense we can't fault David for demanding the return of his legitimate wife, it seems this wasn't one of his finer moments.

Unions based on political expediency don't relate to our experience, but they've characterized much of history. Perhaps the connection to our lives comes in contrast. The expression in 1 Samuel 18:20 of Michal's having been in love with David stands alone in the Bible, the concept of falling in love anachronistic to the times. Pause to consider the opportunity for love-based marriage as a manifestation of God's grace in some sense unique to recent history. Are you grateful for this God-ordained provision for our lives?

Post-ponderings: What part does love, and more specifically being in love, play in your marriage? How have the specifics changed from one stage of your marriage to another?

MICHAL:
A WIFE'S SCORN

"When a woman thinks her husband is a fool, her marriage is over. They may part in one year or ten; they may live together until death. But if she thinks he is a fool, she will not love him again."
—PHILIPPA GREGORY

"Michal daughter of Saul came out to meet [David] and said, 'How the king of Israel has distinguished himself today, going around half naked in full view of the slave girls of his servants as any vulgar fellow would.' David said to Michal, '... I will celebrate before the LORD. I will become even more undignified than this, and I will be humiliated in my own eyes. But by these slave girls you spoke of, I will be held in honor.'" (2 Samuel 6:20–22)

Read 2 Samuel 6.

The ark of the covenant, captured earlier by the Philistines, had been retrieved by Israel. David was on a joyous mission: to return this sacred object to the Jerusalem tabernacle. He didn't travel incognito. It seems that "all the king's men"—thirty thousand, to be exact—accompanied him for this less than stealthy operation. David was outrageously happy, and his particular brand of enthusiasm was raucous and untamed. The king wore a linen ephod, a close-fitting, sleeveless pullover of hip length, maximizing freedom of movement as he leaped and danced and bellowed his way forward.

Enter Michal. Well, not exactly *enter*. David's wife chose to observe the spectacle from behind the shadow of a palace window. How did she react to her husband's unrestrained display? The account minces no words: Michal "despised him in her heart." The author of Samuel doesn't fill in the gap between chapters 3 and 6, but it's apparent the situation between David and Michal hadn't improved since their awkward reunion. The Philippa Gregory quote, above, seems right on. A level of mutual respect that transcends this kind of thinking or name-calling is vital to the survival of a relationship.

Post-ponderings: Where do you and your spouse draw the line in terms of the "rules" governing disagreement?

David and His Family:
A Father Blesses His Household

"No matter what you've done for yourself or for humanity, if you can't look back on having given love and attention to your own family, what have you accomplished?"
—ELBERT HUBBARD

"Then all the people left, each for their own home, and David returned home to bless his family." (1 Chronicles 16:43)

Read 1 Chronicles 16:1–3, 37–43.
David was functioning in a priestly role in blessing the people, and blessing his family ("household" in 2 Samuel 6:20) fell naturally in line. The apostle Peter speaks much later of what we now know as the priesthood of all believers: "You are a chosen people, a royal priesthood, a holy nation, God's special possession, that you may declare the praises of him who called you out of darkness into his wonderful light" (1 Peter 2:9).

I find myself intrigued by that turn of phrase "bless his family." The closest synonym to "bless" in this context seems to be "sanctify," which can mean to consecrate, purify, or dedicate. Priests, as we know, also intercede—a beautiful example appears in Job 1:5: "When a period of feasting had run its course, Job would make arrangements for [his children] to be purified . . . thinking, 'Perhaps my children have sinned and cursed God in their hearts.' This was Job's regular custom."

Our responsibility to our families begins with the love and attention Hubbard cites but goes far beyond making engagement with them a high priority. We in our priestly role have a primary obligation to our families that incorporates in one way or another all of the above functions, very much including testimony about the One who has called us out of darkness, along with heartfelt declaration of his praise.

Post-ponderings: In what ways do you consistently bless your family?

A Place to Call Home:
Security in Israel

"Home is a notion that only nations of the homeless fully appreciate and only the uprooted comprehend."
—WALLACE STEGNER

""I will provide a place for my people Israel and will plant them so that they can have a home of their own and no longer be disturbed."" (2 Samuel 7:10)

Read 2 Samuel 7:1–10.

The verse above isn't typically the focus of this pivotal salvation passage, but it lends itself to the theme of biblical families and households. As we recall from the reflection on 1 Samuel 30, David and two of his wives had experienced an itinerant, tent-dwelling season. As the Stegner quote suggests, anyone who has endured homelessness appreciates the notion of one's own, undisturbed and inviolable, place of respite. I can't help but wonder whether this recollection would in part spur David to rue God's continued tabernacle residence—a concern God assured his servant he did not share.

We as Christians already enjoy that ultimate home of our own. In the words of Richelle E. Goodrich, "Life is a love story, with every character yearning for permanent refuge in someone's heart." Make that "Someone's," and the point is clear. As fleshed out in the reflection on John 14:5–23; 15:1–17, our position in Christ affords us a movable refuge, an inviolate, carry-along security.

Post-ponderings: Where is your home of your own—the one from which, come what may, you can never be uprooted? Do your children know it too?

GOD'S FAMILIAL
PROMISE TO DAVID

"God never made a promise that was too good to be true."
—DWIGHT L. MOODY

"'If my house were not right with God, surely he would not have made with me an everlasting covenant, arranged and secured in every part; surely he would not bring to fruition my salvation and grant me my every desire.'" (2 Samuel 23:5)

Read 2 Samuel 7:11–29; 1 Chronicles 17:1–15.
How like our God to turn the tables on our best-laid plans for his glory, showering us in the process with unexpected and unmerited blessing! Paul's rhetorical question in Romans 8:32 comes to mind: "He who did not spare his own Son, but gave him up for us all—how will he not also, along with him, graciously give us all things?"

David's awed response to this grace beyond reason provides a model for us as parents and family members: "Who am I, Sovereign LORD, and what is my family, that you have brought me this far?" Who, we might ask, are we and *our* families that you should include us in your covenant of grace? That you should have chosen us from among all the families of earth as adoptees into your own family, destined for eternal joy! Do our children understand the implications of God's establishing *his* kingdom in part through *our* estate?

Post-ponderings: Reread and ponder David's words in 2 Samuel 23:5, allowing the pronouns "my" and "me" to apply not to David but to yourself (and, by extension, your family). Then thank God for his promise keeping to you and yours.

DAVID AND MEPHIBOSHETH:
DAVID KEEPS HIS PROMISE

"Promise only what you can deliver. Then deliver more than you promise."
—AUTHOR UNKNOWN

"David asked, 'Is there anyone still left of the house of Saul to whom I can show kindness for Jonathan's sake?'" (2 Samuel 9:1)

Read 2 Samuel 9.
We aren't told why David waited this long to inquire about survivors of the house of Saul, but we aren't surprised at his promise keeping. Mephibosheth's lameness disqualified him for a bid for the throne; still, David found it expedient to keep him on a short leash. Ziba, Saul's former steward, and his sizable entourage had been administering Mephibosheth's holdings, supposedly on his behalf, but it's difficult to know the extent of Ziba's loyalty or trustworthiness (see the reflection on 2 Samuel 16:1–4; 19:24–30).

Keeping an unconditional promise, especially an open-ended one, can entail unanticipated complications. Mephibosheth's self-assessment as a "dead dog" indicates the societal implications of a physical disability that rendered an individual incapable of sustaining himself. There's an interesting juxtaposition here between God's eternal promise to David two chapters early and David's fulfillment of his own promise to show kindness to Jonathan's family. How can you and your family "pass along" God's marvelous grace?

Post-ponderings: The *NIV Study Bible* footnote on 2 Samuel 9:8 points out the author's use of the "dog" or "dead dog" motif. Take the time to look up the relevant passages: 1 Samuel 17:43; 24:14; 25:3 ("Calebite" means "dog"); and 2 Samuel 16:9.

DAVID AND BATHSHEBA: IDLE EYES

"Boredom can be a lethal thing on a small island."
—CHRISTOPHER MOORE

"David had done what was right in the eyes of the LORD and had not failed to keep any of the LORD's commands all the days of his life—except in the case of Uriah the Hittite." (1 Kings 15:5)

Read 2 Samuel 11.

The opening verse of this sordid chapter portends trouble: "In the spring, at the time when kings go off to war, . . . David remained in Jerusalem." This sounds innocent enough, but the picture is skewed. We aren't told why David elected to take a hiatus from his annual rhythm, but his self-imposed idleness boded no good. David, the king God would prevent from building his temple because of the warrior blood on his hands (1 Chronicles 22:8–9), during this interim had time on his hands—and it didn't belong there!

The adage "idle hands are the devil's workshop," trite as it may sound, has a basis in truth. And idle eyes invite trouble just as certainly. The point can be made that pornography (the modern variation on David's roof-peeking) wouldn't be such an issue without the underlying problem of tedium. As Paul reminds us, "You should mind your own business and work with your hands [or eyes, depending on the nature of your job] . . . so that your daily life may win the respect of outsiders" (1 Thessalonians 4:11–12).

Post-ponderings: In what areas do your eyes—or hands, as the case may be—get you into trouble? How does boredom, or inactivity, affect your kids during their "off" seasons?

NATHAN'S PARABLE:
ON-THE-MARK INCRIMINATION

"Nothing that grieves us can be called little: by the eternal laws of proportion a child's loss of a doll and a king's loss of a crown are events of the same size."
—MARK TWAIN

"'The poor man had nothing except one little ewe lamb he had bought. He raised it, and it grew up with him and his children. It shared his food, drank from his cup and even slept in his arms. It was like a daughter to him.'" (2 Samuel 12:3)

Read 2 Samuel 12:1–14.
"The fact of storytelling hints at a fundamental human unease, hints at human imperfection," reflects Ben Okri. "Where there is perfection there is no story to tell." An effective story requires a protagonist (the good guy), an antagonist (the guy who antagonizes the good guy), and a crisis. Take any riveting Bible story and you've got these elements.

I can't help but admire Nathan's skill. The prophet's emphatic "You are the man!" reverberates in our ears. The same line (substitute "that person" to drive this home) could be affixed to every parable. It's so comfortable to ease ourselves off the hook as we recognize other people in the Bible's deceptively simple parables. But that "fundamental human unease" is intended to afflict each of us. If we're willing to take a closer look, *we're there* in every case. Ask God for the courage to point the finger in your own direction when you engage with this or any other biblical parable.

Post-ponderings: Try putting yourself in the place of the rich man in Nathan's story. In what subtle ways might your family be exploiting the less fortunate? This story and its aftermath (verse 1 through the beginning of verse 7 would be sufficient) offer excellent material for family devotions.

DAVID AND HIS INFANT SON: STRAINING TOWARD REUNION

"We never know the love of our parents for us till we have become parents."
—HENRY WARD BEECHER

"'Now that [my son] is dead, why should I go on fasting? Can I bring him back again? I will go to him, but he will not return to me.'" (2 Samuel 12:23)

Read 2 Samuel 12:15–25.
"Where there's life, there's hope." Clichéd as this may sound, it's the principle on which David operated during his son's illness. Yet he embraced a far more certain hope, the assurance that he would one day rejoin the newborn where *he* was.

The Bible tells us little about our anticipated heavenly reunions. God speaks through his prophet in Isaiah 65:17: "See, I will create new heavens and a new earth. The former things will not be remembered, nor will they come to mind." On my initial encounter with this verse, I'll admit that my heart sank; I didn't want to forget. A note from the *NIV Study Bible* suggests, though, that the reference to memory has to do not with the people we've lost but with the associated pain and sorrow (included in the "old order" of things).

God hasn't seen fit to reveal in his Word the detail we crave, but a proliferation of recent reports of near-death experiences seems to reinforce the validity of David's anticipation as expressed in 2 Samuel 12:23. The following is excerpted from *90 Minutes in Heaven* by Don Piper: "Joy pulsated through me as I looked around, and at that moment I became aware of a large crowd of people. . . . As they surged toward me, I knew instantly that all of them had died during my lifetime. Their presence seemed absolutely natural."

Post-ponderings: Do you consider it possible that these reports of near-death experiences constitute revelation from God on a subject of universal interest to Christians?

AMNON AND TAMAR:
BECAUSE HE COULD

"The human race tends to remember the abuses to which it has been subjected rather than the endearments. What's left of kisses? Wounds, however, leave scars."
—BERTOLT BRECHT

"But he refused to listen to her, and since he was stronger than she, he raped her. Then Amnon hated [Tamar] with intense hatred. In fact, he hated her more than he had loved her." (2 Samuel 13:14–15)

Read 2 Samuel 13:1–19.
We have no way of knowing how much David's older children understood of what had transpired with Bathsheba and Uriah, but they must have surmised enough. It seems that David, following his conversation with Nathan, came to terms with his failings and their fallout. But residual guilt remained, along with a diminished sense of entitlement to discipline his children.

Amnon's scheme was anything but adroit; beyond arranging an opportunity to be alone with his half-sister he wasted no energy in forethought. And the fact that he raped Tamar *because he could!* does nothing for his reputation. His reaction to his victim following his assault is telling. Amnon may have realized the futility of any illusion of benefit from his action. It may be that Tamar's "accusing" presence posed an impediment to any positive future he could foresee. Or that the reality behind his flight of fancy failed completely to live up to his unrealistic expectations.

The natural consequences of parental indiscretion visiting itself on later generations is all too real. Loss of respect for a parent leads at the least to envelope pushing. Shaken trust in Dad or Mom diminishes kids' self-esteem and lowers their standards for personal expectation and behavior.

Post-ponderings: Self-fulfilling prophecies, for good or ill, often have their basis in childhood. Whom do you know who has "lived down to" low self-expectations based on a parent's failings?

ABSALOM AND AMNON:
A BROTHER AVENGES

"They say that blood is thicker than water. Maybe that's why we battle our own with more energy and gusto than we would ever expend on strangers."
—DAVID ASSEL

"Absalom never said a word to Amnon, either good or bad; he hated Amnon because he had disgraced his sister Tamar." (2 Samuel 13:22)

Read 2 Samuel 13:20–38.

I get a fascinating image of that wailing band of princes trotting home on their donkeys. The unthinkable has happened, and they're dazed and clueless. How interesting that David had declined Absalom's invitation. Since Absalom's action was clearly premeditated, he must have banked on this response. David evidently understood the invitation to be a formality and made no attempt to feign busyness. The truth was, just as he expressed it, that his presence would have been a burden. David was understandably suspicious of Absalom's mention of inviting his older brother, to whom he hadn't spoken in two icy years. Perhaps it was in an attempt to allay his misgivings that David sent not merely Amnon but all the younger princes as well.

David loved his dashing and charismatic second son, but he seems to have had a lot more trouble being decisive with his offspring than with his military or servants. Perhaps he felt that he deserved the estrangement that was to follow Amnon's murder; still, as we learn, he "longed to go to Absalom, for he was consoled concerning Amnon's death." The king's emotional paralysis was deep-seated, and the father/son standoff seemed intractable.

I'm struck by the similarity between this father's inaction and Jacob's centuries earlier, back when the patriarch perceived the escalating crisis among his own sons but unwisely opted to "keep the matter in mind" (Genesis 37:11). There's "a time to be silent and a time to speak" (Ecclesiastes 3:7). Both of these biblical fathers missed the moment for action; with headstrong and impulsive youth the window of opportunity can be narrow.

Post-ponderings: Think of a time in your life when your good intentions were sabotaged by your resentment over a lack of recognition on the part of someone you wanted to impress. What was the outcome?

CHAPTER 11

Early Kingship—David, Part 2

CHAPTER
INTRODUCTION

A theme in the life of David beginning with the Bathsheba incident toward the end of the last chapter is the natural and at times generational consequences of evil, even for the repentant sinner. Prior to that point David had been a heroic character, a protagonist with whom the reader is pleased to relate. His remorse and repentance are real and appropriate, and God forgives his sexual indiscretion and subsequent murder, but David's family story after that point is rife with tragedy, slipping steadily downhill.

DAVID AND ABSALOM:
A PROBLEM IGNORED

"Ignoring a problem isn't the same as being ignorant of it."
—JAROD KINTZ

"The woman said, '... Like water spilled on the ground, which cannot be recovered, so we must die. But that is not what God desires; rather, he devises ways so that a banished person does not remain banished from him.'" (2 Samuel 14:13–14)

Read 2 Samuel 13:38—14:33.
"'Why have I come from Geshur?'" seethed this son left by his father in anguished limbo. "'It would be better for me if I were still there! Now then, I want to see the king's face, and if I am guilty of anything, let him put me to death.' So Joab went to the king and told him this. Then the king summoned Absalom, and he came in and bowed down with his face to the ground before the king. And the king kissed Absalom."

Absalom expected more from David than this overdue and formulaic gesture. This intense young man wanted full disclosure between father and son, a no-holds-barred confrontation—and, hopefully, reconciliation. He yearned for his dad to address the whole sordid train of events, from incest to a murder put off until it became clear that the father had no intention of acting. David's insipid embrace—far too little and woefully too late—served only to fan the flames of Absalom's outrage.

The words of the wise woman were Spirit inspired. God desires neither our death nor our banishment from himself. And he was willing to pay the ultimate sacrifice of his own Son to eliminate the need for the agony of estrangement. He understands in his Father heart the ache of isolation, just as Jesus knows the agony of abandonment, however temporary, by the Father.

Post-ponderings: Avoidance in a family context is never a wise or effective response. When have you endured isolation on the basis of someone else's unwillingness to confront a problem? Did you ever find resolution, or was the issue allowed to blow over or burn out?

ITTAI'S CHOICE:
IMMIGRANTS RETURN TO WANDERING

"History shows that it is not only senseless and cruel, but also difficult to state who is a foreigner."
—CLAUDIO MAGRIS

"The king said to Ittai the Gittite, 'Why should you come along with us? Go back and stay with King Absalom. You are a foreigner, an exile from your homeland. You came only yesterday. And today shall I make you wander about with us, when I do not know where I am going? Go back, and take your people with you.'"
(2 Samuel 15:19–20)

Read 2 Samuel 15:19–22.

The king's displacement would have far-reaching consequences for many individuals and families; David's sensitivity to this new Philistine immigrant is touching. Ittai's response in verse 21 reminds me of Ruth's when her Israelite mother-in-law intervened to release her from a sacrificial commitment (Ruth 1:16).

Parenthetically, it appears that this émigré was a man of some consequence to David, despite his recent appearance on the scene: "The king commanded Joab, Abishai and Ittai, 'Be generous with the young man Absalom for my sake'" (2 Samuel 18:5).

Nearly all of us in North America come from immigrant stock, and the argument can be made that our melding together, despite the inevitable problems, has resulted in unique strength and mutual resolve. We can take our cue for acceptance and tolerance from God's ready incorporation of aliens and foreigners into full membership in his chosen race from its earliest beginnings.

Post-ponderings: Think back on what you know of Old Testament history and identify some examples of foreigners being grafted into Israel. What does this say about God's inclusivity?

ZIBA'S STORY:
FACT OR FABRICATION?

"Your heart desire will come, but when it comes, you desire for another, and
when it comes again, you still aspire for another, that shows your level of
ingratitude."
—MICHAEL BASSEY JOHNSON

*"The king then asked [Ziba]. 'Where is your master's grandson?' Ziba said to him,
'He is staying in Jerusalem, because he thinks, "Today the Israelites will restore to
me my grandfather's kingdom."' Then the king said to Ziba, 'All that belonged to
Mepibosheth is now yours.'" (2 Samuel 16:3–4)*

Read 2 Samuel 16:1–4; 19:24–30.
This anecdote is a head-scratcher; we have no idea whether Ziba is telling
the truth. Why would Mephibosheth have entertained thoughts of restor-
ing his grandfather's kingdom when Absalom, David's son, had declared
himself king?

There *was* evidently a faction still loyal to Saul's dynasty. Listen to Shimei as he curses the fleeing David and pelts him with stones: "'Get out,
get out, you murderer, you scoundrel! The LORD has repaid you for all the
blood you shed in the household of Saul, in whose place you have reigned.
The LORD has given the kingdom into the hands of your son Absalom. You
have come to ruin because you are a murderer!'" How did Shimei come to
believe David had been responsible for the termination of Saul's reign?

Even in David's confrontation with Mephibosheth upon his return to
Jerusalem the king is unable to sort out the conflicting claims and divides
Mephibosheth's former holdings between Ziba and Mephibosheth. The
reader is left hanging. If there was any truth in Ziba's accusation against
Mephibosheth, the situation leaves us shaking our heads in disbelief at
the ingratitude of Saul's grandson. Perhaps Mephibosheth, still feeling
wronged, was wearing blinders with regard to David's over-the-top generosity. One way or another, we question why the historian would include
this unresolved anecdote in his account. Is there a conclusion he wanted
us to draw?

Post-ponderings: Consider the extent of your gratitude toward those who
have gone out of their way to support you—whether your family members
or others.

DAVID:
CALAMITY, REMORSE, AND PAINFUL DUTY

"Death is lighter than a feather, but Duty is heavier than a mountain."
—ROBERT JORDAN

"'You have made it clear today that the commanders and their men mean nothing to you. I see that you would be pleased if Absalom were alive today and all of us were dead.'" (2 Samuel 19:6)

Read 2 Samuel 17:24–29; 18:19—19:8.
This moving scene is packed with pathos. David, the bereft father now deprived of any opportunity to resolve the issue with Absalom, grieves not only over the loss of this promising young man but over the missed opportunity to rectify the glaring wrong. His thrumming heartstrings are torn between the call of grief and the pull of duty. "Too late!" has been called the saddest cry known to humankind.

This charismatic son had captured David's heart and wasn't about to let go. Though we read that David had grieved over Amnon, we get the sense that his current angst is much stronger—that his inconsolable grief has strayed beyond the bounds of reason: "O my son Absalom! My son, my son Absalom! If only I had died instead of you." And so David's grief was passed, as though by osmosis, along to the victorious, but now subdued and bewildered army: "The men stole into the city that day as men steal who are ashamed when they flee from battle."

Post-ponderings: When, if ever, have you found yourself in a situation that called for different responses based on your differing roles? On another note, when have you found it necessary to temper your response to tragedy or heartbreak for the good of your family?

BARZILLAI:
THE POIGNANT REALITIES OF OLD AGE

"His mind has become a refuge for old thoughts, idle, indigent, with nowhere else to go. He ought to chase them out, sweep the premises clean. But he does not care to do so, or does not care enough."
—J. M. COETZEE

"Barzillai answered the king, 'How many more years will I live, that I should go up to Jerusalem with the king? I am now eighty years old. Can I tell the difference between what is enjoyable and what is not? Can your servant taste what he eats and drinks? Can I still hear the voices of male and female singers?'" (2 Samuel 19:34–35)

Read 2 Samuel 19:31–38.

Old age, so significant a life passage, is a focus of much of the end of 2 Samuel. We're aware of the irony that some people become embittered with the diminishing effects of age, while others mellow. "Remember your Creator in the days of your youth," invites the Teacher in Ecclesiastes, "before the days of trouble come and the years approach when you will say, 'I find no pleasure in them'" (Ecclesiastes 12:1).

Some aging individuals grapple for a return to the past. Barzillai, recognizing the futility of this approach, has reverted to despair, rejecting any future prospect of pleasure or purpose. Other fortunate souls revel in the now. I can't help but contrast the perspective of the eighty-year-old Barzillai with that of Jean Renoir: "The advantage of being eighty years old is that one has had many people to love." Still others transition with age to an eager hope for a glorious forever fast approaching: "If the infinity of the sea may call out thus," muses Henryk Sienkiewicz, "perhaps when a man is growing old, calls come to him, too, from another infinity still darker and more deeply mysterious; and the more he is wearied by life the dearer are those calls to him."

Grief for the elderly is progressive, with individual and family losses coming incrementally but inevitably. For the fortunate believer who opts for a heightened sense of God's presence, along with ever more vibrant faith and hope, homesickness can gradually shift its direction. The beauty for us as Christians is that it's often God's face in those waning years we yearn most to see.

It's ironic that David himself is hardly a young man. And he's seen more than his share of disillusionment. Yet despite the tragedy he is even now enduring he more than transcends Barzillai's fatalistic approach. For a further glimpse of David in his old age, see the reflection on 2 Samuel 21:15–17. For David's final words concerning Barzillai's sons, see 1 Kings 2:7.

Post-ponderings: How do you view your eventual passage to heaven? Does the prospect make you anxious? Anxious as in anxiety, or as in anticipation?

The Fate of
the Concubines

"As long as you're scared you're on the plantation."
—CORNAL WEST

"When David returned to his palace in Jerusalem, he took the ten concubines he had left to take care of the palace and put them in a house under guard. He provided for them but had no sexual relations with them. They were kept in confinement till the day of their death, living as widows." (2 Samuel 20:3)

Read 2 Samuel 20.

Fascinating—and disturbing—as this chapter is, the reflection focuses solely on the verse above. Think back a few chapters to Ahithophel's advice to the aspiring Absalom in 2 Samuel 16:21: "Sleep with your father's concubines whom he left to take care of the palace. Then all Israel will hear that you have made yourself obnoxious to your father, and the hands of everyone with you will be more resolute.'" It's certain these women had no choice in the matter, making David's consequence seem harsh.

God had prepared the king for this very development: "The sword will never depart from your house, because you despised me and took the wife of Uriah the Hittite to be your own. . . . Before your very eyes I will take your wives and give them to one who is close to you, and he will sleep with your wives in broad daylight. You did it in secret, but I will do this thing in broad daylight before all Israel" (12:10–12).

Old Testament law prohibited a man sleeping with his father's wife (Leviticus 18:8), whether or not she was his mother, and David considered these concubines to have been defiled. Sexual sin within the context of a family or extended family entails a heightened element of tragedy, as well as long-lasting, in-your-face consequences for all involved.

Post-ponderings: This sordid story (the verse in focus or the larger, and largely unrelated, story) is unlikely to impinge upon your life. But sexual lust, even if never acted upon, may have been a problem for you. Acknowledge any such incident, pray for forgiveness if you haven't already done so, and thank God for his deliverance.

RIZPAH:
THE FIERCENESS OF A MOTHER'S LOVE

"In the grey of the morning my mind becomes confused, between the dead and the sleeping and the road that I must choose."
—THE MOODY BLUES

"Rizpah daughter of Aiah took sackcloth and spread it out for herself on a rock. From the beginning of the harvest till the rain poured down from the heavens on the bodies, she did not let the birds touch them by day or the wild animals by night." (2 Samuel 21:10)

Read 2 Samuel 21:1–14.

Of all the bizarre Old Testament accounts, this is one of the more extreme. This bereaved concubine of Saul was in her own way protesting the indignity of her sons' and nephews' deaths and the exposure of their bodies, honoring their memory until some sort of satisfaction might be offered. And her quiet gesture was so effective that David "listened" and acted.

In our day, following the slaying or otherwise preventable death of a child, a bereft parent may devote the rest of her life to seeking justice or attempting to prevent the kind of criminal activity that caused the tragedy. Similarly, the parents of children who have succumbed to orphan or untreatable diseases may campaign tirelessly for a cure. Impossible though it is to measure the compounded benefits of such efforts, we acknowledge resulting changes in the criminal code and medical research.

Another matter is the refusal of parents to let go of the memory of a lost child. How sad for themselves and surviving family members when grieving moms and dads fixate on keeping the remembrance of their child alive. When humans build "shrines" to the departed and continuously commemorate their existence, the grief process may be stalled and healing prevented. Such memorializing is unnecessary for those of us with access to the comfort afforded by our faith and hope in Christ. Indeed, our trust in God's promises both compels and propels us to move forward—joyfully, even. How beautiful this tacit testimony to a baffled world!

Post-ponderings: All of us know believers who have lost a child. What testimony of grace and triumph has come to your attention from such parents?

PASSAGE:
DAVID'S LAST BATTLE

"Quite a lot of our contemporary culture is actually shot through with a resentment of limits and the passage of time, anger at what we can't do, fear or even disgust at growing old."
—ROWAN WILLIAMS

"David went down with his men to fight against the Philistines, and he became exhausted.... Then David's Men swore to him, saying, 'Never again will you go out with us to battle, so that the lamp of Israel will not be extinguished.'"
(2 Samuel 21:15, 17)

Read 2 Samuel 21:15–17.
David's men weren't his sons, but they were acting in that role, urging the reluctant king to forego an activity that had become too much for him. Comparable situations in our lives might be counseling a parent to give up his driver's license or sell her home and move into a care facility.

Listen to David's poignant words subsequent to this experience: "'[The LORD] reached down from on high and took hold of me; he drew me out of deep waters. He rescued me from my powerful enemy, from my foes, who were too strong for me'" (22:17–18). That must have been hard for this lifelong warrior to admit. Compounding confusion at this life stage may be a stubborn image of oneself as someone much younger. Oscar Wilde put it this way: "The tragedy of old age is not that one is old, but that one is young."

The transition for the next generation may require some adjustment as well. When we've relied on a parent or parents all our lives, it may jolt us to realize that the tables have slowly—or suddenly—turned. "We grow up," observes Kevin Mccarty, "to see that people who once had our best interests in mind need our best interests now."

This changing of the guard is not only appropriate and God-intended but can be beautiful, just as old age itself can be. I love this quote from André Marois: "An old man, having retired from active life, regains the gaity and irresponsibility of childhood. He is ready to play, he cannot run with his son, but he can totter with his grandson. Our first and last steps have the same rhythm." As will be the case for many of us as our lives come full circle.

Post-ponderings: Depending on which generation you represent, what has been your experience of the limitations brought on by aging? What adjustments have been natural or difficult for you?

BLUEPRINT FOR SOLOMON'S TEMPLE

> "[L]eadership is more like a baton than a trophy. You keep a trophy, but you hand off a baton. In a race, if you don't hand off the baton, you lose."
> —BRUCE MILLER

> "David said, 'My son Solomon is young and inexperienced, and the house to be built for the LORD should be of great magnificence and fame and splendor in the sight of all the nations. Therefore I will make preparations for it.'"
> (1 Chronicles 22:5)

Read 1 Chronicles 22.
Did David, we wonder, have a hard time passing the baton? Could the king be accused of over-engineering here, based on lack of confidence in his son, or was his blueprint God's design? It would appear that David *was* aligned with God's desire: "Then David gave his son Solomon . . . the plans of all that the Spirit had put in his mind" (28:11–12).

Still David seems reluctant, to the point of publicly voicing his reservations about Solomon's ability to follow through: "My son Solomon, the one whom God has chosen, is young and inexperienced. The task is great, because this palatial structure is not for man but for the LORD God" (29:1). David was asking for support; still, his words suggest a hint of resignation, perhaps even an implied questioning of God's clear choice.

"Knowing when it is over is the beginning of a new life and the end of an old one!" observes an unknown author. David's earthly life wasn't past, though his strength was waning. The fact that God allowed him to engineer the project suggests that he was already using David in a new, supportive role—a clear change for this "go to it" personality.

Post-ponderings: What might God's gentle transitioning in David's life have to say to us as we or the generation ahead of us face the end of our lap in life's relay?

ABISHAG:
THE WARMTH OF CARING

"What finally became of Abishag is not recorded, and perhaps it is just as well. This sad story makes it clear that in peace as well as in war there's no tragic folly you can't talk a nation's youth into simply by calling it patriotic duty."
—FREDERICK BUECHNER

"When King David was very old, he could not keep warm even when they put covers over him. So his attendants said to him, 'Let us look for a young virgin to serve the king and take care of him. She can lie beside him so that our lord the king may keep warm.'" (1 Kings 1:1)

Read 1 Kings 1:1–4.
The use of a human body—that of a vibrant young woman, no less—to keep an old man warm sounds suspect in our ears, but there's beauty in it too. The author's presentation of Abishag is nothing but positive. Her loyalty to her lord, the king, is unquestioned. Rather than focusing on the strangeness of this cultural practice—if it was such—I prefer to reflect briefly on its imagery and possible associations for us. Abishag wasn't serving the aged king in an aloof, duty-motivated manner. David in his last days was no longer attractive. As a dedicated and caring nurse, Abishag was evidently able to overcome her natural revulsion at the sight of the wasted old man or to his involuntary sounds and smells. But she did so much more, nestling close to him in an effort to transfer some of her overflowing warmth and vitality.

Old age, like any other life passage, has its stages, of varying duration based on the individual's physical, mental, and emotional circumstances. This final stage, which we might associate with a lingering death, is no longer about the person's attitudes or choice of activity. The primary players in these final months or minutes are his or her caregivers. As our loved ones face their final earthly passage, we can make all the difference in the quality of the experience—for them, for us, and even for our watching children.

Post-ponderings: Have you personally experienced the gradual passing of an aged parent or grandparent? Were you actively involved in the caregiving process? If so, what did the experience mean for you?

ADONIJAH:
THE UNADMONISHED SON

"I'm not the boss of my house. I don't know how I lost it, I don't know when I lost it, I don't really think I ever had it. But I've seen the boss's job . . . and I don't want it!"
—BILL COSBY

"Now Adonijah, whose mother was Haggith, put himself forward and said, 'I will be king.' So he got chariots and horses ready, with fifty men to run ahead of him. (His father had never rebuked him by asking, 'Why do you behave as you do?' He was also very handsome and was born next after Absalom.)" (1 Kings 1:5–6)

Read 1 Kings 1:5–10.

Amnon, Absalom, and now Adonijah. David's oldest three, all born and at least partially raised *before* David's adultery with Bathsheba. Three strikes against David comes to my mind when I look at these promising young men with their dismal failings. Their formative years had taken place in the palace—the early years in which David should have systematically trained them in the ways of the Lord.

We aren't clued in as to why David, even as a young father, seems to have had a problem administering discipline. But he may have been aware of his deficiency in this area. If he were clueless he might well *have asked* in exasperation, "Why do you behave as you do?" As it were, had he pronounced these words they would have constituted a self-indictment.

Was David a hands-off kind of dad, too busy with affairs of the kingdom to attend to the formative needs of his children? Was it their mothers (mothers in the plural may have been a part of the problem) who spoiled them, or their nurses? Did they resent lack of attention on the part of those whose opinions mattered most? David was an interesting combination of "man's man" and sensitive poet. But preoccupied he may well have been. Painfully evident is the reality that children raised without discipline—which they must internalize as a necessary step in maturation—won't produce a good outcome.

Post-ponderings: If you're actively parenting, to what degree does preoccupation with other concerns limit your attention or the effectiveness of your discipline?

Bypassed:
The Ultimate Affront

"Be there with your loved one, as fully present as you've ever been. Let him or her share with you the fear and the wonder, the strangeness and the beauty revealed at the end of life."
—KATHLEEN DOWLING SINGH

"'My lord the king, the eyes of all Israel are on you, to learn from you who will sit on the throne of my lord the king after him.'" (1 Kings 1:20)

Read 1 Kings 1:11–40.
Bathsheba's words must have cut David deeply. It seems evident that his active involvement in the things of the kingdom had become awkward and cumbersome, a time-consuming hiccup in a process that seemed to run along well enough without it—at least most of the time. But treason didn't fall into the "most of the time" pot. In this case everything depended on David's knowledge and decisive follow-up. Being sidestepped in the matter of succession was unconscionable. Once again Nathan's timely intervention played a pivotal role in the working out of God's salvation plan.

Throughout the last chapters of Samuel we've witnessed David's slow slide into age-related debility. But despite the king's frailty his mind remained alert. How tragic for any leader or family head when physical decline is assumed to go hand-in-hand with mental incapacitation.

Those last months or minutes with a bedridden but lucid father or mother can be magical for a family willing to overlook and look beyond bodily constraints to appreciate the reminiscences and spiritual insights their loved one may feel inclined to share. And what a blessing for that parent/grandparent to be taken seriously, loved and identified with, as opposed to having to observe the family's gradual withdrawal in preparation for goodbye.

Post-ponderings: What has been your experience in terms of the passage of loved ones? If you were able to communicate with them prior to the transition, what memories have you carried with you?

CHAPTER 12

LATER KINGSHIP—
SOLOMON TO EXILE

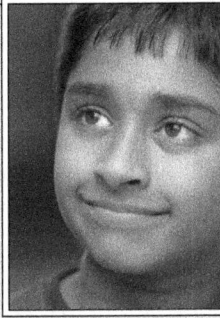

CHAPTER
INTRODUCTION

While the reign of Solomon represents Israel's glory days, the situation for the divided kingdom to follow represents a downhill trajectory ending for both kingdoms in free fall. Solomon's instructive story encompasses nearly half of this chapter; while there is much to admire in this initially wisest of men, irremediable mistakes during his reign point to consequences that will fall after his death.

The remainder of the chapter covers isolated stories centering around interactions of the prophets Elijah and Elisha with specific families, as well as family-related vignettes from the lives of selected kings of Israel and Judah. As was the case with chapter 7, there are accounts here that, despite family-related content, are too horrendous to have any intersection with our lives. For this reason I have bypassed the following:

Elisha Is Jeered (the parent/child influence in terms of attitudes) (2 Kings 2:23–25)

The Cannibalizing of Children during Samaria's Siege (2 Kings 6:24–31)

SOLOMON WITH ADONIJAH: EARLY EVIDENCE OF WISDOM

"Family life is too intimate to be preserved by the spirit of justice. It can be sustained by a spirit of love which goes beyond justice."
—REINHOLD NIEBUHR

"Solomon replied, 'If he shows himself to be worthy, not a hair of his head will fall to the ground; but if evil is found in him, he will die.'" (1 Kings 1:52)

Read 1 Kings 1:41–53.

The stakes were high when it came to allowing a potential rival to the throne to survive. Solomon was under no obligation to show such grace to his older brother, who could well become a threat again (borne out almost immediately in 3:13–25).

I can't help but acknowledge a degree of wisdom in Solomon *before* his request to God for this very quality (see the reflection on 1 Kings 3:1–15; 2 Chronicles 1). Like some of the memorable characters in the children's classic *The Wizard of Oz*, it can take the possession of the very quality one most desires to instill that inner longing. We aren't acquainted with Solomon prior to these early chapters of Kings, but our initial impression is one of both wisdom and humility—qualities that invariably reside together in the heart of an individual possessing one or the other!

Neibuhr makes the excellent point that it takes more than justice to nurture and preserve family life. Solomon could have extended the same mercy he did to his brother to anyone else who had wronged him, dangling before the culprit that second chance that could, if rightly used, channel the situation toward good. Yet it's especially in the context of family that the benefit of the doubt can become an all-around benefit. What more was at stake for this troubled family than Solomon's security?

Post-ponderings: Siblings can lose their moorings, perspective, and will to maintain connection once their parents are gone. What efforts have you made to keep the brother/sister ties strong in your family of origin?

A FATHER'S CHARGE:
THE GOD WHO WILL BE FOUND

"Of course God does not consider you hopeless. If He did, He would not be moving you to seek Him (and He obviously is) . . . Continue seeking Him with seriousness. Unless He wanted you, you would not be wanting Him."
—C. S. LEWIS

"'And you, my son Solomon, acknowledge the God of your father, and serve him with wholehearted devotion and with a willing mind, for the LORD searches every heart and understands every desire and every thought. If you seek him, he will be found by you; but if you forsake him, he will reject you forever.'" (1 Chronicles 28:9)

Read 1 Kings 2:1–12; 1 Chronicles 28:5–10.
David's charge to Solomon articulates a legacy any believing parent would do well to bequeath to their offspring. I'm particularly intrigued by the concept—repeated several times in the Old Testament—of God's *allowing himself to be found.* Have you ever watched a toddler playing Hide and Go Seek? He'll squirm impatiently in his hiding place but will soon jump out, squealing "Here I am!" It's as though the suspense is beyond his ability to bear. If you pretend momentarily not to see or hear him, he'll run to you in triumph, exhilarated at having been found.

First Chronicles 28:9 and 2 Chronicles 15:2 use identical phraseology: "If you seek him, he will be found by you." And Jeremiah 29:13–14 personalizes the concept: "'You will seek me and find me when you seek me with all your heart. I will be found by you,' declares the LORD." Notice that God neither promises to search out our hiding place nor assures us that we'll eventually stumble upon his. No, God *wills* himself to be discovered by us.

In the case of the delinquent Israelites, God would go further still: "I revealed myself to those who did not ask for me; I was found by those who did not seek me. To a nation that did not call on my name, I said, 'Here am I, here am I'" (Isaiah 65:1). This seeking and finding process revolves continuously in a gracious circle. In the words of a beloved old song, "I sought the Lord, and afterward I knew he moved my soul to seek him, seeking me."

Post-ponderings: Our part as parents with regard to this seeking/finding continuum is threefold: we're to train our children, pray for them, and entrust them to the care of the Father who goes beyond patient waiting to active invitation. If you find yourself agonizing over a child's spiritual disinterest, how can God's words through Isaiah afford you comfort?

SOLOMON'S REQUEST:
THE WISDOM OF A "CHILD"

"There are many more layers to innocence than one might ever imagine,
and we are ever unaware of them until each barrier is breached."
—PAULA REED

*"'Now, LORD my God, you have made your servant king in place of my father David.
But I am only a little child and do not know how to carry out my duties. . . . So give
your servant a discerning heart to govern your people and to distinguish between
right and wrong.'" (1 Kings 3:7, 9)*

Read 1 Kings 3:1–15; 2 Chronicles 1.
What is there about the innocence of a little kid that walks hand-in-hand
with wisdom, goodness, and faith? It's as though they're wise—and good
and trusting—because they haven't yet acquired the sophistication to be
otherwise. In Psalm 51:5 David articulated the innate sinfulness of a human
being from the point of conception, going on to express that God teaches
wisdom already within "that secret place." No temptations or negative influences there in the womb, but sin—and the beginnings of wisdom—all
the same. "I want to protect innocent people from sin by locking them in
cages, where the evil can't get them," expresses Jarod Kintz. Trouble is, sinfulness is a genetic condition—unlike wisdom, which is learned and subject
to loss.

Solomon metaphorically referred to himself as a little child (likely an
idiomatic expression), citing this as a rationale for his need for wisdom. But
it occurs to me that he may have had this backward. Could it be that God
had in some sense extended the natural wisdom of childhood to accom-
modate this wise request? As Jesus would make clear, there's something
poignant and unique about a child heart. "To express nostalgia for a childhood we no longer share is to deny the actual significance and humanity
of children," reflects Perry Nodelman. But to desire a continuation in our
adult lives of some of the best traits of those magical early years makes
sense for us.

Post-ponderings: What bits and bytes of childhood wisdom hold a special
place in your memory?

SWITCHED AFTER BIRTH: AMBUSHED BY LOVE?

"Sometimes when you pick up your child you can feel the map of your own bones beneath your hands, or smell the scent of your skin in the nape of his neck. This is the most extraordinary thing about motherhood—finding a piece of yourself separate and apart that all the same you could not live without."
—JODI PICOULT

"The woman whose son was alive was deeply moved out of love for her son and said to the king, 'Please, my lord, give her the living baby! Don't kill him!'"
(1 Kings 3:26)

Read 1 Kings 3:16–28.
We don't know how the birth of a child would have affected the life of a prostitute in that day, but it's hard to imagine parenting would have been easier for her then than today. It's possible that competition between the two women for the "prize" of a living child was a factor, but much of the background of this strange story remains a mystery.

I've chosen to focus on the emotional response of a brand new mother toward her child. Some first-time moms enter their new station tentatively, resignedly, resentfully, or in fear, while others find fulfillment in that first hungry gaze into the little face. Rajineesh reminds us, though, of one constant: "The moment a child is born, the mother is also born. She never existed before. The woman existed, but the mother, never. A mother is something absolutely new."

And that absolutely new mom might react or respond in ways that surprise even herself, and with feelings that are subject to development. The will is involved, but there's also the letting it happen, particularly when feelings are ambivalent or wildly fluctuating in synch with hormonal leaps. The writer of Kings tells us that the mother of the live child was deeply moved with love. What we don't know is whether this was an immediate response or a surprise, perhaps realized in full only after the prospect of potential loss. All kinds of factors, physiological, practical, and emotional, come into play in terms of that bonding experience.

Post-ponderings: If you're a mom, what feelings do you recall shortly after your first child's birth? Did some progression take place in terms of bonding, or were you smitten from first sight, if not already long before the birth event?

Staying Home

"Stay, stay at home, my heart, and rest. Home-keeping hearts are happiest."
—HENRY WADSWORTH LONGFELLOW

"During Solomon's lifetime Judah and Israel, from Dan to Beersheba, lived in safety, everyone under their own vine and under their own fig tree." (1 Kings 4:25)

Read 1 Kings 4:20–28.

The expression "everyone under their own vine and under their own fig tree" seems to have been Old Testament shorthand—or longhand—for "at home and at peace" (see also Micah 4:4; Zechariah 3:10). Vernon Joseph Baker, a United States Army Medal of Honor recipient for his actions in 1945 in Italy, performed with valor far from home or peace. Yet his later words tell us where his heart resided during his deployment: "Home is where the heart can laugh without shyness. Home is where the heart's tears can dry at their own pace."

Staying home may not be the most exciting thing a person can do, but it has throughout history been the choice of so many who've known a happy home. In this sense Solomon's reign was in stark contrast to David's, which was marked by continuous strife. A war-weary people, as we know so well, can become cynical. Staying home for you, though, probably doesn't revolve around reprieve from political unrest. We Westerners are a restless people, spurred by the prospects of adventure and new experience. When have you been pleasantly surprised while sticking close to base—perhaps spending a family vacation rediscovering the pleasures of that world in the micro you call home?

Post-ponderings: To what degree do you associate home with rest and happiness?

PRIORITIES OF THE HEART

"When we put God first, all other things fall into their proper place or drop out of our lives. Our love of the Lord will govern our claims for our affection, the demands on our time, the interests we pursue, and the order of our priorities."
—EZRA TAFT BENSON

"The temple was finished in all its details according to its specifications. He had spent seven years building it. It took Solomon thirteen years, however, to complete the construction of his palace." (1 Kings 6:38—7:1)

Read 1 Kings 6:38—7:12.
Something tells me that procrastination and burnout weren't problems delaying Solomon's palace building. Nor were his priorities in the wrong place in terms of sequence. Yet that seemingly innocuous "however" speaks volumes. Have you ever hurried through necessary duties before launching with relish into your personal pet project? You couldn't be faulted in terms of duty fulfillment. But it matters where our heart is. A related passage from Haggai reflects a more serious variation on the theme: "Then the word of the LORD came through the prophet Haggai, 'Is it a time for you yourselves to be living in your paneled houses, while this house remains a ruin?'" (Haggai 1:3–4).

Priorities are hard to hide because they reside in the heart. We might go through the motions of fulfilling our obligations, all the while focusing on how we *really* want to be spending our time—or money or energy or . . . And that will show, either in the quality of our work or in our attitude while we're engaged in it. What a shame when God has to broach the subject of our misplaced priorities, gently (or with some vehemence; it's hard to tell from the Haggai quote) asking a question rather than barking a command. Ask yourself, "Is it the time for me to. . . , while . . . ?" If there's an issue—for you personally or as a family matter—your conscience will find it immediately.

Post-ponderings: Where is your heart? No matter how diligently you serve the Lord, is it focused more on God? Or more on you?

SOLOMON AND HIS HAREM:
WISE VERSUS WIVES

"Knowing others is intelligence; knowing yourself is true wisdom. Mastering others is strength; mastering yourself is true power. If you realize that you have enough, you are truly rich."
—LAO TZU

"Was it not because of [foreign] marriages . . . that Solomon king of Israel sinned? Among the many nations there was no king like him. He was loved by his God, and God made him king over all Israel, but even he was led into sin by foreign women." (Nehemiah 13:26)

Read 1 Kings 11:1–13.

Solomon's self-assessment in Ecclesiastes 2:8–9 closes on a note of dissonance: "I amassed silver and gold for myself, and the treasure of kings and provinces. I acquired male and female singers, and a harem as well—the delights of a man's heart. I became greater by far than anyone in Jerusalem before me. In all this my wisdom stayed with me." *Come again on that last sentence*, we want to object. First Kings 11:4 diagnoses the problem Israel's king was ignoring: "As Solomon grew old, his wives turned his heart after other gods, and his heart was not fully devoted to the LORD his God."

Solomon didn't exactly turn his back on God. It was simply a matter of opening the door—perhaps he would have said opening his mind—to some backup support from his wives' gods. Yet how could this wisest of men not have recognized that he was dealing with the jealous Creator God who brooks no rivals? Solomon's one thousand-to-one odds present such a lose-lose situation it sounds ludicrous in our ears. But the truth is that it takes only one; one heels-dug-in, godless spouse or significant other can take the "fight"—or the faith—out of almost anyone. True, the result can be beautifully opposite, but is it worth the risk?

Post-ponderings: Whether the situation has to do with us as we mellow or our kids as they toy with relationships holding the potential for spiritual ruin, the issue is serious. Especially when we assume that our own wisdom and persistence will result in a God-honoring outcome for all involved. How has this issue touched your family?

REHOBOAM:
PEER CONFIRMATION

"Few are willing to brave the disapproval of their peers, the censure of their colleagues . . . Moral courage is a rarer commodity than bravery in battle or great intelligence."
—ROBERT KENNEDY

"'My little finger is thicker than my father's waist. My father laid on you a heavy yoke; I will make it even heavier. My father scourged you with whips; I will scourge you with scorpions.'" (1 Kings 12:10–11)

Read 1 Kings 11:26—12:24; 2 Chronicles 10.

Bigger. Badder. Meaner. These qualities were the king's prerogative, and Rehoboam had yet to make a name for himself. To borrow from the Robert Kennedy quote, his grandfather had been characterized by bravery in battle and his father by superior wisdom. What was to be Rehoboam's legacy?

Solomon's advisors offered careful, balanced counsel. As a king he had been demanding; perhaps the time had come to alleviate some of the burden. But that idea didn't sound strong enough to Rehoboam or to the blustery friends with whom he'd grown up. He was ready to flex his muscle, not come off as flabby. And his dream was to gain the respect, not the love, of the populace. It probably didn't take much convincing for this aspiring young man to follow the advice he had wanted in the first place to hear. Peer influence in Rehoboam's case was closely aligned to peer confirmation.

Hand in hand with confirmation came conformity; in the words of Ralph Waldo Emerson, "A man must consider what a rich realm he abdicates when he becomes a conformist." What a mark Rehoboam could have made had he opted for the moral high road.

Post-ponderings: To what degree do you seek confirmation for courses of action you've already decided to follow? Do you discuss with your children the issue of peer influence?

Abijah's Untimely End:
The Death of a Child

"When I lay these questions before God I get no answer. But a rather special sort of 'No answer.' It is not the locked door. It is more like a silent, certainly not uncompassionate, gaze. As though He shook His head not in refusal but waiving the question. Like, 'Peace, child; you don't understand.'"
—C. S. LEWIS

"'As for you, go back home. When you set foot in your city, the boy will die. All Israel will mourn for him and bury him. He is the only one belonging to Jeroboam who will be buried, because he is the only one in the house of Jeroboam in whom the Lord, the God of Israel, has found anything good.'" (1 Kings 14:12–13)

Read 1 Kings 14.

It's hard to know what to feel or say when a child dies what seems from our perspective to be prematurely. There's something seemingly incongruous and incomplete about a life cut short at some point along the developmental milestone spectrum. We've heard the reflection that God has "taken" a little one to himself to spare that child inevitable hardship. And such a scooping up may indeed be a sign of his grace.

The prophet's declaration in Ezekiel 18:32 affords a degree of comfort: "'I take no pleasure in the death of anyone, declares the sovereign Lord. Repent and live!'" It's possible that the Lord postpones this passage for some, allowing a longer opportunity for repentance. Might such a delay be circumvented for a little person who is already, or still, close to the Lord? Listen to Isaiah's ringing affirmation about the future for God's people: "'Never again will there be in [Jerusalem] an infant who lives but a few days . . . They will not labor in vain, nor will they bear children doomed to misfortune'" (Isaiah 65:20, 23).

"Now we see only a reflection as in a mirror," observes Paul in 1 Corinthians 13:12, going on to proclaim that "then we shall see face to face. Now I know in part; then I shall know fully, even as I am fully known." Fully known—whether *I'm* a stillborn infant, toddler, adolescent, or adult. Fully known, and fully engulfed in God's all-consuming love.

Post-ponderings: Does this reflection hit home for you in some personal way? If so, have you found your way to—and into—the comfort only God can afford?

AHAB AND JEZEBEL:
A WICKED KING FURTHER CORRUPTED

"A wicked wife, a false friend, a saucy servant and living in a house with a
serpent in it are nothing but death."
—CHANAKYA

"Ahab son of Omri did more evil in the eyes of the LORD than any of those before
him. He not only considered it trivial to commit the sins of Jeroboam son of Nebat,
but he also married Jezebel daughter of Ethbaal king of the Sidonians, and began
to serve Baal and worship him." (1 Kings 16:30–31)

Read 1 Kings 16:29–33.
The author of Kings leaves no doubt as to the corrupting influence of Jezebel on her impressionable husband. In fact, Jezebel's infamy has been
swept forward through history to the point that Merriam Webster defines
her name as representative of "an impudent, shameless, or morally unrestrained woman." Jesus himself, through John, cites her in his address to
the church in Thyatira: "Nevertheless, I have this against you: You tolerate
that woman Jezebel, who calls herself a prophet" (Revelation 2:20).

Ahab, following in Omri's footsteps, was bad in his own right. This
gullible man seemed to trip all over himself in his haste to fall into sin; still
Jezebel, the shrewd manipulator, lurked behind the scenes as a puppeteer.
"Evil influence," reflects E. A. Bucchianeri, "is like a nicotine patch, you
cannot help but absorb what sticks to you." Jezebel was certainly the canny
one; I can't help but wonder whether Ahab could, without her, have been
influenced for good. We'll never know, of course, but Jezebel, not Ahab,
captures the biblical focus. (For further discussion of this couple's relational dynamic, see the reflection on 1 Kings 21).

Post-ponderings: Whom do you know who has been influenced by a Jezebel?

ELIJAH, A WIDOW, AND HER SON: FAITHFULNESS REWARDED

"The most sublime act is to set another before you."
—WILLIAM BLAKE

"A father to the fatherless, a defender of widows, is God in his holy dwelling."
(Psalm 68:5)

Read 1 Kings 17:7–24.

There's an interesting play on death in this tightly woven two-act story, reflected by the widow's words to Elijah: "I am gathering a few sticks to take home and make a meal for myself and my son, that we may eat it—*and die*" and later "What do you have against me, man of God? Did you come to remind me of my sin and *kill my son?*" (emphasis added in both quotes).

It seems incredible that this widow, a foreigner, would be so willing to trust the prophet—or his God—as to feed him first. We could pass this off as courtesy, as resignation, or even as a forcing of the inevitable, assuming as she did that this was to be the family's final meal. And we aren't surprised by the outcome.

It's the boy's later death that strikes us as a disconnect. *Where did this come from?* we want to ask. This unforeseen loss *following* the miraculous survival must have seemed the ultimate in capricious cruelty—some sort of sadistic "divine comedy," perhaps not unexpected from a god like Sidon's. This distraught mother might never have recognized the ramifications of God's reward for faithfulness had not this miracle showcased his power and goodness.

Post-ponderings: Think back to a time in your life, or in that of someone you know, in which God demonstrated his power and love by resolving a problem in a manner that couldn't be explained in any other way.

AHAB'S CONCESSION:
A STUDY IN SKEWED PRIORITIES

"Only you know your circumstances, your energy level, the needs of your children, and the emotional demands of your other obligations. Be wise during intensive seasons of your life."
—CHIEKO N. OKAZAKI

"The king of Israel summoned all the elders of the land and said to them, 'See how this man is looking for trouble! When he sent for my wives and my children, my silver and my gold, I did not refuse him.'" (1 Kings 20:7)

Read 1 Kings 20:1–12.
Ahab agreed to sacrifice some of his wives and children to save his own skin. His attitude afterward toward Ben-Hadad was one of outrage: "I readily conceded to give him my wives and children. *Now* what does he want?" None of us would blatantly or with such cavalier disinterest treat our family members as expendable. Yet our lifestyles can leave that precise impression—particularly on the vulnerable loved ones involved, or who long for us to be more involved.

Stephen Covey expresses the ideal situation: "You have to decide what your highest priorities are and have the courage—pleasantly, smilingly, nonapologetically—to say 'no' to other things. And the way to do that is by having a bigger 'yes' burning inside." The crucial point for us as Christians is that the bigger yes must first be to God and the things of the kingdom. Our family priorities must then fall into line—not an automatic assumption!—as part of that kingdom priority package.

Post-ponderings: How would you rate your top five priorities, from highest to lowest? Is some readjustment in order?

JEZEBEL AND AHAB:
THE TOXIC SPOUSE

"She was like a master builder who could bend materials like stone and steel and clay to her will . . . except her materials were flesh and spirit."
—NEAL SHUSTERMAN

"(There was never anyone like Ahab, who sold himself to do evil in the eyes of the Lord, urged on by Jezebel his wife.)" (1 Kings 21:25)

Read 1 Kings 21.
My picture of the petulant king sulking in his royal bed, lips tightly compressed against the intake of food, is comical. Jezebel's response—"Is this how you act as king over Israel? Get up and eat!"—sounds right on, until she goes on: "I'll get you the vineyard of Naboth the Jezreelite." She would be only too happy to sweep away the impediment, no doubt indicative of a damaging pattern.

What's amazing to me isn't God's pronouncement against the house of Ahab but the postponement of his sentence based on the king's sheepish repentance. Ahab comes off in this vignette as more pathetic than wicked, though we know he was also very much the latter. What was there about this disobedient despot that made him so malleable in the fingers of his wife?

When it comes to maturity, life's timetable has a way of tossing in throwbacks. Each of us may be, at any given time, a child or an adult, based in part on where we are and whom we're with. Have you ever had the disconcerting experience of finding yourself feeling—or acting—like a much younger you when in a situation you associate with your childhood? The set of circumstances pulls you back into a life stage chronologically long past. Ahab's immaturity was nurtured not by a place association but by a person. Jezebel, the silver-tongued, cunning manipulator, epitomizes the toxic spouse.

Post-ponderings: Who in your life never fails to bring out your most negative qualities? Why do you think this is true?

ELISHA, ANOTHER WIDOW, AND HER SONS: ENTITLEMENT

"Entitled people consider their own needs and problems more important than others', so a good deed done for them is often quickly forgotten."
—COFFEE GUY

"'Go, sell the oil and pay your debts. You and your sons can live on what is left.'"
(2 Kings 4:7)

Read 2 Kings 4:1–7.
While on first glance Elisha's encounter with this Israelite widow seems reminiscent of Elijah's with the widow of Zarepheth (see the reflection on 1 Kings 17:7–24), the differences are pronounced. Elijah approaches a foreigner on her turf with a seemingly audacious request, while this home-grown widow, the wife of a fellow prophet, comes to Elisha expecting assistance. Both women experience the miraculous multiplication of their oil, but "Elijah's widow" gives unstintingly—everything she has—*before* trusting the unknown prophet and his God. "Elisha's widow" complies in anticipation of a solution.

I don't mean to minimize her predicament; widows and orphans were poised on one of the lowest rungs of the social ladder, and the potential loss of her sons to slavery loomed large. Still, this encounter has the feel to me of a business transaction. There's generosity—undeserved and unexpected—and then there's benevolence with entitlement based on a person's inner-circle identity, status, and credentials. Paul calls upon Christians to take care of their own (Galatians 6:10), and the *NIV Study Bible* note on 1 Timothy 5:8 cites provision for one's relatives as a norm. *Which of these two women*—that sounds so like the beginning of a Jesus question, doesn't it?—do we suppose was the more convicted and changed by her experience of blessing?

Post-ponderings: What standards does your church use to determine benevolence disbursements to members versus needy but unaffiliated individuals or families?

Naaman and the Slave Girl: From Where Did the Love Come?

"So much of what is best in us is bound up in our love of family, that it remains the measure of our stability because it measures our sense of loyalty. All other pacts of love or fear derive from it and are modeled upon it."
—DANIEL LONG

"She said to her mistress, 'If only my master would see the prophet who is in Samaria! He would cure him of his leprosy.'" (2 Kings 5:3)

Read 2 Kings 5:1–6.

Moses had clearly delineated to a new generation of Israelites following the forty years in the wilderness the curses for disobedience, including this: "Your sons and daughters will be given to another nation, and you will wear out your eyes watching for them day after day, powerless to lift a hand" (Deuteronomy 28:32). Second Kings 5:2 speaks of one such young girl who'd been swooped up and carried away by Amamean raiders.

The Bible is replete with the wistful and wishful expressions of God's people, often prefaced with sighs like "If only . . ." or "Oh, that . . ." Young people are resilient, and we have no reason to suspect that Naaman or his wife had mistreated this girl. Still, I find it amazing that she cared so deeply about the well-being of her master!

Daniel Long rightly asserts that our mature ability and inclination to love are byproducts of our early experience with the love of family. It seems to me, though, that an element of learned love too often falls between the cracks as we push our children in the direction of ever-expanding knowledge and skills sets in a competitive and often unkind world. That element is compassion. It's a quality, a force, a gift that needs to be extended beyond the confines of family (though it begins there) in a wide and generous swathe of concern for humanity, both individually and as a whole.

Post-ponderings: If you're a believing parent, how deliberately are you teaching—and modeling—the limitless compassion of the Christ you serve?

AHAZIAH AND ATHALIAH: MATERNAL ENCOURAGEMENT IN WICKEDNESS

"I hold that a strongly marked personality can influence descendants for generations."
—BEATRIX POTTER

"[Ahaziah] too followed the ways of the house of Ahab, for his mother encouraged him to act wickedly. He did evil in the eyes of the LORD, as the house of Ahab had done, for after his father's death they became his advisers, to his undoing."
(2 Chronicles 22:3–4)

Read 2 Chronicles 22:1–9.
The history of Israel and Judah, intertwined here through marriage, is difficult to follow. For clarification, I'm including the cast of characters: Judah's king Ahaziah was the son of Jehoram of Judah and Athaliah of Israel, the daughter of Ahab who had married Jehoram in a political alliance. Jehosheba, Jehoram's (and Athaliah's?) daughter and Ahaziah's sister, was married to the chief priest, Jehoiada. This couple secreted away Ahaziah's young son Joash, Jehosheba's nephew, at the time of Athaliah's massacre of Judah's royal family (we aren't apprised of why Jehosheba was passed over).

Jehoram, the son of Jehoshaphat, one of Judah's best kings, had been influenced for evil by Athaliah and her family. And Ahaziah followed suit (it's encouraging to read in the next reflection that Jehosheba did not!). Given free rein in a family, evil can proliferate at an alarming rate; it can take only one "marked personality" to allow Satan to infiltrate. And he doesn't waste his opportunities. "Don't walk in my head with your dirty feet," warns Leo Buscaglia. This cautionary note can apply to any individual in any family. We as Christians can never be too careful about the influences insinuating themselves upon our own minds and hearts and those of our children.

Post-ponderings: What, if any, strongly negative influences have played a role in your family history? If this has not been an issue, even in your extended family, pause to thank the Lord for his faithfulness!

ATHALIAH:
THE CORRUPTING INFLUENCE OF POWER

"Woman is the salvation or the destruction of the family. She carries its destiny in the folds of her mantle."
—HENRI FREDERIC AMIEL

"When Athaliah the mother of Ahaziah saw that her son was dead, she proceeded to destroy the whole royal family. But Jehosheba, the daughter of King Jehoram and sister of Ahaziah, took Joash son of Ahaziah and stole him away from among the royal princes, who were about to be murdered. . . . He remained hidden with his nurse at the temple of the LORD for six years while Athaliah ruled the land." (2 Kings 11:1, 3)

Read 2 Kings 11:1–16.
This vignette is part of a complicated story told over the course of multiple chapters in 2 Kings and 2 Chronicles. It makes for fascinating reading; the portion in 2 Kings 11 in particular reads like a fairytale. Depraved women have a reputation for being particularly ruthless when it comes to the hunger for power. Perhaps a basis is the disconnect between what society expects of a woman—stereotypically the nurturer—and the reality of those who don't fit the mold. Television has picked up on the theme of the black widow or designing woman because it makes for fascinating and counterintuitive drama.

The contrast between expectation and reality is even more pronounced when a controlling woman intends harm to her own child or grandchild. "Power attracts the corruptible," observes Frank Herbert. "Suspect any who seek it." You and I would never knowingly endanger our children, though we all as fallen humans at times inflict unintentional harm. But we're wise to curb any impulse to control or manipulate family members to our advantage.

Post-ponderings: If we're honest with ourselves, most of us have impulses to control. What is it that motivates you in this direction?

"What You See . . .":
An Uncle's Temporary Influence

"It should always be kept in mind that what you are after with your child is not that he should learn obedience but that he should learn to govern himself."
—AUTHOR UNKNOWN

"Joash did what was right in the eyes of the LORD all the years of Jehoiada the priest. Jehoiada chose two wives for him, and he had sons and daughters."
(2 Chronicles 24:2–3)

Read 2 Kings 11:17—12:21; 2 Chronicles 23–24.
Our hopes for little Joash, beginning anew with a clean slate during baby-hood, run high. The account of the seven-year-old's ascension to the throne and his promising early years under the tutelage of his uncle and mentor, Jehoiada, is heartwarming. All is well until the old priest's death; it seems as though the adage "out of sight, out of mind" defines Joash's heart- and mindset after that. It would appear that, for whatever reason, Joash failed to internalize the goodness he'd seen modeled in his uncle; once Jiminy Cricket slid down from his shoulder, his conscience ceased to operate.

It's important for us as parents to make certain our children at some point take over as arbiters of their own attitudes and behaviors, that we let go the reins enough to allow *their* wills to appropriate that vital role. How that looks will vary, but unless the baton of control is at some point passed along to the young person's nascent self, compliance to moral standards will remain external and arbitrary.

Post-ponderings: What do you see as the advantages and disadvantages of tight control over a child's behavior, especially during the adolescent years?

EXILE, AFTERMATH, AND RETURN

CHAPTER
INTRODUCTION

Ezra and Nehemiah contain some minimal material applicable to the theme of family dynamics. In contrast, the book of Esther, the last of the Old Testament historical books, includes a good deal of theme-related material. Like Ruth a literary masterpiece (which is not to disparage the authenticity of either account), this short book is a tightly choreographed account that, despite its lack of mention of God's name, unmistakably declares his providence.

The first half of chapter 13 is devoted to Ezra and Nehemiah, books chronicling the situation for the returnees from exile. Esther, again in contrast, relates the account of a family electing to remain in Persia (formerly Babylon), its adopted home.

The Family Trees
of 1 Chronicles

"In all of us there is a hunger, marrow deep, to know our heritage—to know who we are and where we came from. Without this enriching knowledge, there is a hollow yearning. No matter what our attainments in life, there is still a vacuum, an emptiness, and the most disquieting loneliness."
—ALEX HALEY

"Jabez was more honorable than his brothers. His mother had named him Jabez, saying, 'I gave birth to him in pain.' Jabez cried out to the God of Israel, 'Oh, that you would bless me and enlarge my territory! Let your hand be with me, and keep me from harm so that I will be free from pain.' And God granted his request."
(1 Chronicles 4:9–10)

Skim 1 Chronicles 1–9; 23:7–23.
Much attention was given a few years ago to the prayer of Jabez, and it isn't my intention to cover that territory here. What does fascinate me is the intermittent attention in these lengthy genealogies to seemingly random details (see also 7:21–24 for an interesting vignette). These anecdotes provide a poignant personal touch to what would otherwise be wooden lists of names.

These genealogies were vital to the returning exiles addressed in 1 and 2 Chronicles—that displaced second and third generation of the captives who were desperate to latch on to the threads of personal history, to pick up those dangling ends and begin anew the weaving of an interrupted legacy. The Chronicler's cryptic backdrop encapsulates something of both the significance of these lists and the stakes involved in getting it right with this new start: "All Israel was listed in the genealogies recorded in the book of the kings of Israel and Judah. They were taken captive to Babylon because of their unfaithfulness" (1 Chronicles 9:1).

Post-ponderings: "No one remembers the former generations," laments the Teacher in Ecclesiastes, going on, "and even those yet to come will not be remembered by those who follow them" (Ecclesiastes 1:11). How does reflection on his verse make you feel?

AWKWARD ANONYMITY:
THE LOSS OF CONNECTION

"I do have a sense of displacement as constant instability—the uninterrupted
existence of everything that I love and care about is not guaranteed at all.
I wait for catastrophes."
—ALEKSANDAR HEMON

*"The following came up from the towns of Tel Melah, Tel Harsha, Kerub, Addon and
Immer, but they could not show that their families were descended from Israel."*
(Ezra 2:59)

*"These searched for their family records, but they could not find them and so were
excluded from the priesthood as unclean." (Ezra 2:62)*

Skim Ezra 2.
I'm reminded of the chaos in Europe following WWII when people, many
of whom had lost their personal records, were attempting to reconnect with
lost loved ones and reestablish a place for themselves. The loss of family
connectedness can leave people feeling adrift in anonymity. We all want
to belong to something or someone else and will latch on to whatever or
whomever we can if that linkage is displaced—or information on it misplaced, as following the Judahite exile or the twentieth-century holocaust.

"God sets the lonely in families" (Psalm 68:6). This connection seems
to apply as much to a felt need for continuity (even if family members are
no more) as to present attachments. Membership of one kind or another is
a basic drive of humans—a vital part of bearing the image of God.

Our anonymous, mobile Western society includes an ever-increasing
number of disconnected souls bravely going it alone, people who live out
their lives with no sense of attachment to or claim upon affection. This
problem is so endemic that the chances are your own neighborhood includes an assortment of nondescript and invisible loners. What can you do
as a member of God's family to reach out to at least one such individual?

Post-ponderings: Even if you find yourself surrounded by members of immediate and/or extended family, pause briefly to assess what you would lose
without the family of believers, particularly those of your own congregation.

INTENSE AMBIVALENCE: GRANDDAD'S MEMORIES

"Memories are bullets. Some whiz by and only spook you. Others tear you open and leave you in pieces."
—RICHARD KADREY

"And all the people gave a great shout of praise to the LORD, because the founda-tion of the house of the LORD was laid. But many of the older priests and Levites and family heads, who had seen the former temple, wept aloud when they saw the foundation of this temple being laid, while many others shouted for joy. No one could distinguish the sound of the shouts of joy from the sound of weeping, because the people made so much noise. And the sound was heard far away."
(Ezra 3:11–13)

Read Ezra 3.
What a hauntingly beautiful picture! We can almost see the gathered fami-lies, little ones on shoulders or propped on hips, the slightly older children wide-eyed and incredulous, stimulated but uncertain about the contagious excitement. But it's the grandpas and grandmas, those well beyond the age of seventy (surprisingly, there seem to have been more than a few), who are the most moved. Because only they among the gathered congregation have a ref-erence for comparison. Sadly, the present reality falls dishearteningly short.

Sometimes it's life's most exquisite recollections, subtly retouched by time, that haunt us the most, especially in contrast to a present, less ex-travagant reality. Our perception is skewed to begin with by the disparity between reality past and our recollection of it, colored by personal associa-tion. "We don't see things as they are, we see them as we are," notes Anaïs Nin. Or as we *were* . . .

I'm intrigued by the mingling of sounds emanating from that scene. From keening to cheers, the clamor must have been a startling punctuation of the silence of a sparsely populated area. What message was conveyed to the people "far away" who strained to make sense of the noise?

One thing is certain: that foundation, despite its truncated dimensions and bleak backdrop, was beautiful to God. Beauty involves so much more than the physical. In this case the beauty of worship, intentionality, hope, and a new beginning, not to mention the noise erupting from God's people, added to the mystique. In the words of Malcolm de Chazal, "The beautiful remains so in ugly surroundings." And sometimes those surroundings are intrinsic to its allure.

Post-ponderings: What significant new start has punctuated your life or that of your family or worshiping community? Did it have to do with an event or with an internal development or change of heart?

UNDER THE WEATHER

"My mom says that when it rains you never feel like you should be anywhere but home."
—ELISE BROACH

"On the twentieth day of the ninth month, all the people were sitting in the square before the house of God, greatly distressed by the occasion and because of the rain." (Ezra 10:9)

Read Ezra 9:1—10:17.

"By the occasion and because of the rain"—I've always admired this author's success in painting a complete picture with the barest economy of words. It doesn't matter where the camera pans: once again (reminiscent of the previous reflection) they're all there—men, women, and little ones—all bedraggled and sniffling and equally miserable. Under the weather in the most literal sense.

And that particular situation, often more so than any overt disaster, can try our individual and collective souls. Moods and bugs are, after all, about equally transmittable within the family context. And all it can take is one of us, sneezing or scowling, to transform the bunch of us into an anything but cohesive unit.

No, the occasion for the assembly wasn't auspicious or joyous. That didn't help. But the relentless, drilling downpour and the discomfort of other selves pressing drenched tunics into thoroughly chilled bodies was uppermost in many minds. How often, after all, isn't it the niggling concerns that take priority in our consciousness over the issues truly needing to be addressed? That's the way we're wired, and it affects our family life in the most negative of ways.

The intermarriage debacle affected relatively few families, and we can easily see the others shaking their heads, truly saddened but convicted that these fellow returnees had it coming. It was their wives and kids who were the innocents. Another story . . . Infinitely more serious, yes! Universal, no.

Post-ponderings: When was your "twentieth day of the ninth month"—you know, when you last allowed that misnomer "a bad day" to impact not only you but your entire family? What was the problem . . . if you can remember? In the overall scheme of things, how important was it?

SOLIDARITY IN CRISIS

"Energy is the basis of everything. Every Jew, no matter how insignificant, is engaged in some decisive and immediate pursuit of a goal . . . They are the most perpetual people of the earth."
—JOHANN WOLFGANG VAN GOETHE

"Shallum son of Hallohesh, ruler of a half-district of Jerusalem, repaired the next section with the help of his daughters." (Nehemiah 3:12)

Read Nehemiah 3.
How refreshing to read this acknowledgment of the assistance of Shallum's girls! From Zelophehad's daughters to Naaman's wife's servant girl, the Old Testament repeatedly honors the spirit and pluck of stalwart young women.

"So we rebuilt the wall till all of it reached half its height, for the people worked with all their heart," records Nehemiah (4:6). The roster of the workers in chapter 3 may strike us as superfluous, but the participation of each one mattered. This joint effort was not only necessary but cemented a badly needed cohesion in this ragtag band of assorted returnees. The work mattered, and each individual represented by those busy hands and straining backs mattered.

Sometimes a forced togetherness in time of crisis can create a solidarity and community bond that could never otherwise have existed. America's relatively recent history has been punctuated in this way by such events as the Great Depression; two world wars; and, on a smaller scale I've personally experienced, 9/11. Despite hardship and tragedy, it can be gratifying to watch those threads of humanity pulling together (despite the inevitable drifting apart once again after the status quo has been restored).

Post-ponderings: Can you suggest long-range benefits of societal cycles revolving around tragedy of one kind or another? Might these times of insecurity in some sense serve as a force for good?

THE LAMENT OF THE POOR:
LIFESTYLE PROMOTION OF GOD'S HONOR

"There is no trust more sacred than the one the world holds with children. There is no duty more important than ensuring that their rights are respected, that their welfare is protected, that their lives are free from fear and want and that they can grow up in peace."
—KOFI ANNAN

"'Although we are of the same flesh and blood as our fellow Jews and though our children are as good as theirs, yet we have to subject our sons and daughters to slavery. Some of our daughters have already been enslaved, but we are powerless, because our fields and our vineyards belong to others.'" (Nehemiah 5:5)

Read Nehemiah 5.
Not only was the moneyed class's treatment of these fellow returnees inhumane; it was tarnishing God's reputation among his enemies. This is the same concern Moses expressed at Sinai when God threatened to wash his hands of his people after the golden calf incident. Listen to snippets of the exchange between God and Moses on that occasion: "Now leave me alone so that my anger may burn against them and that I may destroy them. Then I will make *you* into a great nation" (Exodus 32:10, emphasis added). "Why should the Egyptians say, 'It was with evil intent that he brought them out, to kill them in the mountains and to wipe them off the face of the earth'?" (verse 12). Nehemiah's appeal to the people on God's behalf follows the same line of thought: "Shouldn't you walk in the fear of our God and avoid the reproach of our Gentile enemies?" Reproach to *God* was at issue.

Kofi Annan's quote is convicting for us as representatives of Christ's body, especially when we substitute "Church" for "world" in the first sentence. The family of God has a responsibility both to uphold God's honor through individual and corporate lifestyle choices that glorify him and to promote the well-being of those fashioned in his image.

Post-ponderings: Pause to reflect on these beautiful yet sobering words from this chapter: "I also shook out the folds of my robe and said, 'In this way may God shake out of their house and possessions anyone who does not keep this promise. So may a person be shaken out and emptied.'" What does this imagery mean to you?

VASHTI AND XERXES: A QUEEN'S REBUFF

"Taught from infancy that beauty is women's scepter, the mind shapes itself to the body, and roaming around its gilt cage, only seeks to adorn its prison."
—MARY WOLLSTONECRAFT

"On the seventh day, when King Xerxes was in high spirits from wine, he commanded the seven eunuchs who served him . . . to bring before him Queen Vashti, wearing her royal crown, in order to display her beauty to the people and nobles, for she was lovely to look at. But . . . Queen Vashti refused to come." (Esther 1:10–12)

Read Esther 1.
To set the scene, the Medes and Persians have overtaken Babylon. The Jewish remnant has returned to Judah; those remaining have acclimated, choosing to stay on as transplants in Persia. Act One opens in the final stretch of Xerxes' decadent, ostentatious banquet; the royal wine has flowed unabated for a week. Drunkenly magnanimous, Xerxes decides to flaunt the asset he hasn't yet shared: his stunning queen. But Vashti, either herself under the influence or recoiling in disgust, opts to reveal the one quality she has dutifully kept under wraps—a mind of her own!

Aghast, Xerxes consults his wise men and is given to understand that all women in the kingdom will follow suit, despising and disobeying their husbands. Dispatches are rushed to the ends of the empire: Vashti is deposed, and every man, by royal decree, is to rule his own household. Blatant, capricious male domination is foreign to many in Western society and in the Church, but it's very much alive—often in guardedly private manifestations—all around us. Once again, the issue affects us not as participants but as caring representatives of Christ.

Post-ponderings: Abuse of women by husbands and significant others, though largely camouflaged or overlooked, is endemic in Western culture. What can you, as an individual or in league with other Christians, do to combat this disgrace?

MORDECAI AND ESTHER: "HEART RESONANCE"

"Family is the first social unit for developing the qualities of the heart. . . . Whether a biological family or an extended family of people attracted to each other based on heart resonance and mutual support, the word 'family' implies warmth, a place where the core feelings of the heart are nurtured."
—DOC CHILDRE AND HOWARD MARTIN

"Mordecai had a cousin named Hadassah, whom he had brought up because she had neither father nor mother. This young woman, who was also known as Esther, had a lovely figure and was beautiful. Mordecai had taken her as his own daughter when her father and mother died." (Esther 2:7)

Read Esther 2:1–15.
We don't often think of extended families as reflecting personalities, but in contemplating our own most of us could come up with a roughly consistent composite profile. We wouldn't ordinarily think of identifying family traits from a sampling of two, but Mordecai and Esther seem to have been all there were. A winning combination of modesty, loyalty, and courage melded with caution, impeccable timing, and sound judgment—these traits, reflected in "father" and "daughter"—worked together to make this nontraditional adoptive family ideal candidates for the physical salvation of the Jews in Persia.

We don't know the age difference between the two (or whether or not they were first cousins)—only that Mordecai was a third-generation exile and that the roughly seventy years of captivity had run their course. This beautifully crafted book never mentions God's name, but his presence permeates its pages. And the unpretentious joint protagonists are obviously godly.

Post-ponderings: Think of some adoptive families in your circle of acquaintance. Can you identify character traits at least some of the non-biologically-related members share in common? How do you account for this?

Selfless Beauty: A Disconnect?

"They may talk of a comet, or a burning mountain, or some such bagatelle;
but to me a modest woman, dressed in all her finery, is the most tremendous
object of the whole creation."
—OLIVER GOLDSMITH

*"Now the king was attracted to Esther more than to any of the other women, and
she won his favor and approval more than any of the other virgins." (Esther 2:17)*

Read Esther 2:16–18.
Remove "modest" and the Goldsmith quote loses its meaning. The word
seems, if you'll pardon the obvious word play, too modest for the context.
But that incongruity makes the picture alluring. It took more than physical
beauty for Esther to win the favor of everyone who saw her. The admiration, maybe, but her gentle and humble (not self-effacing) demeanor must
have caught people off guard in that competitive setting. A haughty woman
dressed in finery might turn eyes, yes, but Esther turned hearts . . . and not
just romantically.

As expressed in 1 Samuel 16:7, people look at the outward appearance,
while God looks at the heart. But there's another layer. We expect success
from the individual with the attractive physical package, and we may envy
them on that account. But we humans can be more heart-perceptive than
we realize. The sad truth is that we don't expect physical and heart beauty
together. Israel's Golda Meir, in reflecting back on her exemplary life, made
an astute observation: "Not being beautiful was the true blessing. Not being beautiful forced me to develop my inner resources. The pretty girl has
a handicap to overcome."

Post-ponderings: How sad that exceptionally beautiful people *do* often
lose their heart for others. When have you suspected some "drop-dead gorgeous" but thoughtful and giving woman—perhaps a Christian woman, an
involved mother in your congregation—of putting on a show? Deep down,
did you wonder why she bothered with caring?

At God's Disposal:
Available and Willing

"Availability is better than ability to God."
—AUTHOR UNKNOWN

"'I will go to the king, even though it is against the law. And if I perish, I perish.'"
(Esther 4:16)

Read Esther 4.
I'm impressed by the character of all three players in this chapter, very much including Hathak. It occurs to me how easily he could have sabotaged the plan. The go-between in an intensely private family conversation, this Persian servant was used by God in a mighty way and stands out in his Word as an example of trustworthiness.

The father/daughter interaction through Hathak is poignant. Neither flinches in terms of the opportunity God has placed at Esther's feet—or the inherent danger in her following through. God grants ample opportunity for us to accomplish good in his name. When have you found yourself in the right place at the right time in terms of performing a service for God? Did you, like Esther, rise willingly to the occasion?

"People are like stained-glass windows," reflects Elisabeth Kübler-Ross. "They sparkle and shine when the light is out, but when the darkness sets in their true beauty is revealed only if there is light from within." That inner light would shine brightly in and through Esther's actions to follow. Perhaps that very light would predispose her erratic husband to act on the Jews' behalf.

Post-ponderings: Assess both the opportunities for good God has opened for you and your current level of response.

THE CONTROLLING SPOUSE—THE ROLE
OF WHIM IN A DOMINATED MARRIAGE

"The true essence of a dictatorship is in fact not its regularity but its unpredictability and caprice; those who live under it must never be able to relax, must never be quite sure if they have followed the rules correctly or not."
—CHRISTOPHER HITCHENS

"When [the king] saw Queen Esther standing in the court, he was pleased with her and held out to her the gold scepter that was in his hand. So Esther approached and touched the tip of the scepter." (Esther 5:2)

Read Esther 5:1–8.
We've seen this dynamic in the opening of the book. In the reflection on Esther 1 we dealt with it primarily in the context of ancient royalty, making application to spousal abuse in our culture. But there's a softer side to the issue that finds expression in too many marriages, including those in the Church. The dynamic is of one-sided submission to a domineering spouse (typically the husband) operating on the basis of whim or emotion. This is what's going on when she waits for him to be in a good mood before requesting a favor for herself or one of the kids—who learn to play the game as well. Because miscalculation can bring unforeseen repercussions, everyone remains wary.

Not having been called for by Xerxes for thirty days, Esther is leery. As God would have it, she catches him in a magnanimous and even tender frame of mind. (He can be a great guy, the relieved wife reassures herself when met with this kind of response.) The chapter revolves around a subtle but all-important symbol—the point of a scepter. The matter at hand is often trivial, but in Esther's case the outcome could have been life or death!

Post-ponderings: Can your spouse and children depend on you for a considered response, independent of how your day is going?

ZERESH AND HAMAN: BACKHANDED MANIPULATION

"There isn't a wife in the world who has not taken the exact measure of her husband, weighed him and settled him in her own mind, and knows him as well as if she had ordered him after designs and specifications of her own."
—CHARLES DUDLEY WARNER

"His wife Zeresh and all his friends said to him, 'Have a pole let up . . . Then go with the king to the banquet and enjoy yourself.' This suggestion delighted Haman, and he had the pole set up." (Esther 5:14)

Read Esther 5:9–14.
If the previous reflection hit harder on husbands, this one points the finger at wives—not all wives (the quote takes that too far), any more than the last discussion implicated all husbands, but those who tend toward manipulation. We've encountered the Zeresh type already more than once; to varying degrees Sarai, Rebekah, and Jezebel fall within this category, at least at given points in time.

Zeresh may not have stood to gain personally from her plan, any more than Jezebel had by arranging for Ahab to obtain Naboth's vineyard (see the reflection on 1 Kings 21). The intention of both seems to have been to placate petulant husbands. As dominant in their way as the mood-driven Xerxes of the last reflection, such wives maneuver impressionable husbands as putty in their hands.

At the risk of overgeneralizing, it would seem that men are more likely to be direct about calling the shots in a relationship; women tend to be backhanded, circling around an issue before moving in for the thrust. Either approach can be damaging to a union, particularly if it describes a repeated mode of operation.

Post-ponderings: To what degree do mutual trust and respect define your marriage? Do both of you practice full disclosure, no matter what the issue?

CHAPTER 14

THE PSALMS

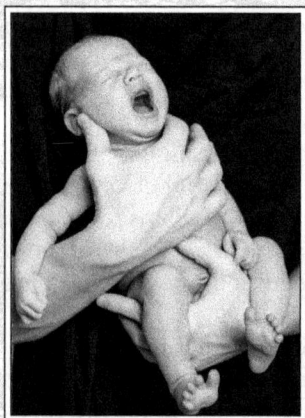

CHAPTER
INTRODUCTION

C hapters 14, 15, and 16, covering the psalms, wisdom literature, and the prophets, respectively, complete the portion of this book related to the Old Testament. My focus in treating non-historical (non-story) material—including the epistles and Revelation—is to reflect on the writing as it relates to family dynamics.

THE CHOSEN FAMILY

"Where would you be without friends? The people to pick you up when you need lifting? We come from homes far from perfect, so you end up almost parent and sibling to your friends—your own chosen family."
—JENNIFER ANISTON

"But you, LORD, are a shield around me, my glory, the One who lifts my head high." (Psalm 3:3)

Read Psalm 3.
How tragically deficient the world's recourses and resources for uplifting! And the lifts people do get are often temporary, disappointing—even hazardous to their health. It's easy for us who have grown up in the supportive environment of well-functioning Christian homes to relate to and expect the kinds of props that have shored us up throughout life. But Jennifer Aniston's quote reminds us that it isn't that way for everyone.

As the single mother of three daughters, all adopted at older ages, I know Aniston's statement to be anything but farfetched. My younger daughters, both of whom came to me after failed adoptions, knew the tragedies of dual disruptions, and the issues with which they struggle will be life-long. My youngest at seven, shortly after joining our family, made the wistful comment that, prior to that point, she "didn't know there was love in the world." Nor will I ever forget the evening I was to introduce her to her soon-to-be older sisters. A thunderstorm and flash flooding had nearly derailed our plans, and before attempting the crosstown trip to pick her up for the evening I called the disrupting adoptive home to make sure I should still come. The strange response was chilling: "Well, *we* don't want her!"

Despite years of Christian education both of these girls, now thirty-three and twenty-nine, struggle with their faith, finding it hard to accept God the Father as their shield, glory, and lifter. I'm struck by the poignant contrast between Aniston's "own chosen family" and your and my inclusion as cherished children and siblings in God's forever family of choice.

Post-ponderings: Following the structure of Aniston's quote, where would you be without God? The One who picks you up when you need lifting?

Full-on Glory

"You have set your glory in the heavens. Through the praise of children and infants you have established a stronghold against your enemies, to silence the foe and the avenger." (Psalm 8:1–2)

Read Psalm 8.

I'm fascinated by God's response in Exodus 33:22–23 to Moses' request for a glimpse of his glory: "When my glory passes by, I will put you in a cleft in the rock and cover you with my hand until I have passed by. Then I will remove my hand and you will see my back."

A few years ago my then five-year-old granddaughter and I, whiling away some travel time on an afternoon errand, were exploring synonyms to describe the overcast day: "cloudy" versus "dark," "windy" versus "blustery" (she preferred the latter, based on its familiarity from a Winnie the Pooh book). Moments later the pulsing sun infiltrated a break in the clouds, transforming the landscape on their underside. Taken aback, she marveled, "That looks like heaven, Granna. *I think I just saw God!*" I'm not at all sure Addie was wrong. Those clouds were the perfect counterpoint—the ideal foil to shield us from full-on glory.

I can only imagine that such childlike reflections leave Satan dumfounded. How could he counter the force of such full-out praise? God had indeed set his glory in the heavens, and an impressionable little one had seen and responded. Satan works most effectively with those of us who are pliable based not on innocence or inexperience but on that oh-so-adult openness to cynicism and doubt. The unwavering faith of the very young eludes him, because it's impervious to his wiles.

Post-ponderings: When was the last time you were convicted of God's presence by the trusting comment of a child? When did you last see—or hear, smell, taste, or touch—God?

THE DESIRE OF THE AFFLICTED

"Poverty is taking your children to the hospital and spending the whole day waiting with no one even taking your name—and then coming back the next day, and the next, until they finally get around to you."
—JANICE BRADSHAW

"You, LORD, hear the desire of the afflicted; you encourage them, and you listen to their cry, defending the fatherless and the oppressed, so that mere earthly mortals will never again strike terror." (Psalm 10:17–18)

Read Psalm 10.
Whether the context is trying to cash a check (the privilege of owning an account isn't for everyone); working with a cut-rate auto dealership (the kind that remotely disables the vehicle's ignition if payment is late); housing an entire family in a hotel room because less expensive, lower-end rental units are inaccessible due to credit problems; or employment that subjects the worker to the indignity of standing along the roadside in a silly costume waving at drivers—degradation comes in many forms. A friend of my daughter wasted more than sixty hours attempting to cold sell a product door to door, his remuneration (he never received a dime) contingent on his making a designated number of presentations within the week. Having trudged for hours through an icy rain, he not only ended up physically sick but was assaulted by a severe bout of his chronic depression.

All around us policies are operative that relentlessly and methodically strike terror into human beings. What makes these situations so insidious is that they happen in the context of business as usual. It behooves us as Christ's representatives to walk through life with our antennae up, doing whatever we can to encourage, listen to, and defend those subjected by circumstance to lives of dysfunction, oppression, and despair. Those "invisible" sufferers are all around and among us, but it takes eyes anointed by the Spirit to identify them and hearts filled with love to effectively respond.

Post-ponderings: If you live in a city, what is your response—including your emotional reaction—to panhandlers or to those homeless, mentally ill or addicted individuals shuffling along with their belongings down the street?

CAST UPON GOD

"Birth is the sudden opening of a window, through which you look out upon a stupendous prospect. For what has happened? A miracle. You have exchanged nothing for the possibility of everything."
—WILLIE DIXON

"Yet you brought me out of the womb; you made me trust in you, even at my mother's breast. From birth I was cast on you; from my mother's womb you have been my God." (Psalm 22:9–10)

Read Psalm 22:1–10.
Besides being traumatic, the birth experience must be, well, eye-opening. It's too bad none of us can remember back to those preverbal days when every experience and encounter was amazing and unprecedented. It's thought-provoking to recognize that newborns come equipped with full intelligence, needing only to learn through trial and error to effectively engage it.

Nineteenth-century British novelist William Makepeace Thackeray made the provocative statement that "mother is the name for God in the lips and hearts of little children." Before we're able to pronounce "Ma—" or even to differentiate that seemingly omnipresent, omniscient force that comforts us as being separate from ourselves, we recognize her voice and burrow ourselves into Love and Peace.

Psalm 139 deals extensively with incubation and birth, but David's take on the subject in the two verses above is different. I'm intrigued by the image of being cast upon God—quite literally from the birth canal. Typically our mother's embrace constitutes our first impression of God's everlasting arms. What a privilege that God entrusts to us as their parents and his delegates the nurture of these precious little ones.

Post-ponderings: Thinking back as far as you can, what early memories of your mother come to mind?

NEVER FORSAKEN:
ETCHED IN HIS HANDS

"If it comes down to a choice of being unloved and being vulnerable and sensitive and emotional, then you can just keep your love."
—CHUCK PALAHNIUK

"Do not reject me or forsake me, God my Savior. Though my father and mother forsake me, the LORD will receive me." (Psalm 27:9–10)

Read Psalm 27; Isaiah 49:13–18.

"Can a mother forget the baby at her breast and have no compassion on the child she has borne?" asks Isaiah. "Though she may forget, I will not forget you! See, I have engraved you on the palms of my hands." The prophet's opening question sounds rhetorical. But his ensuing statement reflects his recognition that every rule has its exceptions. Unfortunately, in our society there are too many. This unthinkable kind of abandonment happened to each of my three daughters prior to their separate adoptions at older ages. And I've watched one of them make the same choice. Depressed and overwhelmed by the demands of three babies, she simply walked away, first repeatedly and then finally. Whether the abandonment is physical or emotional, the results often are devastating and lasting. This applies even if the rejection happened in earliest infancy; sadly, attachment issues and other insecurities on the parts of children often catch adoptive parents by surprise.

Isaiah's point is that God will not—indeed, based on the integrity of his nature *cannot*—forget them, or us. An analogy to engraving someone's name on our palm is a tattoo. But God hasn't engraved our *names*, or those of our children, on the palms of his hands; he has permanently etched *us* there. That makes each of us enduringly—indelibly—unforgettable to him! Engraving us and our children in his hands cost God something, just as the nails in his palms cost his Son. Such pricey love is eternal and unforgettable.

Post-ponderings: Do your children understand and appreciate the depths of God's love, and the incalculable value of Christ's sacrifice, for them?

The Arms of Love

"The arms of love encompass you with your present, your past, your future, the arms of love gather you together."
—ANTOINE DE SAINT-EXUPÉRY

"May your unfailing love be with us, LORD, even as we put our hope in you."
(Psalm 33:22)

Read Psalm 33:12–22.
To borrow from Saint-Exupéry, God's unfailing arms gather us *together* in a communal sense (the "us" and "we" of the psalmist's prayer), and they gather each of us "together"—present, past, and future—integrating and defragging our broken lives. The arms of love effect for us both union with others and reunion within our selves, with the wholeness that had so briefly been the native condition of humankind.

Our God is a promise keeper, embracing his own through generations and millennia within his encompassing covenant: to be God to us and to our believing children after us. His embrace is as wide and long as history, enveloping you, me, yours, ours, and mine in his everlasting arms. For those of us so blessed as to come from a long line of believers, this realization lends special meaning to our family tree, offering both security and hope.

So what are we to think about those family members we have reason to believe haven't been grafted into the true vine (John 15:1–17), or for whom the graft hasn't apparently taken? Jesus exhorts us to remain in his love. It's our job to love and obey him, to hope in him, and to be both faith-filled and faithful. And he offers an invitation: "Ask whatever you wish, and it will be done for you" (verse 7). It isn't up to us to determine what God should do with those branches that seem to be casualties. We can and must continue in prayer for those loved ones who have yet to make a decision. Beyond that, we can do nothing better than to relax in God's arms, knowing that he holds it all together and that he can and will do infinitely more than all we can ask or begin to imagine.

Post-ponderings: How, specifically, does this issue hit home for you?

Prayer: Hardship Tactic?

"You say to God, 'I have never seen you provide for me.' God says to you, 'You have never trusted me.'"

—CORALLIE BUCHANAN

"I was young and now I am old, yet I have never seen the righteous forsaken or their children begging bread." (Psalm 37:25)

Read Psalm 37.
Like the general wisdom principles in Proverbs, David's declaration, above, doesn't constitute a hard and fast rule. It is, however, a ringing affirmation of God's eagerness to care for his own. And perhaps, just perhaps, if we would pray *expecting provision*, we would be surprised at the outcome: "Cast your cares on the LORD and he will sustain you; he will never let the righteous be shaken" (Psalm 55:22). Fickle people that we are, when we experience trouble or hardship we toy with different avenues in our quest for a solution. A season of prayer—even earnest, sincere prayer—may be one of them. But when resolution isn't immediate, we're tempted to cut our losses and try a more proactive approach.

When it comes to prayer, our kids have a lot to teach us. Young children have no trouble calling up delight, and their trust quotient is enormous. Their knowledge of God—their *knowing* him—is unhampered by caveats, and they're surprisingly undeterred by delayed gratification. The concept of God disappointing them, or the presumption of expecting him to prove himself, is beyond them. They know they aren't in control, and questioning the Power that is doesn't occur to them. God doesn't pass or fail, exist or cease (or fail) to exist, based on our assessment of his performance. The more we delight in him, just as he is, the more likely that our desires will align with his will and wisdom for our lives.

Post-ponderings: When have you—or you and your spouse—tried prayer before moving along to a different tactic?

Sandbox Wisdom

"Original sin, therefore, appears to be a hereditary depravity and corruption of our nature, diffused through all the parts of the soul, rendering us obnoxious to the divine wrath and producing in us those works which the scripture calls 'works of.'"

—JOHN CALVIN

"Surely I was sinful at birth, sinful from the time my mother conceived me. Yet you desired faithfulness even in the womb; you taught me wisdom in that secret place." (Psalm 51:5–6)

Read Psalm 51:1–6.
Our sin nature is original and hereditary, but David reminds us that God's grace is operative from our earliest days too. We don't know at what point God begins teaching wisdom to our nascent hearts, but the little one old enough to knowingly disobey is not too young to catch inklings of right and wrong. These words of Jean Paul remind us of the privilege and opportunity God has granted us to reinforce those inklings: "The conscience of children is formed by the influences that surround them; their notions of good and evil are the result of the moral atmosphere they breathe."

While God's Spirit instills wisdom in the hearts of believers' children, it's vital for us to work with him on the endeavor. The environment of a little child is in many ways closed and cocooned. When she's very small we may limit her exposure to germs by keeping her from crowds. And we'll incrementally regulate her exposure to evil for years to come.

The acquisition of wisdom is a lifelong process. Still, in the familiar words of Robert Fulghum, "Wisdom was not at the top of the graduate-school mountain, but there in the sandpile at Sunday School." While we as Christian parents would endorse his point, I have no doubt most of us would move up the beginnings of that learning by a few years and substitute the image of a parent's knee.

Post-ponderings: The reflection on 1 Kings 3:1–15; 2 Chronicles 1 also refers to Psalm 51:5, stressing God's imparting of wisdom starting even earlier, *from conception onward.* Pause to consider this offsetting grace in light of our hereditary sin nature. What does this say to you about the viability of those waiting to be born?

RESOLUTION FOR LONELINESS

"[I]f you meet a loner, no matter what they tell you, it's not because they
enjoy solitude. It's because they have tried to blend into the world before,
and people continue to disappoint them."
—JODI PICOULT

"A father to the fatherless, a defender of widows, is God in his holy dwelling.
God sets the lonely in families." (Psalm 68:5–6)

Read Psalm 68:1–6.

I've quoted this verse at least twice before, but it's one of my favorites, and
I view it as worth repeating in a book devoted to biblical familiar dynamics. Our world is characterized for many by insecurity, instability, and isolation. For good or ill, many seek solace in intimate relationships outside
the "nuclear" family that has offered safe boundaries until recent decades.
From live-in relationships to group homes to gangs to cults to foster families, adults and kids desperately seek to fulfill their God-given need to belong to another human being. Many others look for relief to inanimate
objects or passions. Maya Angelou poignantly reflects that "music was my
refuge. I could crawl into the space between the notes and curl my back to
loneliness."

Our Lord does set the lonely in families. He did it for me not through
marriage and childbirth but via adoption. Yet regardless of our family situation, we Christians can affirm a sense of belonging and entitlement unknown to a pining world. Elizabeth Gilbert relates God's "words" as the
Spirit spoke them to her: "I'm here. I love you. I don't care if you need to
stay up crying all night long, I will stay with you. There's nothing you can
ever do to lose my love. I will protect you until you die, and after your death
I will still protect you. I am stronger than Depression and I am braver than
Loneliness and nothing will ever exhaust me."

Post-ponderings: Are you lonely? Whether or not you're surrounded by
loved ones? Or are you relishing your inclusion in God's forever family? If
so, remember that he's there for you. And so are the rest of us if you'll only
reach out.

FILTERED-DOWN SHAME

"Once they know they've got a hold of your shame, they can shake it out and hold it up for all the world to see. And you become less than it. You become something disgusting."

—KIRSTY EAGAR

"May those who hope in you not be disgraced because of me. . . . For I endure scorn for your sake, and shame covers my face. I am a foreigner to my own family, a stranger to my own mother's children." (Psalm 69:6–8)

Read Psalm 69:1–12.
David didn't want his sinful actions or their consequences to reflect poorly on the rest of God's people. It's the same issue we face when the moral lapse of a pastor, priest, or televangelist comes to light or when Christians in the media are caught behaving badly. Has your reputation or that of your family ever suffered on the basis of something a relative did or failed to do? Did family members reject or distance themselves from the offending individual? If so, you can empathize with David's angst.

When this happens we do well to recall that God is bigger than our conception of him. Human righteousness is based for each of us on the intersection of grace and faith. And God is remarkably inclusive. Each person, whether or not they are—or are currently—"his," is precious in his sight. Not all will come to repentance and salvation, but that hope remains alive from our side for as long as the person does. God doesn't treat any of us as our sins deserve (103:10). And it isn't up to us to make a value judgment on anyone else—let alone the person's family. There but for the grace of God, as the adage reminds us, go we.

Post-ponderings: Approaching this issue from an opposite angle, has your opinion of another family taken a nosedive on the basis of the indiscretion of one member?

INFINITE, ETERNAL HOPE

"An infinite God can give all of Himself to each of His children. He does not distribute Himself that each may have a part, but to each one He gives all of Himself as fully as if there were no others."
—A. W. TOZER

"For you have been my hope, Sovereign LORD, my confidence since my youth. From birth I have relied on you; you brought me forth from my mother's womb."
(Psalm 71:5–6)

Read Psalm 71:1–8.
Our mental paradigm is that God has to spread himself thin to have enough of himself to go around. Perhaps especially those of us who grew up in large families consider it presumptuous to ask for more than our "share," preferring to hold back and accept the amount he feels is reasonable. We find ourselves continuously assessing our level of need in comparison to that of others, invariably coming up short. When, if ever, will it legitimately be our turn? And so we bide our time, waiting for that moment of fulfillment.

The reality is that a shortage mentality reflects the very antithesis of God, who is all about liberality and unstinting blessing. We worry about spoiling our little ones with too much of any good thing, but we ourselves are in no danger of being spoiled by our Father's indulgence. Nothing is too good from the God who is himself the personification of goodness.

I'm drawn back to a lovely song that played a big role in nudging me through those dark weeks and months following my mother's death when I was eleven. Some of those precious lyrics: "His love has no limits, His grace has no measure, His power has no boundary known unto men; For out of His infinite riches in Jesus He giveth, and giveth, and giveth again." The psalmist was so right in harking back to life's inception when it comes to embracing the goodness of God. Truly the Lord is our hope and confidence . . . all the way from womb to tomb and infinitely beyond.

Post-ponderings: What role do you suspect your childhood background has played in your perception and expectations of God?

UNFINISHED TOUCH?

"Children ... are our legacy. Our responsibility. They are our destiny and we are theirs. The extent to which we fail as parents, we fail as God's children."
—DIRK BENEDICT

"He decreed statutes for Jacob and established the law in Israel, which he commanded our ancestors to teach their children, so the next generation would know them, even the children yet to be born, and they in turn would tell their children." (Psalm 78:5–6)

Read Psalm 78:1–8.
"Look at this, Granna" (holding up a Play-Doh sculpture). "It's a finished touch!" *Unlike you and me*, I thought to myself with a rueful smile that day a few years back. The day of completion will come, but as the saying goes "God isn't finished with me yet." Or with my granddaughter. And I'm not either. My every touch—physical, verbal, emotional, intellectual, relational, and spiritual—leaves an impression on Adelyn, now eight. As John Keats expressed with spare eloquence, "Touch has a memory." And such touching is one of those awesome, intimidating privileges and responsibilities of parenting—or, in my case, of grandparenting.

The Indian philosopher and spiritualist Jiddu Krishnamurti observed that "in our relationship with children and young people, we are not dealing with mechanical devices that can be quickly repaired, but with living beings who are impressionable, volatile, sensitive, afraid, affectionate." And the applicable adjectives go on and on. In the words of Ralph Nader it's our responsibility, in this case spiritually and by example, to be "good ancestors." What more significant accountability for us as believing predecessors?

Post-ponderings: What kind of spiritual legacy are you working to leave?

NUMBERING OUR DAYS

"If I'd known I was gonna live this long, I'd have taken better care of myself."
—EUBIE BLAKE AT AGE 100

"Our days may come to seventy years, or eighty, if our strength endures; yet the best of them are but trouble and sorrow, for they quickly pass, and we fly away." (Psalm 90:10)

Read Psalm 90.
I had occasion recently to uncover a black-and-white photo of my grandma in her early sixties—shortly before her death—an amiable little lady with wire rims, waist-length gray hair braided and bobby-pinned around her head, and a sensible print dress. Fine and good—until it occurred to me that I'm nearly sixty-three. We're hearing a lot these days about the increasing number of octogenarians inhabiting the planet, and there can be no doubt that a heightened awareness of health maintenance and improving health care are playing significant roles.

Checking the context of the above verse, I'm taken aback by those that flank it: "All our days pass away under your wrath; we finish our years with a moan" and "If only we knew the power of your anger! Your wrath is as great as the fear that is your due." Heavy stuff, isn't it? I'll have to concede that the author, Moses, an old man when he wrote this psalm, had seen his share of God's anger.

Moses comes to the point in verse 12: "Teach us to number our days, that we may gain a heart of wisdom." Ah, there's the issue. How am I doing at numbering my days? At gaining that heart of wisdom? If I'm to be one of those who lives to an extreme age, what does God want me to do with those bonus years? These are questions worth pondering as I inch my way toward old age, twenty-first-century style.

Post-ponderings: If your family history points to long life, what will you do with your later years?

DUST MOTES RISING

"It is true that we are made of dust. And the world is also made of dust. But the dust has motes rising."
—MUHAMMED IQBAL

"As a father has compassion on his children, so the LORD has compassion on those who fear him; for he knows how we are formed, he remembers that we are dust."
(Psalm 103:13–14)

Read Psalm 103.
"Beauty is everlasting and dust is for a time," reflects Marianne Moore. Most household dust, as you already know, is comprised of sloughed-off skin cells. And I learned as a girl that our body replaces *all* its cells every seven years (I'll admit to not having checked out the reliability of that statistic). Our physical bodies are a part of our "package" (we'll have them for eternity), but in their current condition they change on a moment-by-moment basis. Not so our spirits. Within each of us is a core, untouchable "me" that remains remarkably intact throughout life. We come to understand ourselves differently, and hopefully better, as time goes by, but the continuity is never disrupted.

"It appears to me impossible," reflected Mary Wollstonecraft, an eighteenth-century British philosopher and feminist, "that I should cease to exist, or that this active, restless spirit, equally alive to joy and sorrow, should be only organized dust." She's right, of course, despite an absence of Christian faith to back her statement—or infuse it with hope. How comforting to know that our Father God has compassion not only on the generations of those who fear (revere or reverence) him but on all who bear his image—that he implants within each human psyche a core intuition pointing in the direction of truth.

Post-ponderings: Thank God for his concern for your own and your family members' physical vulnerability. Then express your gratitude for your undying, indomitable spirits.

HERITAGE AND REWARD

"Children are a heritage from the LORD, offspring a reward from him." (Psalm 127:3)

Read Psalm 127.
It doesn't take much digging to come up with "children are" quotes. A sampling: "Children are the living messages we send to a time we will not see"
(John W. Whitehead) or "Children are the hands by which we take hold of
heaven" (Henry Ward Beecher). Perhaps that's because the human race has
been trying since the births of those first squirmy replicas of ourselves to
pin down the enigma of these intriguing creatures. "A baby," reflects Carl
Sandburg, "is God's opinion that the world should go on." These little ones
are the channel through which God passes along the faith. The quality of
each generational baton exchange is critical to the outcome of the race . . .
and to the well-being of the Church.

This psalm can be bittersweet to those who long for a child but find
their arms empty. If you fall within the ranks of Christian parents, take
seriously the trust God has seen fit to assign you. If you feel passed over in
this area, remember that God entrusts each upcoming generation not simply to the parents but to his bride, the Church. The children with which the
Lord blesses his Church are indeed a heritage, not to mention a privilege,
an opportunity, and a responsibility—for all of us!

Post-ponderings: Come up with a "children are . . . " statement that is meaningful to you.

THE FATHER'S LOVE:
CONCEPTION AND BEYOND

"I praise you because I am fearfully and wonderfully made . . . My frame was not hidden from you when I was made in the secret place, when I was woven together in the depths of the earth. Your eyes saw my unformed body; all the days ordained for me were written in your book before one of them came to be." (Psalm 139:14–16)

Read Psalm 139:13–18.

"In pregnancy," marvels Joan Raphael, "there are two bodies, one inside the other. Two people live under one skin. . . . When so much of life is dedicated to maintaining our integrity as distinct beings, this bodily tandem is an uncanny fact."

Running for the phone, already on the fourth ring, I heard my then five-year-old granddaughter already in conversation, announcing matter-of-factly, "I don't have a dad." The caller was Right to Life, and, moved (and amused) as I was by her poignant admission, I couldn't help but shudder at the thought that this vibrant little girl could have been the casualty of a young mother's decision to abort based on disappointment, shame, or shattered dreams and hopes.

As I watch Adelyn, now eight, dance and sing her way through life, I'm struck by the reality that today—like every other of her days—was specifically ordained for her. Not only that, but she's becoming acquainted with her heavenly Daddy, the same Abba who will never leave her fatherless.

Post-ponderings: Take the time to read through this beautiful psalm in prayer mode, being profuse in your praise.

CHAPTER 15

WISDOM LITERATURE

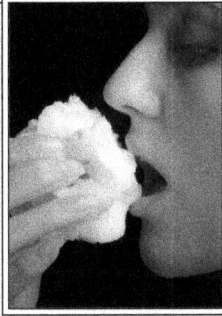

CHAPTER
INTRODUCTION

Most of the reflections included in this chapter relate to nuggets of wisdom from the book of Proverbs; the final two are gleaned from Ecclesiastes and Song of Songs, respectively. Itself a compilation, with a given verse frequently unrelated thematically to those around it, Proverbs is a largely disjointed book that must be assimilated as bytes of wisdom.

Incidental Learning

"I believe that what we become depends on what our fathers teach us at odd moments, when they aren't trying to teach us. We are formed by little scraps of wisdom."

—UMBERTO ECO

"Listen, my sons, to a father's instruction; pay attention and gain understanding. I give you sound learning, so do not forsake my teaching. For I too was a son to my father, still tender, and cherished by my mother." (Proverbs 4:1–3)

Read Proverbs 1:1–9; 4.

When we're in the company of a child, it's amazing how much learning goes on. I spend a good deal of time with my eight-year-old granddaughter. In part because there are only two of us, we tend to engage in easy, rambling conversation. Periodically I find myself listening in on us and chuckle at how much teaching is going on, usually in both directions—scraps and snippets of information and advice for living. We talk about word meanings and God and etiquette and share how to's and why not's. Subjects from dealing with a friend's quirks to methods for mental subtraction to fashion statements to bullying to adult behavior to the relative nature of gifts and talents—any and every topic is fair game.

I hope, though, that matters of the heart are getting fair representation. I try to teach, and hopefully model, compassion. The need of children to just talk—or, better, *really* talk—is too often overlooked. That's one of the main reasons I enjoy sitting with first-graders at Adelyn's school listening to them hone their reading skills. So many opportunities come up, both in terms of the subject matter of the books and the matters on their minds. Uninhibited, they bring up anything and everything, opening the door of opportunity to so much incidental learning.

It's that, I hope, that will stay with them—just as my own childhood experiences of this kind have stayed with me! "Above all else, guard your heart, for everything you do flows from it," urges the writer of Proverbs 4:23. I can't imagine a more apropos concept to instill within a child.

Post-ponderings: What conversation with a parent or other adult from your childhood do you recall as though it were yesterday? Did you internalize the concept to the point that it still guides your behavior?

THE DISCIPLINE/DELIGHT CONNECTION

"You cannot catch a child's spirit by running after it; you must stand still and for love it will soon itself return."
—ARTHUR MILLER

"The LORD disciplines those he loves, as a father the son he delights in."
(Proverbs 3:12)

Read Proverbs 3.
Again focusing on the child/parent connection, we all thrive on liberal doses of love, often expressed as mutual enjoyment of one another. And, ironically, on the discipline that accompanies and enables it. As the writer of the above verse reminds us, God's discipline of us and ours of our kids are natural and necessary offshoots of love. As God would have it, the pleasure in both cases flows in two-directional streams: "Discipline your children, and they will give you peace; they will bring you the delights you desire" (29:17).

Proverbs 3 lets us in on an extended heart-to-heart conversation between a dad and an adolescent or young adult son. The discipline stage, at least in the direction of parent to child, has run its course; the time has come for the young man to internalize the precepts and run with them. The baton is being passed, along with some summation to make sure the points are clear.

In similar fashion God reminds us in his Word of his directions for our life, beginning with the Ten Commandments and branching in countless elaborations from there before coming back together in Jesus' wrap-up in Luke 10:27.

Post-ponderings: Paul makes clear in Romans that the believer is no longer bound by the letter of the Law as spelled out in the Ten Commandments. And yet in love and gratitude—and because the moral law is written upon our hearts—we rightly strive to keep each one. What is your relationship as a Christian to this Old Covenant list of commands?

Marital Fidelity: One's Own Cistern

"When I say 'I will be true to you' I am drawing a quiet space beyond the reach of other desires."
—JEANETTE WINTERSON

"Drink water from your own cistern, running water from your own well. Should your springs overflow in the streets, your streams of water in the public squares? Let them be yours alone, never to be shared with strangers. May your fountain be blessed, and may you rejoice with the wife of your youth." (Proverbs 5:15–18)

Read Proverbs 5.
Adultery isn't only sinful, it's unhealthy. Not just physically but emotionally and spiritually as well. To a certain degree the same can be said of any sin—though this isn't to be our primary reason for shunning evil. But sexual sin, along with any other that involves lack of personal restraint, is perpetrated against our own bodies, God's temples.

The startling words of Proverbs 9:16–18 drive home in a particularly graphic manner just how unhealthful sexual sin is: "To those who have no sense [Folly] says, 'Stolen water is sweet; food eaten in secret is delicious!' But little do they know . . . that her guests are deep in the realm of the dead." Death—whether physical or spiritual! That's the epitome of unhealthy, isn't it?

I'm drawn to the imagery in the Jeanette Winterson quote. That quiet, impermeable space surrounding a couple's sexuality reminds me of a protective mote or an electric fence. The clear intent and message are "Private Property. Keep Out!" More to the point, though, is the internalized impetus to "Keep In!" Because sexual sin, despite the reality of temptation, flows from the inside out.

Post-ponderings: If temptation toward sexual sin, even in the fantasy area, is an issue for you, what steps can you take to avoid it?

THE "LIVED IN" HOUSE

"Marrying is easy, it's housework that's hard."
—PROVERB

"The wise woman builds her house, but with her own hands the foolish one tears hers down." (Proverbs 14:1)

Read Proverbs 14:1–11.

"Like plowing," observes Letty Cottin Pogrebin, "housework makes the ground ready for the germination of family life. The kids will not invite a teacher home if beer cans litter the living room. The family isn't likely to have breakfast together if somebody didn't remember to buy eggs, milk, or muffins." Any house can be a home, but that transition is never automatic or a foregone conclusion. The euphemism "lived in" can reflect that comfortable human touch difficult to achieve through an interior decorator—or a state of unrelenting turmoil. When it comes to stressors, clutter can be a major offender—enough to keep everyone on edge and a frustrated spouse away from home.

The fact is that our home building has a lot to do with homemaking. If your partner is stumbling over toys or riffling through overflowing stacks in quest of the bank statement, it may be time to adopt new habits.

Post-pondering: When it comes to housekeeping, at what point in your opinion does relaxed move full circle into highly stressful?

THE FAMILY THAT DINES TOGETHER

"The act of nutrition is not a purely physiological event. . . . The family meal is a formality that cultivates in us . . . a capacity for sharing, generosity, thoughtfulness, a talent for civilized conversation."
—FRANCINE DU PLESSIX GRAY

"Better a small serving of vegetables with love than a fattened calf with hatred."
(Proverbs 15:17)

Read Proverbs 15:1–17.
In all fairness to the vegetable, meat was an extravagance in the Israelite diet. But whether a family was eating in luxury or in poverty, Solomon's point was that love and togetherness are the mealtime factors that count. He was probably able to take for granted that families sat down and ate together. Encouragingly, I learned in a newscast a few weeks ago that the American family dinner remains at least a somewhat intact institution. Whether the fare is fast-food pizza, grilled cheese sandwiches, or serious meat and potatoes (and other veggies), the opportunity afforded in the evening for family members to face one another around and across a table can go a long way toward cementing cohesion and promoting respect and understanding.

As an addendum, one of the byproducts of real family dinners is the passing along of manners, whether in terms of table etiquette or of basic civilities—like taking turns, making sure everyone is served before taking a second helping, and refraining from reaching across the table or interrupting. This principle goes beyond mouthing the right words to making appropriate statements that require empathy, emotional investment, and simple human kindness. "In some families," reflects Margaret Laurence, "*please* is described as the magic word. In our house, however, it was *sorry*."

Post-ponderings: In what context does your family commune together? Is God included?

GENERATIONAL APPRECIATION

"I have often thought what a melancholy world this would be without children, and what an inhuman world without the aged."
—SAMUEL TAYLOR COLERIDGE

"Children's children are a crown to the aged, and parents are the pride of their children." (Proverbs 17:6)

Read Proverbs 17:1–6.
We Boomers (just apply that to me if it doesn't fit you) are "coming of age." How typical of this generation to do it twice! We've tackled life with gusto and, despite a desire to remain engaged and active, are looking toward or enjoying retirement.

Probably more than any of our predecessors, we hang our dreams on our grandchildren. Wiling away some time with my granddaughter in a McDonald's Playplace some time ago, I couldn't help but notice that the adults present could have organized a grandparents' club. The majority of us, I gathered from conversational snatches, were killing, or filling, time before picking up our own "kids" from work. Boomers waiting for our Boomerang kids . . .

What bothers me about the arrangement is the entitlement mentality characterizing so many of the young adults who rely on continued "hands-on" parenting for themselves, not to mention a kind of grandparental involvement with their offspring that looks a lot like parenting. With regard to the first clause of Solomon's observation, well and good—or at least real (though "aged" might better apply to great-grandparents). But what of the second? In our societal context, the notion of parents being the pride of their kids doesn't necessarily ring true.

Post-ponderings: No matter what generational group you represent, how well does this verse apply to your situation? Have we lost something along the way? The Lord expects intergenerational honor.

"Disregarded Entities"

"The poverty in the West is a different kind of poverty—it is not only a poverty of loneliness but also of spirituality. There's a hunger for love, as there is a hunger for God."

—MOTHER TERESA

"The poor are shunned by all their relatives—how much more do their friends avoid them!" (Proverbs 19:7)

Read Proverbs 19:1–8.

A few years ago I was browsing a tax form when I was stopped in my visual "tracks" by a sentence beginning something like "If you are a disregarded entity . . ." This was my first exposure to that disconcerting term, which immediately called to mind the unfortunate Tom Hanks character in the movie *The Terminal.* Curious, I pulled it up on the internet. I now know that this descriptor refers to "a business entity that chooses to be disregarded as separate from the business owner for federal tax purposes." Well, okay . . . sort of.

A saying popular a couple of decades ago still speaks: "God doesn't make junk." Oh, there's plenty of junk around. But it's manmade (or should I say human-made?). Human beings, though tragically sin-marred, have never been castoffs in God's sight. For my part, I'm going to renew my efforts to view all people through his eyes.

"When you say a situation or a person is hopeless," notes Charles L. Allen, "you are slamming the door in the face of God." If God has yet to give up on any of those "marginal" others populating the planet alongside me, I as a caring Christian have no business doing so either. Two words to expunge from my vocabulary when it comes to human beings: *disregarded* and *entity.*

Post-ponderings: How much would you and your family be willing to invest—and risk—to invite some interaction with "down-and-out" individuals in your area? "God does not love us because we are valuable," reminds Martin Luther. "We are valuable because he loves us."

PLIP PLOP: THE NAGGING WIFE

"Lady Middleton resigned herself. . . . Contenting herself with merely giving her husband a gentle reprimand on the subject, five or six times every day."
—JANE AUSTEN

"A quarrelsome wife is like the constant dripping of a leaky roof." (Proverbs 19:13)

Read Proverbs 19:9–13.

"Three things drive a man outdoors; smoke, a leaking roof and a scolding wife." So declares a proverb from an unknown source. The problem is different from that of the scheming wife we've already discussed (Jezebel comes to mind). Not to aggrandize that much more subtle habit, nagging is unimaginative and tedious to the point of being insufferable. The badgering spouse belittles with each repetition. And the browbeaten partner learns to cover over the scars with indifference—the only available defense.

We can, of course, fall into the same pattern with our children, the result being sons and daughters who agree to our faces but do their own thing when our backs are turned. "*Yeah, yeah!*" We can almost hear the longsuffering, dismissive groans.

In all fairness, most nagging wives and mothers—for some reason we see this as a woman thing—don't develop the trait out of the blue (the habit has a cause, though not a valid reason!). But the more continuously people hear the same thing, the less likely they are to listen or respond. Practical James offers a directive rich in common sense: "Everyone should be quick to listen, slow to speak and slow to become angry" (James 1:19). How much more impact our words would have if each of us would practice this approach.

Post-ponderings: If you suspect nagging may be an issue in your marriage or parenting, talk to your spouse before taking it to God.

RECIPROCATING LOVE

"Love, it has been said, flows downward. The love of parents for their children has always been far more powerful than that of children for their parents; and who among the sons of men ever loved God with a thousandth part of the love which God has manifested in us?"
—AUGUSTUS HARE

"Whoever robs their father and drives out their mother is a child who brings shame and disgrace." (Proverbs 19:26)

Read Proverbs 19:19–29.
"Children have a heart problem," notes John MacArthur. "They are constitutionally sinful. Like their parents, and like the rest of the Adamic race, they are fallen. What they need most are regenerate hearts. This is the most fundamental issue in parenting. It's not ultimately about behavior; it's all about the child's heart."

Consideration for others, very much including parents, doesn't come naturally to kids. It, like everything else they learn, needs to be taught . . . and modeled. The parent who gives endlessly and sacrificially, without asking anything from the child in return, unwittingly transmits an entitlement mentality that will skew that child's perspective on life and produce a demanding adult continuously unhappy and unfulfilled without the least idea why.

While it's true that God loves us more than we love him, he does expect our reciprocation. As the author of 1 John reminds us, much of our love for God is manifested through our love for others: "This is love: not that we loved God, but that he loved us . . . If we love one another, God lives in us and his love is made complete in us" (4:10, 12). Yes, loving our children is included in the mandate, but we do them a disservice if we fail in the process to pass along the principles of and tools for loving.

Post-ponderings: To what degree do your children understand Christ's call to mutual, reciprocal love?

CONDUCT MOTIVATION

"A true hero is not someone who thinks about doing what is right, but one that simply does what is right without thinking!"
—KEVIN HEATH CEO

"Even small children are known by their actions, so is their conduct really pure and upright?" (Proverbs 20:11)

Proverbs 20:1–11.

Not being musically inclined, I'm mystified by the concept of sight-reading. I've had enough piano lessons to grasp the basics of notes and time signatures, but the concept of "reading" ahead makes no sense to me. My need would be to figure out each note or combination of notes when I came to it, necessitating a total disregard for timing. Much as I enjoy singing and listening to music, the mechanics aren't "in me."

On a related note (no pun intended), it's important for us as parents to teach our children not a calculating, what's-in-it-for-me? code of ethics but spontaneity in doing what's intrinsically right. Where would any of us be if we had to pause anew to assess pros and cons before making a moral decision, if we lacked the capacity to subconsciously "read ahead" before opting for that which we already know to be right? Life with its continuous bombardment of options and opportunities simply moves too fast.

Our kids don't come to us prewired in terms of moral values and autonomic conscience engagement. Some of the most basic principles that govern my behavior were given to me by my mom when I was two or three. Certain engrained principles are still reflexive for me six decades later. "Don't means don't," "You cannot hide from God," "Do to others as you want them to do to you," "There's no such thing as a white lie," and "Be sure your sins will find you out" come immediately to mind. If we want our children's conduct, in Solomon's words, to be "really [as in actually] pure and upright," it's up to us to plant the seeds.

Post-ponderings: What principles of conduct you learned as a young child still guide you?

THE JUICIEST MORSELS

"If minutes were kept of a family gathering, they would show that 'Members not Present' and 'Subjects Discussed' were one and the same."
—ROBERT BRAULT

"Without wood a fire goes out; without a gossip a quarrel dies down. . . . The words of a gossip are like choice morsels; they go down to the inmost parts." (Proverbs 26:20, 22)

Read Proverbs 26:20–28.
Rehashing family quirks is as natural at a get-together as noshing snacks. When we engage as a group in humorous self-critique, the result can be cathartic. How long does it take, though, when someone isn't present, to turn the focus to their personal shortcomings or habits? Gossip within a family is usually a frame for competition, an attempt at one-upmanship, a scrambling for status. Who among us doesn't want to be the favored—at least while the foible that isn't ours is under discussion? And why doesn't it occur to us that our own shortfall will come up soon enough once we step away?

Speaking of framing, we Christians are adept at couching this damaging pastime in euphemistic terms deemed somehow to change its nature. Brian Cleary's assessment may sound uncomfortably familiar: "It's not technically gossip if you start your sentence with 'I'm really concerned about _____.' (fill in the name of the person you're not gossiping about _____)." Mutual caring is one thing if it's expressed *to* the individual; if there's no plan for the group to engage the subject of concern, the activity is gossip.

Post-ponderings: How satisfying for you are verbal family dissections of non-present members? What do you suspect you get out of them?

"Old Friends"

"Neighbors bring food with death and flowers with sickness and little things in between. Boo was our neighbor. He gave us two soap dolls, a broken watch and chain, a pair of good-luck pennies, and our lives. But neighbors give in return. We never put back into the tree what we took out of it: we have given him nothing and it made me sad."
—HARPER LEE

"Do not forsake your friend or a friend of your family." (Proverbs 27:10)

Read Proverbs 27:1–10.
"It takes a long time to grow an old friend," observes John Leonard. Many friendships tend to be seasonal, matters of expediency, proximity, or temporarily shared activities or life circumstances. We would be more than happy to run into one of these old friends (there are *old* friends and then there are *old friends*) on the street, might enjoy some light chitchat or catching up, but to pick up where we left off?—likely not. Either our situations have changed or we have or both. We grow in and out of relationships throughout our lives. This is especially true when one party moves on or when two individuals grow in differing directions or at differing rates.

True friendship doesn't depend on convenience, coincidence, or commonality. It's a constant that transcends change, and that's precisely what makes it so precious in an uncertain world. Even so, as the verse above suggests, such relationships need to be tended and cultivated. I failed to do that with a best friend whose company I had enjoyed in church and neighborhood and school from our church nursery days through high school. She and I and another mutual friend from those early years struck up an email relationship fifteen or twenty years ago. I knew she had struggled through bouts of cancer but wasn't aware until a "chance" conversation a few years later that she had passed away after we had once again drifted apart and lost touch. Jeannie peopled my dreams for a while after that with some regularity. If only I had made more of an effort to treasure our re-acquaintance!

Post-ponderings: Who are your old friends, your tried and true friends? Thank God for each one individually.

KING LEMUEL:
THE TEACHINGS OF HIS MOM

"My mother is a poem I'll never be able to write, though everything I write
is a poem to my mother."
—SHARON DOUBIAGO

"The sayings of King Lemuel—an inspired utterance his mother taught him."
(Proverbs 31:1)

Read Proverbs 31:1–9.

If we're honest with ourselves, there's a lot of Mom in most of us who have
had good mothers—in the way we view the world and frame our thoughts
about it, in our personal moral compass and system of values, and in our
faith. Possibly as early as our in utero days, mother was present in our
consciousness as an extension of ourselves—we were egocentric even then.
Later on she became the first human outside ourselves of whose presence
we were aware.

Both Kings Lemuel and David acknowledge their mothers in a beautiful
way. Listen to David's tribute, spoken of her to God: "Show your strength
in behalf of your servant; save me, because I serve you just as my mother
did" (Psalm 86:16). And the apostle Paul in a letter to young Timothy refers to two generations of matriarchal faith transmission: "I am reminded
of your sincere faith, which first lived in your grandmother Lois and in
your mother Eunice and, I am persuaded, now lives in you also" (2 Timothy 1:5). Godly mothers serve as first evangelists for their little ones, gently
introducing them from a tender age to the Creator/Father from whom they
came and to whom they belong.

Post-ponderings: If you remember back to your early days with a believing
mother, what faith-related memories come to mind? Can you recall your
own early feeling toward Mom—and God?

THE NOBLE WIFE
AND MOM

"There is no doubt that it is around the family and the home that all the greatest virtues, the most dominating virtues of human society, are created, strengthened and maintained."
—WINSTON CHURCHILL

"Her children arise and call her blessed; her husband also, and he praises her: 'Many women do noble things, but you surpass them all.'" (Proverbs 31:28–29)

Read Proverbs 31:10–31.
Those of us who are moms do well to take our sacred calling seriously. In a world where making a living consumes so much of our resources, it's easy to feel guilty about a lack of time and energy expenditure on our kids. The fact is, though, that being the recipients of our undivided attention isn't their greatest need. An observation by Mother Teresa rings true: "Love begins at home, and it is not how much we do . . . but how much love we put in that action." The wife and mother of Proverbs 31 was busy too, using artificial illumination, as we do, at both ends of the dark/light cycle. (It took years for me as a kid to figure out that "both ends" in that saying refers to the darkness and not the candle!)

My guess is that the biggest difference between motherhood in our day and in previous generations is that so much of our energy is expended in isolation from our children. When we're together we need to maximize the quality of our interaction. Reciprocal giving, accepting, and sharing are mutually satisfying and effective. My own stay-at-home mom taught me all kinds of skills in my very early years. In many cases technology matured much faster than I did (I don't, for example, spend time dampening and rolling men's hankies for ironing). But those early moments with a mom who died when I was eleven remain dear to me. They're a big part of how I remember her love.

Post-ponderings: Putting yourself in the same remembering mode as after the last reflection, identify a cherished childhood recollection in which your mom is central.

THE OPTIMISM OF YOUTH

"Youth is happy because it has the capacity to see beauty. Anyone who keeps the ability to see beauty never grows old."
—FRANZ KAFKA

"You who are young, be happy while you are young, and let your heart give you joy in the days of your youth. Follow the ways of your heart and whatever your eyes see, but know that for all these things God will bring you into judgment. So then, banish anxiety from your heart and cast off the troubles of your body." (Ecclesiastes 11:9)

Read Ecclesiastes 11:7—12:14.
The author of Ecclesiastes was in memory mode. And as we see from 12:2–8, that mode was bittersweet. Solomon had seen his share of living. And he'd made mistakes, big ones, which he now rued. Those idealistic early days were long past, but they were the highpoint of his memory life, a point to which nostalgia frequently transported him back.

That carefree, sky's-the-limit quality of life on the cusp of adulthood holds a hindsight appeal to all of us who've known it. For many of us "If only we'd known" isn't our sentiment, looking back, as much as "What we didn't know then!" Part of the mystique of that unique time lies in the illusion of continuing, unabated beauty. It's as though to a certain degree we indulge the young, allowing them to embrace that mindset, knowing that when they need the maturity for disillusion they'll be ready for it.

As Kafka reminds us, though, disillusionment doesn't deserve the last word. While youthful idealism makes room for mature realism, appreciation for life doesn't need to fade. Nothing is sweeter than a mellowed, experience-based gratitude for beauty, for God, and for his eternal goodness.

Post-ponderings: What memories of youthful optimism are dear to your heart?

THE SONG OF SONGS COUPLE

"To find someone who will love you for no reason, and to shower that person with reasons, that is the ultimate happiness."
—ROBERT BRAULT

"Place me like a seal over your heart, like a seal on your arm; for love is as strong as death, its jealousy unyielding as the grave. It burns like blazing fire, like a mighty flame." (Song of Songs 8:6)

Read Song of Songs 8:5–7.
Most of us find it difficult to relate to the writing style of Song of Songs. We may find it a little hard to keep a straight face when the lover informs his beloved that her teeth are like a flock of sheep or her nose like the tower of Lebanon. Strange similes aside, Song of Songs is a beautiful and uninhibited expression of the sensual love between husband and wife.

The infatuation of energetic young love fades, eventually giving way to the more mellow satisfaction of comfortable companionship. (Which is not to suggest that a spouse is ever too old for romancing.) I suspect, though, that the danger of losing touch lies not so much in youth or old age as in those middle years when couples become overextended, too preoccupied to show their love romantically or too complacent to see the need for it.

In terms of marriage, in what life passage do you currently find yourself? If you've found that someone willing to love you "for no reason" (not that they don't have their own reasons!) and your love is standing the test of time, are you proactively stoking the flame in endless small ways?

Post-pondering: On a romantic level, might you be taking too much for granted at this stage of your marriage?

CHAPTER 16

THE PROPHETS

CHAPTER
INTRODUCTION

Like the material in chapters 14 and 15, the reflections here comment on verses or passages in this final section of the Old Testament that themselves comment on matters related to family life. Some of the material is story-related (the reflection on Hosea 1:1—3:5, for example); portions of some of the prophetic books are historical in nature and lend themselves to this approach. Considering the vast amount of Old Testament material covered by this chapter, it is disproportionately brief.

"Oh Give Me a Home"

"'After all,' Anne had said to Marilla once, 'I believe the nicest and sweetest days are not those on which anything very splendid or wonderful or exciting happens but just those that bring simple little pleasures, following one another softly, like pearls slipping off a string.'"
—L. M. MONTGOMERY

"My people will live in peaceful dwelling places, in secure homes, in undisturbed places of rest. Though hail flattens the forest and the city is leveled completely, how blessed you will be, sowing your seed by every stream, and letting your cattle and donkeys range free." (Isaiah 32:18–20)

Read Isaiah 32.
I'm irresistibly drawn to Isaiah's word pictures, above. The passage speaks of undisturbed rest in the midst of a decidedly disturbed situation. The allusions to devastation most likely refer to Assyria's destruction of nearby Israel (Judah is basking in prosperity, oblivious to the more distant threat of Babylonia). Yet the *NIV Study Bible* points out that verse 20, beginning with "how blessed . . . ," despite falling in the middle of a sentence leaps ahead to the "day of the LORD" so prominent in the prophetic writings—a day of reckoning or of rejoicing, depending on one's perspective. Despite the characteristic jumping of Isaiah's images in terms of chronology, these verses form a cohesive thought. It's as though the prophet were stretching a "before and after" statement across a time barrier from one phase of human history into another.

What comfort we can derive from this picture of home as the safe haven in a turbulent world! In the words of Jesus of all who love and obey him, "My Father will love them, and we will come to them and make our home with them" (John 14:23). Now there's a picture of peace! A picture that, though changing in its particulars, applies both to the now and to the later.

Post-ponderings: What qualities make your home a place of refuge? To what degree is Christ's presence a factor in this?

IN HIS ARMS:
SHARING GOD'S STRENGTH

"[God] doesn't expect you to run the mile but HE promises to give you
strength to go the distance."
—AZGRAYBEBLY JOSLAND

*"Even to your old age and gray hairs I am he, I am he who will sustain you. I have
made you and I will carry you; I will sustain you and I will rescue you." (Isaiah 46:4)*

Read Isaiah 46.
Did you notice how beautifully Isaiah weaves into this passage the metaphor of carrying or being carried? (See also the reflection on Deuteronomy
1:26–46 for this theme.) The prophet begins by portraying weary exiles
bent nearly double as they stumble along under dead-weight idols. The contrast comes quickly, signaled by an up-tempo in verse 3. God *has carried us*
since our birth and will continue to do so.

In some sense our lives come full circle in terms of our physical need to
be hefted by God. It's during our middle years, when we take our seemingly
boundless strength for granted, that we need to be reminded of our reliance
on his sustaining power. "It is God who arms me with strength," enthuses
David in his prime (2 Samuel 22:33), going on to boast of his physical ability to run, stand, and bend a bow. In verse 37 he cites a softer example of
God's sustenance: "You provide a broad path for my feet, so that my ankles
do not give way."

Sounds to me like a parent clearing the path of obstacles that might
otherwise impede the lunging progress of a wobbly but enthusiastic toddler. Yes, the little one is moving beyond the need for being carted every-
where. But he is also hurtling into far greater risk. We're wise to bear in
mind that God continues throughout our lives to uphold (carry) us—in
whatever way we currently need.

Post-ponderings: How does your present situation affect your perspective
on your need for sharing, or borrowing, God's strength?

GO WITH THE FLOW?
SEEKING GOOD IN BABYLON

"It is a sweet thing that we serve a dissatisfied God who has destinations in mind for us that we would never choose for ourselves. It really is a good thing that he will not be satisfied until he has gotten us exactly where he created us and re-created us to be."
—PAUL DAVID TRIPP

"This is what the LORD Almighty, the God of Israel, says to all those I carried into exile from Jerusalem to Babylon: '. . . Marry and have sons and daughters; find wives for your sons and give your daughters in marriage, so that they too may have sons and daughters. Increase in number there; do not decrease. Also, seek the peace and prosperity of the city to which I have carried you into exile. Pray to the LORD for it, because if it prospers, you too will prosper.'" (Jeremiah 29:4, 6–7)

Read Jeremiah 29:1–23.

Two well-loved Bible promises come together for this reflection! The first: "'For I know the plans I have for you,' declares the LORD, 'plans to prosper you and not to harm you, plans to give you hope and a future.'" Those plans will continue for us without a hiccup even if the "worst," from a human perspective, should befall. And the second: "We know that in all things God works for the good of those who love him, who have been called according to his purpose" (Romans 8:28). Notice that Paul doesn't say here that all of life's exigencies in themselves *are* good.

Judah's captivity wasn't the best possible scenario for the generation experiencing it. But God sees and acts in big-picture mode; a single life-span is miniscule from the perspective of the eternal One who transcends time. "Adapt," he urged his people through the prophet, "and adopt the customs of your home away from home. I'll be with you there."

Hebrews 11, too, is well known and loved, but its final verses are often overlooked: "These were all commended for their faith, yet none of them received what had been promised, since God had planned something better for us so that only together with us would they be made perfect." Their reward, their hope and their future, their all-things-working-together-for-the-good not only didn't come during the lifetimes of these Old Testament faith heroes but still hasn't been realized. God's better plan will find fruition for all of us together after Christ returns. Hallelujah!

Post-ponderings: It doesn't always take generations of hindsight to see the good in unexpected changes of plan. When have God's purposes for you and your family differed from what you had anticipated? Do you have enough perspective on the situation now to identify benefits?

THE REKABITES:
UNQUESTIONED OBEDIENCE

"Does it make sense to pray for guidance about the future if we are not obeying in the thing that lies before us today? How many momentous events in Scripture depended on one person's seemingly small acts of obedience?"
—ELISABETH ELLIOT

"Then Jeremiah said to the family of the Rekabites, 'This is what the LORD Almighty, the God of Israel, says: "You have obeyed the command of your forefather Jehonadab and have followed all his instructions and have done everything he ordered. Therefore this is what the LORD Almighty, the God of Israel, says, 'Jehonadab son of Rekab will never fail to have a descendant to serve me.'"'" (Jeremiah 35:18–19)

Read Jeremiah 35.
While we might view the Rekabites as a fanatic and reclusive sect pulled by circumstances into the main city but not the mainstream, God approved of their loyalty. The Rekabites didn't question their inherited nonconventional lifestyle; they followed it because they'd been instructed to—generations in the past. True, the clan had of necessity relinquished their tent-dwelling lifestyle, but that hadn't tempted them in the direction of other concessions. Here the Lord through Jeremiah showcased their obedience as an object lesson for his rebellious people.

Why do we obey, and teach our children to do the same? And what amount of slippage do we see taking place in this area as time goes by? Scriptural understandings change; letter-of-the-law adherence, for example, to old "Sunday rules" has been replaced by a focus on the Sabbath as a day of rejuvenation and worship, whatever the specifics may look like for a given individual, family, or group.

Moral and ethical slipping occurs not when traditions are relaxed but when standards for obedience to God become lax, when we begin to lose our sensitivity toward what pleases God, looking instead to what we can get away with. The Rekabites weren't tempted in this way, despite the situation-driven alteration of one standard of conduct. Obedience will not always look the same as it has in the past. But unless we've relaxed to the point that our consciences have become jaded, we'll know when we've crossed the line.

Post-ponderings: Describe briefly what obedience to God looks like for you. How is your own life, or that of your family, different because you obey?

DEPRIVATION OF THE VERY YOUNG

"I saw the world I had walked since my birth and I understood how fragile it was, that the reality was a thin layer of icing on a great dark birthday cake writhing with grubs and nightmares and hunger."
—NEIL GAIMAN

"My heart is poured out on the ground because my people are destroyed, because children and infants faint in the streets of the city. They say to their mothers, 'Where is bread and wine?' as they faint like the wounded in the streets of the city, as their lives ebb away in their mothers' arms." (Lamentations 2:11–12)

Read Lamentations 2:8–13.

Life isn't fair. We've heard that so often it has become clichéd; humans are in some sense engineered to view themselves as missing out on their share of the goods. There's an element of truth to the observation, of course— more than a small one—but we as adults do have some control, if not over our circumstances at least over our grace of response.

Not so with the millions of helpless little ones getting their first taste of life . . . and experiencing it only as hunger, squalor, and desperation. The author of Lamentations was acutely attuned to their distress; his heart was "poured out on the ground" because the lives of his people were being poured out.

As we know so well, sin's curse is an equal-opportunity reality. But so is the commonality of God's grace, dispensed both through himself and through us his servants in this world. That grace may indeed seem at times to be only a thin icing, but it can make life palatable in the fleeting here and now. Fragile as the forces of good may at times feel, God wants us to overspread the globe with the message of his love for its wounded, offered through word and action.

Post-ponderings: How, specifically, might God be calling you and your family to respond to this world's "little ones" living in deprivation?

A Private Sorrow

"Grief is at once a public and a private experience. One's inner, inexpressible disruption cannot be fully realized in one's public persona."
—MEGHAN O'ROURKE

"The word of the LORD came to me: 'Son of man, with one blow I am about to take away from you the delight of your eyes. Yet do not lament or weep or shed any tears. Groan quietly; do not mourn for your dead.'... So I spoke to the people in the morning, and in the evening my wife died." (Ezekiel 24:15–18)

Read Ezekiel 24:15–27.

This vignette has no parallel in biblical history, other than perhaps Moses' God-ordained mandate to Aaron and his remaining sons not to grieve openly over the fiery deaths of the older two (see the reflection on Leviticus 10). We know little about the relationship between Ezekiel and his wife, other than that she was his delight. A word picture borrowed from Milan Kundera suggests what her loss may have meant: "When his wife was at his side, she was also in front of him, marking out the horizon of his life. Now the horizon is empty; the view has changed."

It's tempting for us to critique the expression, depth, and duration of another's grief. Too much or too little? Too open or too closed? Too brief or too prolonged? Too glib or too dramatic? The truth is, though, that while grief follows to some degree its "prescribed" stages, its expression is as individual as we are.

When we stifle the mourning process natural to someone else, we may unwittingly stunt their ability to grow through and beyond the experience, leaving them trapped in their devastation. "Every man has his secret sorrows which the world knows not," observes Henry Wadsworth Longfellow, "and often times we call a man cold when he is only sad."

Post-ponderings: If you've lost a loved one, what did your grief look like and how did it progress? Did you receive unsolicited advice for coping with your pain? Was it helpful or guilt-inducing?

HOSEA AND GOMER:
THE LONGSUFFERING SPOUSE

"Her only thought was of getting away, as if she were carrying a live grenade from inside the house, so that when it exploded, it would destroy just herself."
—JENNIFER EGAN

"'Go, marry a promiscuous woman and have children with her, for like an adulterous wife this land is guilty of unfaithfulness to the LORD.'" (Hosea 1:2)

Read Hosea 1:1—3:5.

We have no idea how Gomer felt or what torments drove her. The Jennifer Egan quote may or may not capture some of her angst, but there can be little doubt that she was hurting and conflicted. Of Hosea's feelings we know nothing. As with the death of Ezekiel's wife, Hosea's marriage was used by God as an object lesson for his people. It's difficult to fathom God's modus operandi in these cases. It has no equivalent in our lives, other than perhaps his call to take a path we might not have chosen.

You or I wouldn't knowingly unite with a morally loose or otherwise difficult spouse, but it's possible to find ourselves in a marital relationship very different from the one we had anticipated. When we take our vows seriously we try to do whatever it takes to make it work. Our hurt may stretch into long suffering—longer than we imagined ourselves capable. We may have to stack forgiveness on forgiveness, finally achieving a less than comfortable truce.

If you've found yourself in an untenable marriage from which you felt it necessary to move on, you no doubt did so as a reluctant last resort. But if you're learning to accept long suffering as a way of life, know that your Lord is hurting—and ultimately triumphing—with you and on your behalf. You've chosen to stay in it for the long haul, relying on Christ's love that is immeasurably wide and long and high and deep (Ephesians 3:18).

Post-ponderings: Do you find yourself profoundly disappointed in marriage—or is there someone close to you for whom this is a reality? If so, what comfort can you derive or offer from Paul's words in Ephesians 3:14–21?

LED, NOT PUSHED

"You don't have to say everything to be a light. Sometimes a fire built on a hill will bring interested people to your campfire."
—SHANNON L. ALDER

"'I led them with cords of human kindness, with ties of love. To them I was like one who lifts a little child to the cheek, and I bent down to feed them.'" (Hosea 11:4)

Read Hosea 11.
The opening four verses of this beautiful chapter are gentle with imagery depicting the relationship between an inquisitive toddler and his attentive dad. Harking back to Israel's early days in Egypt, we get a picture from God's side of unconditional, doting love. No coercion. No pushing or herding from behind. Only tender leading through mild tugs at the heartstrings. Oh, there were conditions affecting Israel's outcome; the current situation reflected the people's stubborn adolescent rebellion, but the love factor had never waned.

Speaking of unions, Simone Signoret points out that "chains do not hold a marriage together. It is threads, hundreds of tiny threads which sew people together through the years." Neither partner pushing. Neither pulling. No ulterior motives. Only gentle leadership, based in love and trust. What a beautiful example for all relationships we find in our Creator, Lover, and Lord.

Created in God's image, we're called to lead in his name. The most obvious application is parenting, but Christ also wants us to pique the interest of others in the things of God. The more effectively we can employ a soft-sell approach in our invitations, the less intimidated others will feel. When we beckon through kindness and concern, others, intrigued, will be motivated to search out for themselves what it is we have.

Post-ponderings: What is your preferred leadership style, with your children or others? To what style do you most readily respond?

HISTORICAL MEMORY:
PASSING ALONG THE HARD STUFF

"The worst part of holding the memories is not the pain. It's the loneliness
of it. Memories need to be shared."
—LOIS LOWRY

*"Hear this, you elders; listen, all who live in the land. Has anything like this ever
happened in your days or in the days of your ancestors? Tell it to your children, and
let your children tell it to their children, and their children to the next generation.
What the locust swarm has left the great locusts have eaten . . . " (Joel 1:2–3)*

Read Joel 1:1–12.
We hear a lot about once-in-a-lifetime natural events, the droughts or
floods or heat waves or cold snaps that occur on average once in a hundred
years. Rare comets or asteroid showers grab our attention in part because
we get just one chance to view them. The tide of human history, too, is
cyclical; we take note of the D-days and moon landings and 9/11s and so
many other events, both positive and negative, we recognize as pivotal century markers.

From where does our compulsion come to share the deep hurts and
joys we ourselves or our ancestors have experienced? When it comes to the
pain, to some degree it's the lessons learned. How we'd like to spare those
following behind the same kind of angst, particularly if the event points
directly back to human sin. The sheer excitement—or other emotion—
associated with an experience remains with us too; this highpoint (or low
point) in our lives seems significant enough to invite vicarious "memory"—
a memory of the hearing—in the young. But there's another aspect to sharing an emotion-laden recollection. Lois Lowry catches the loneliness aspect
of remembering in her insightful quote.

When I was a girl in the fifties my grandmother spent a fair amount
of time with my brother and sisters and me singing tragic Depression era
songs (it seems to me now that she had an amazing repertoire) that never
failed to produce in me a gush of tears. I remember one in particular about
a little girl who lost both legs under a freight train. Why would Grandma
have done this? I didn't think to ask her then and no longer have the opportunity. I can acknowledge, though, that I learned compassion by her side.

Post-ponderings: How much about past decades do your children or grandchildren know, not through school but from your lips and perspective? With
how much of your family's faith history are they familiar?

COWS OF BASHAN: COMPLACENT IN ZION

"None are so empty as those who are full of themselves."
—BENJAMIN WHICHCOTE

"Hear this word, you cows of Bashan on Mount Samaria, you women who oppress the poor and crush the needy and say to your husbands, 'Bring us some drinks!'" (Amos 4:1)

Read Amos 4:1–5; 6:1–7.
I'm sure my associations are different from those of Amos's original audience, but I can't help but chuckle at the imagery in this verse. Can't you just picture a field of ample-bodied cows, contentedly chewing their cuds, the scene punctuated by an occasional, protracted *moooo*? Yes, this bovine imagery is comical to us, but the context and reality are anything but humorous.

If I may legitimately divorce the imagery for the moment from the intended metaphor for Israel, this depiction of a pampered woman would be universally recognizable. My daughter at one point worked for a foreign-born restaurateur who clucked his tongue to signify a desire to have his drink replenished. While his female relatives responded quickly enough, it took the other servers a longer time to "hear" him. Gender aside, he too—or at least his attitude—reminds me of this verse.

But to ignore Amos's application would be to misread the text. The prophet himself offers a concise thematic statement at the beginning of chapter 6: "Woe to you who are complacent in Zion, and to you who feel secure on Mount Samaria." No equivocation there! Nor will any of us in our North American context have trouble on the application end.

Post-ponderings: In what ways is complacency a problem for you personally? For your family? Your congregation? Be as specific as possible.

THE TIME OF CONFUSION: FAMILY DISINTEGRATION

"When there is no enemy within, the enemies outside cannot hurt you."
—WINSTON CHURCHILL

"Now is the time of your confusion. . . . Even with the woman who lies in your embrace guard the words of your lips. For a son dishonors his father, a daughter rises up against her mother, a daughter-in-law against her mother-in-law—a man's enemies are the members of his own household." (Micah 7:4–6)

Read Micah 7:1–7.
Jesus reaffirmed Micah's warning, above, in Matthew 10:34–36: "Do not suppose that I have come to bring peace to the earth. I did not come to bring peace, but a sword. For I have come to turn 'a man against his father, a daughter against her mother, a daughter-in-law against her mother-in-law—a man's enemies will be the members of his own household.'" I had assumed Jesus was referring to the spiritually divided households that would result from isolated individuals responding to his call, but that doesn't appear to have been his primary emphasis.

The immediate result of Jesus' coming would not be peace but upheaval in the world order, as good and bad experienced a head-on clash of proportions never before experienced. This fulcrum point upon which history turns would force the issue of decision-making as sides lined up in a confrontation that could no longer be avoided.

We can relate to Micah's warning and Jesus' confirmation, living as we do in a day of unprecedented family disintegration and dysfunction—a time of global warring, eroded and superficial loyalties, "viral" communication, and rapid-fire change exponentially more frenetic than our world could have imagined only decades ago. The intactness of family—and more especially of the Christian family—is both critical to society and alarmingly in question, difficult to maintain amidst a bombardment of outside influences and temptations. Yet as Churchill assures us—his words apply at a family level too—no enemy can touch us when we're internally cohesive.

Post-ponderings: Now is a time of confusion, yes, but it's also a day of abundant grace for the taking. Does your family know that grace and peace?

THE INSCRIPTION

"The great lesson is that the sacred is in the ordinary, that it is to be found in one's daily life, in one's neighbors, friends, and family, in one's backyard."
—ABRAHAM MASLOW

"On that day HOLY TO THE LORD will be inscribed on the bells of the horses, and the cooking pots in the LORD's house will be like the sacred bowls in front of the altar." (Zechariah 14:20)

Read Zechariah 14.

In 1 Samuel 21:3 David asks the priest at Nob for bread for his ravenous men. His response: "I don't have any ordinary bread on hand; however, there is some consecrated bread here—provided the men have kept themselves from women."

Jesus referred to this event when his disciples were accused of harvesting on the Sabbath by plucking grain from the field to eat, asserting that "the Sabbath was made for man, not man for the Sabbath" (Mark 2:27). Yes, the bread at Nob was consecrated to God and, as such, sacred. And yet it was ordinary bread, made sacred not only for God's honor but for people's spiritual (and in David's case physical) nourishment. The line between sacred and secular appropriately blurs in Scripture. Everything is God's, after all, and it's our place to receive with gratitude every slice of bounty he is pleased to serve.

In terms of our personal and family life, we can do no better than to live sacramentally—in continuous remembrance of Christ and his moment-by-moment, ordinary calls on our lives. In the words of Evelyn Underhill, "Christ risked his reputation for holiness by healing on the Sabbath; he touched the unclean and dined with the wrong people; he accepted the love and companionship of a sinner (that most wonderful of all remedies for the wounds of sin). He loved with God's love and so went straight to the point: What can I do to restore my fellow creature and how?" The physical means God places at our disposal are neutral. It's what we do with them—and teach our children to do with them—that matters.

Post-ponderings: What is your, and your family's, perspective on money and its use?

JESUS—
THE EARLY YEARS

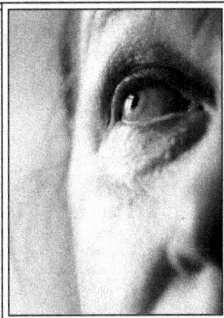

CHAPTER
INTRODUCTION

C hapters 17–20 bring us back into the familiar territory of story, with chapters 21 and 22 together focusing on the New Testament epistles. In terms of the Jesus account in chapter 17 through the beginning of chapter 20, you may notice a jumping around in terms of Gospel references. As I attempted to do in my treatment of the Old Testament books of Samuel through Chronicles, I've organized the reflections in chronological sequence.

Chapter 17 focuses on family-related material from Jesus' infancy to the beginning of his public ministry.

ZECHARIAH AND ELIZABETH:
THE DELIGHT FACTOR

"As much as you want to plan your life, it has a way of surprising you with
unexpected things that will make you happier than you originally planned.
That's what you call God's will."
—AUTHOR UNKNOWN

*"The angel said to him, 'Do not be afraid, Zechariah; your prayer has been heard.
Your wife Elizabeth will bear you a son, and you are to call him John. He will be
a joy and delight to you, and many will rejoice because of his birth, for he will be
great in the sight of the Lord. He . . . will be filled with the Holy Spirit before he
is born.'" (Luke 1:13–15)*

Read Luke 1:5–25.
The delight factor in the angel's message takes me aback. I hardly think
of delight when I reflect on the adult John, whom I picture—perhaps
mistakenly—as severe and dour. Nor would the delight of his parents seem
to have been necessary to the story. Their enjoyment seems to have been
a serendipitous extra, particularly following that long season of yearning
gradually giving way to resignation.

Elizabeth's reflection during the early months of her pregnancy con-
firms what this unanticipated development in her old age meant to her:
"The Lord has done this for me . . . In these days he has shown his favor
and taken away my disgrace among the people" (Luke 1:25). The writer of
Psalm 149 enthuses in verses 4–5 about God's relishing of his own: "The
LORD takes delight in his people; he crowns the humble with victory. Let
his faithful people rejoice in this honor and sing for joy in their beds." It
doesn't take much imagination to picture the aged Elizabeth crooning
praise from her mat during those months of confinement.

We don't know what John's childhood was like or the number of years
he was able to spend in the company of his parents. We do believe, though,
that God made a considered decision in terms of the parentage of this forerunner for his Son. And that, based on the angel's words, Zechariah's faithful prayer played a role in that choice!

Post-ponderings: What delayed or unanticipated gratification in your life
has surprised and delighted you?

THE "RIGHT" QUESTION?

"Some things have to be believed to be seen."
—MADELEINE L'ENGLE

"Zechariah asked the angel, 'How can I be sure of this? I am an old man and my wife is well along in years.'" (Luke 1:18)

"'How will this be,' Mary asked the angel, 'since I am a virgin?'" (Luke 1:34)

Read Luke 1:26–38.
I'm intrigued by the subtle difference between the two short questions, above, in terms of their use of the verb form for "to be": Zechariah's "can . . . be?" versus Mary's "will . . . be?" Would the meanings have been substantively different if Zechariah had asked "How will I be sure?" and Mary "How can this be?" The *NIV Study Bible* notes on these verses confirm that these distinctions *are* meaningful—that Zechariah, unlike Mary, was asking for a sign.

Is this an implied commentary on their respective degrees of faith? In a way it seems to be. God doesn't fault us for our fact-finding efforts in response to his revealed will but does clearly approve of immediate, unquestioned expressions of belief. In the words of the writer to the Hebrews, "Now faith is *confidence* in what we hope for and *assurance* about what we do not see. This is what the ancients were commended for" (Hebrews 11:1–2, emphasis added). Or, in a contemporary take from Elizabeth Gilbert, "Faith is belief in what you cannot see or prove or touch. Faith is walking face-first and full-speed into the dark."

How ready are we to ask the "right" questions when God makes a revelation to us, either through his Word or through the inner prompting of the Spirit? Perhaps it's the difference between "How can I know?" and "Where do I start?"

Post-ponderings: Are there statements or promises in God's Word you find difficult to take at face value or internalize as applicable to yourself?

MARY AND ELIZABETH: "SISTERS" IN EXPECTATION

"Any woman who chooses to behave like a full human being should be warned that the armies of the status quo will treat her as something of a dirty joke . . . she will need her sisterhood."
—GLORIA STEINEM

"'Blessed are you among women, and blessed is the child you will bear! But why am I so favored, that the mother of my Lord should come to me? As soon as the sound of your greeting reached my ears, the baby in my womb leaped for joy. Blessed is she who has believed that the Lord would fulfill his promises to her.'"
(Luke 1:42–45)

Read Luke 1:39–56.

In many ways Elizabeth and Mary couldn't have been more opposite, yet both were anomalies—possibly even the butts of sniggers and snide remarks. Elizabeth's old-age pregnancy no doubt raised eyebrows and elicited knowing smiles—and young Mary's unmentionable "condition" during her and Joseph's period of betrothal, prior to marriage, disgust and ire! How could the good Joseph look the other way in the face of such behavior, and how could Mary so demurely and with such barely concealed elation show her face in public? Both women were overjoyed at the miracle God was working in her, but it would have been too much to expect public support in Mary's situation.

We aren't told why Elizabeth had chosen seclusion for the first five months of her prenatal period, but we do learn that Mary stayed with her much older relative for the next three—almost until Elizabeth's due date. We can only imagine that these two very different mothers-to-be afforded one another mutual support and encouragement during their shared confinement. When no one else would have understood, these cousins clung to one another in a unique sisterhood of dreams, anticipation, hope, and wonder.

Post-ponderings: When has the empathy or fellow feeling of a same-gender friend or family member meant a great deal to you?

Called Forth
to Dignity

"John the Baptist was supposed to point the way to the Christ. He was just the voice, not the Messiah. So everybody's calling has dignity to it and God seems to know better than we do what is in us that needs to be called forth."
—JAMES GREEN SOMERVILLE

"His father Zechariah was filled with the Holy Spirit and prophesied: '... And you, my child, will be called a prophet of the Most High; for you will go on before the Lord to prepare the way for him, to give his people the knowledge of salvation through the forgiveness of their sins.'" (Luke 1:67, 76–77)

Read Luke 1:57–80.
"Everyone who heard [the story of John's birth] wondered about it, asking, 'What then is this child going to be?' For the Lord's hand was with him." As it is with you and me. No, we haven't been called to be the forerunner on Earth of God's Son—that was John's unique calling—but there is something (no, some *things*) within each of us that our Creator has already called or will call forth. Your birth and mine were hardly random, just as none of us is run-of-the-mill, too ordinary to stand out in the crowd.

"I think of all the thousands of billions of steps and missteps and chances and coincidences that have brought me here," muses Lauren Oliver, going on, "Brought you here, and it feels like the biggest miracle in the world." I don't know Oliver's faith stance, but her words, with some qualification, ring true for a person of faith. Not in terms of missteps and chances and coincidences (although it may seem that way from our vantage point), but certainly of those steps, each tread deliberate and certain in the direction of the fulfillment of God's plan that *is* you, me, or your son or daughter. What is there in you that God appears to be calling forth? Consider the same question with each of your children in mind.

Post-ponderings: Briefly compare and contrast the praise songs of Mary and Zechariah.

"Come Quick! We Have a Miracle!"

"A novice master once responded when asked about a life lived in Christian authenticity . . . that to be a Christian was not to know the answers but to begin to live in the part of the self where the question is born . . . He was speaking of an attitude of listening, of awareness of presence, of an openness to mystery."
—WENDY M. WRIGHT

"Mary treasured up all these things and pondered them in her heart." (Luke 2:19)

Read Luke 1:46–56; 2:1–19.

I was filling the dishwasher when I heard the squeal from my computer desk: "Gramma, come quick. We have a miracle!" Understandably intrigued, I hurried to the living room to find that my then five-year-old granddaughter had managed to get the sound working for a kids' application. So much in life seems miraculous to a person who appreciates wonder. Every breath, every mental synapse, every soundless plop of snow on snow, every flower straining toward the sunlight—moment by moment we experience a surfeit of wonder far beyond our capacity to take in. What happened on Christmas Day was, of course, a different story—a miracle the like of which the world had never before witnessed and won't see again until the encore we know is coming. Over and again each Advent we join the shepherds in heralding the news: "Come quickly to the manger! We have a miracle!"

Alfred North Whitehead has an interesting take on the matter of wonder, so closely aligned to the miraculous: "Philosophy begins in wonder. And, at the end, when philosophic thought has done its best, the wonder remains." I love that one short verse in Luke 2, above. Why, I wonder, does Luke pause for breath during a fast-moving narrative (we've just read that the shepherds "hurried off") to tell us about the "but" of Mary, the mother of our Lord, sitting still, wondering? Makes us want to exhale slowly before moving on, doesn't it?

Post-ponderings: Think back to a time when you were overwhelmed with wonder. Why do you think you remember it so well?

INFANTICIDE:
THOSE OTHER MOMS

"It is exactly the fear of revenge that motivates the deepest crimes, from the killing of the enemy's children lest they grow up to play their own part, to the erasure of the enemy's graveyards and holy places so that his hated name can be forgotten."
—CHRISTOPHER HITCHENS

"When Herod realized that he had been outwitted by the Magi, he was furious, and he gave orders to kill all the boys in Bethlehem and its vicinity who were two years old and under, in accordance with the time he had learned from the Magi." (Matthew 2:16)

Read Matthew 2:13–18.
Why did the incarnation of God's Son have to entail the deaths of those other little boys in and around Bethlehem? We don't know, of course, beyond our limited grasp of what this birth must have meant for Satan and his hosts. If the devil had been in some sense complacent during four centuries of God's silence in terms of revelation to his people, that inertia came to an end. Grace abundant marshaled from his side a show of strength!

We live in a world of contrast and paradox. A world in which innocent people, too often children, are victimized, oppressed, and killed. A world in which the triumph of good gets passing notice—as though it's a novelty—while continuously recycling accounts of evil invade our homes and hearts. It's hard for us as Christians, let alone as parents, to know what to do with the account in Matthew 2:16–18, sitting awkwardly as it does in the middle of the Christmas story. Perhaps it serves as a commentary—in case we were tempted to forget—on the reason for Christ's Advent.

As Isaiah reminds us, a different future awaits, the future as God wants it, the future secured for us by Christ's defeat of Satan through his death and resurrection: "'Never again will there be in [Jerusalem, or Bethlehem, its near neighbor] an infant who lives but a few days . . . They will not labor in vain, nor will they bear children doomed to misfortune'" (Isaiah 65:20, 23). The devil is on borrowed time, as he well knows. And history is moving ever closer to its glorious culmination.

Post-ponderings: What comfort do you derive from Isaiah's depiction of the new heavens and the new earth in Isaiah 65:17–25? Do his words help place the tragedies that punctuate history in perspective for you?

Faithful Joseph

"God found the perfect couple to raise His Son—as perfect as He could find among the Jews who had the right lineage at the time. They are wonderful examples of submission to God. Even though His intervention in their lives threw a huge monkey wrench into their personal plans, they selflessly said, 'So be it, Lord. What would You like us to do next?'"

—RICHARD T. RITENBAUGH

"When Joseph and Mary had done everything required by the Law of the Lord, they returned to Galilee to their own town of Nazareth." (Luke 2:39)

Read Luke 2:22–40.

Throughout Matthew's and Luke's accounts of Jesus' early life, we see his stepfather, Joseph, as a one-dimensional figure. Nearly every reference to this understated individual highlights one characteristic—steadfast, unquestioning faithfulness. Joseph obeyed God without suspicion when the reports seemed preposterous, when the instructions involved humiliation, inconvenience, danger, and displacement. No less than four times, directed by an angel in a dream, he immediately complied. We see in Joseph a reliable and righteous middle-aged man. Luke refers to him as Jesus' father; for all practical purposes this obscure descendant of David took on that role without question or grudge. A carpenter by trade, he trained "his" son in the intricacies of his craft.

We don't know to what extent Joseph understood the implications of the virgin birth or grasped the divine identity and mission of the Son of God under his care. Jesus wasn't a "son of man" in a gender-specific sense; still he was, through Mary's genetic contribution, fully human.

By the time of Jesus' public ministry Joseph had faded from sight, presumably having lived out his expected life span and died in humble dignity. Still, this faithful Jewish tradesman was God's agent in one of the most important roles any human has ever undertaken.

Post-ponderings: Reflect on the implications for salvation history of Joseph's unhesitating obedience. What would it look like for you as a Christian parent to emulate him?

LEARNING TO OBEY

"Parents learn the uses of power and its limits. They can insist on certain outward behavior but cannot change inner attitudes. They can require obedience but not goodness—and certainly not love."
—PHILIP YANCEY

"Son though he was, [Jesus] learned obedience from what he suffered."
(Hebrews 5:8)

Read Luke 2:41–52.
It's difficult to imagine God's Son learning obedience, though we recognize that, had it come for him without a struggle, his death could not have been a triumph. The author of Hebrews wasn't talking about Jesus' childhood obedience to his earthly parents but about his submission to the will of the Father in the area of his crucifixion, an issue over which the Savior—from his human side—was at least somewhat conflicted (Matthew 26:39).

Despite the angst his remaining behind in Jerusalem caused his parents, this preteen wasn't disobeying. From earliest childhood Jesus had to learn obedience, yes—but never goodness or love. Jesus had to learn that he couldn't take his parents' understanding of his higher allegiance for granted. In his unique case the attitudes and motivations for obedience were intact; it was the conventions that required reinforcement.

How different the challenges we face as we seek to instill obedience in our sons and daughters. Parenting approaches vary widely but fall into two basic categories: teach the actions and the motivations will follow, or implant the motivations and the actions will fall into line. Because our children do yield to temptation, our parenting will always require incorporation of both emphases. We'll never on our own "get it right," but when we in humility and prayer do our best in this critical area, their and our heavenly Father will reward our efforts.

Post-ponderings: How would you describe your parenting style? If you're actively parenting at this point, how well does your approach seem to be working?

JOHN THE BAPTIST: BORN TO PROMOTE

"True humility is not thinking less of yourself; it is thinking of yourself less."
—C. S. LEWIS

"'The friend who attends the bridegroom waits and listens for him, and is full of joy when he hears the bridegroom's voice. That joy is mine, and it is now complete. He must become greater; I must become less.'" (John 3:29–30)

Read Matthew 3:1–12.

Despite a loyal following of his own, John was eclipsed by his cousin Jesus. To make the situation even more difficult, the crowds didn't automatically transfer their allegiance from one to the other but needed John's prompting to understand the relative significance of his own and Jesus' respective ministries. John understood that he had been born to promote—a designated role that must at times have rankled.

"It is the nature of the ego to take, and the nature of the spirit to share." I resonate with this anonymous proverb—if and only if "spirit" is capped. I have a hard time separating my ego from my spirit (my spirit, that is, sans the influence of the Holy Spirit). I can't imagine an unredeemed human spirit acting opposite a human ego, nor do I view it as naturally inclined toward sharing. Even with the Spirit's help I have to work at it.

I have to acknowledge, though, that Paul's words in Romans 8:5 contradict my take on this issue. Listen: "Those . . . who live in accordance with the Spirit have their minds set on what the Spirit desires." Wow! What a concept—both enabling and ennobling! Do we as Christian men and women dare to believe it's true? More to the point: Do we live as though it is? In the words of Alan Redpath, "Before we can pray, 'Lord, Thy Kingdom come,' we must be willing to pray, 'My Kingdom go.'" If we allow the Spirit to grow within us, to take charge of our desires, inclinations, and actions, others will take notice, both of our selves and of the Christ shining through us.

Post-ponderings: Ask for the power and grace to surrender your agenda and to live out your Spirit enablement.

PLEASURE IN
A FAITHFUL SON

"Deep within, there is something profoundly known, not consciously, but unconsciously. A quiet truth, that is not a version of something, but an original knowing. . . . It is so self-sustaining that our recognition of it is not required. We are [offspring] of such a powerfully divine force—Creator of all things known and unknown."
—T. F. HODGE

"A voice from heaven said, 'This is my Son, whom I love; with him I am well pleased.'" (Matthew 3:17)

Read Matthew 3:13–17.

"Love," reflects Ogwo David Emenike, "springs from the inside. It is the immortal surge of passion, excitement, energy, power, strength, prosperity, recognition, respect, desire, determination, enthusiasm, confidence, courage, and vitality that nourishes, extends and protects. It possesses an internal objective—life." This packed quotation demands a second and third reading, but we as Christians recognize it first as descriptive of the love that resides in—that defines, that *is*—our Creator God. Only secondarily does it remind us of the thrusting inner force with which he has endowed each of us as his child and image bearer.

God's declaration of love for and pleasure in his Son at the time of Jesus' baptism by John resonates with us, calling up in us a longing for the same assurance of love and approval from our mutual Father. Our ears strain for the affirmation and invitation Jesus assured us we can expect when we live in grateful obedience: "'Well done, good and faithful servant! . . . Come and share your master's happiness!'" (25:21).

In the words of John Piper, "Our obedience is God's pleasure when it proves that God is our treasure. This is good news, because it means very simply that the command to obey is the command to be happy in God. The commandments of God are only as hard to obey as the promises of God are hard to believe. The Word of God is only as hard to obey as the beauty of God is hard to cherish."

Post-ponderings: What is there in your Christian life that assures you of God's pleasure and approval?

JESUS—MINISTRY YEARS, PART 1

CHAPTER
INTRODUCTION

Chapters 18 and 19 divide chronological reflections from Jesus' ministry years into two equal groupings. All relate to Jesus' relationship with his own family members, to his interaction with other families or family members, or to his exhortations or parables on family themes.

A Prophet without Honor:
The Myopia of the Home Crowd

"Familiarity so dulls the edge of perception as to make us least acquainted with things forming part of our daily life."
—JULIA WARD HOWE

"'Isn't this the carpenter's son? Isn't his mother's name Mary, and aren't his brothers James, Joseph, Simon and Judas? Aren't all his sisters with us? Where then did this man get all these things?' And they took offense at him." (Matthew 13:55–57)

Read Luke 4:14–30.
The good people of Nazareth hadn't the slightest notion of the history being made that Sabbath in their sleepy synagogue—or of the true identity of the person up front. They'd heard something of the notoriety of this hometown "boy" and would ask soon enough for a demonstration. Their eyes were fastened on him as he read—fastened in curiosity and anticipation of . . . *what?* An exhibition of some sort as this audacious son of Joseph aggrandized himself? The rest of the family was as regular as they come, but this oldest had always been a little different. They'd taken his measure years earlier and knew exactly *who* he was. What this late bloomer was up to now they weren't so sure.

They were settled in comfortably for what might prove to be a good show. And they puffed themselves up a little when he declared the real-time fulfillment of prophecy right there in their midst. There just might be something to this! And it wouldn't hurt Nazareth for the sheen to rub off a bit. Jabs like "Nazareth! Can anything good come from there?" (John 1:46), though commonplace, still rankled. What they didn't expect was to have the tables turned. They were the audience—skeptical, sure, but open to a spectacle—not the target! *Wow* us! they'd dared him with their eyes—the same eyes that now shot daggers.

Post-ponderings: "The better you know someone, the less well you often see them," observes Julian Barnes. "They may be so close as to be out of focus." When have you been totally surprised by someone you thought you knew?

BROTHER DUOS:
SIBLINGS OF ONE MIND

"It takes two men to make one brother."

—ISRAEL ZANGWILL

"As Jesus was walking beside the Sea of Galilee, he saw two brothers, Simon called Peter and his brother Andrew. They were casting a net into the lake, for they were fishermen. 'Come, follow me,' Jesus said, 'and I will send you out to fish for people.' At once they left their nets and followed him." (Matthew 4:18–20)

Read Matthew 4:18–22.

The less demonstrative Andrew was eclipsed by the dominant Peter, and yet we read here of no rift. We know little about Andrew—much more about Peter—but we're impressed that this brother combo without hesitation left their homes and families to follow the One who called. Not only that, but a second brother duo, fellow fishermen, made the same decision when James and John tacitly declared their allegiance. There were to be only twelve disciples who traveled with Jesus throughout his ministry years, and it seems significant that a third of these were brother duos. (It's possible, parenthetically, that James and John were Jesus' first cousins, their mother, Salome, being both the wife of Zebedee and the sister of Jesus' mother, Mary.)

Support from Jesus' own brothers would come later—James and Jude, skeptical during his lifetime, would both emerge as authors of epistles included in the Bible. From the very beginning fellow members of Christ's Church would be known as brothers and sisters, and that identity remains intact—a true picture of our status in relation to our ultimate Father and Brother.

Post-ponderings: If you're a sibling, what shared memories come immediately to mind?

PETER'S MOTHER-IN-LAW: HEALING AND RESPONSE

"In the end, . . . maybe we must all give up trying to pay back the people in this world who sustain our lives. In the end, maybe it's wiser to surrender before the miraculous scope of human generosity and just keep saying thank you, forever and sincerely, for as long as we have voices."
—ELIZABETH GILBERT

"Now Simon's mother-in-law was suffering from a high fever, and they asked Jesus to help her. So he bent over her and rebuked the fever, and it left her. She got up at once and began to wait on them." (Luke 4:38–39)

Read Luke 4:38–44.
This hint of the family life of Peter—quite likely similar to that of Andrew, James, John, and the other eight—leaves intriguing questions. For these two sets of brothers, who was to take over the family businesses during their itinerant years? Was Zebedee, the fisherman father of James and John, still active? What about Peter and Andrew's parents? And Peter's father-in-law? Were there children in the home? The Gospel writer doesn't say, nor do we need to know.

The response of Peter's mother-in-law says something not only about the radical nature of her healing but about her own nature. Service was evidently what this dear woman was all about. It came as naturally to her as breathing; it was the activity she was, in her own mind and heart, healed to resume. Most of us are acquainted with some relative, friend, or fellow church member who, despite continuing physical challenges, rises again and again for selfless service—and in some inexplicable way receives added strength and determination in the process.

There can be little doubt that profound gratitude motivated her as well. What did she have to offer this healer? Her service, from an overflowing heart. "Everybody can be great," asserts Dr. Martin Luther King Jr. "Because anybody can serve. You don't have to have a college degree to serve. You don't have to make your subject and verb agree to serve. You only need a heart full of grace. A soul generated by love."

Post-ponderings: Whose selfless service at some critical point has made a difference in your life?

Co-Incidence

"Life is a gift of God, of the God of Coincidence!"
—MEHMET MURAT ILDAN

"The father realized that this was the exact time at which Jesus had said to him, 'Your son will live.' So he and his whole household believed." (John 4:53)

Read John 4:43–54.
I don't know what this author had in mind by "Coincidence," though the capital C suggests a God thing. God delights, as we know, in startling us with his timing; when two seemingly related events happen at the same moment, they probably *are* related. What such co-incidences are probably *not* is coincidental. And we tend—much of the time correctly—to take them as evidences of God's will and work.

I've had an unforgettable experience of this kind. Between the adoptions of my first and second daughters I waited ten agonizing years (the result of a policy shift in the eighties in the direction of birth-parental rights, leaving many children to languish in foster care). One morning I awoke unaccountably exhilarated; for some inexplicable reason I just knew my second daughter would be coming soon. Reluctant to slow my revving adrenalin, I shared my excitement with a coworker—only to be interrupted by the phone. I should have known: it was my caseworker, announcing, "We have a nine-year-old waiting for you!" The adoption turned out to be a challenge, but that confirmation has meant a great deal ever since that morning in 1991.

Sometimes we need to experience "too good to be true" before daring to acknowledge truth. Natural skeptics that we are, it can take a *what-are-the-chances?* "fluke" to catch our attention and impress us. In this case not only the Roman official but his entire household were both convinced and convicted.

Post-ponderings: What co-incidences in your life have pointed you in the direction of God's will for you and/or your family?

"RACA!": WHAT'S IN A NAME?

"Integrity: A name is the blueprint of the thing we call character. You ask, What's in a name? I answer, Just about everything you do."
—MORRIS MANDEL

"'Anyone who is angry with a brother or sister will be subject to judgment. Again, anyone who says to a brother or sister, "Raca," is answerable to the court. And anyone who says, "You fool!" will be in danger of the fire of hell.'" (Matthew 5:22)

Read Matthew 5:21–26.
We don't really need to know the meaning of *Raca!* (the exclamation point needed to stay to make the point). The word itself is harsh and dismissive. I grew up in the fifties on that now taboo adage "Sticks and stones may break my bones, but names will never hurt me." This saying was employed by a well-meaning mom to stanch the pain of a verbal sideswipe in an effort to thicken our baby skin. We're much more attuned today to the very real hurt of name-calling. But to what degree has that stopped the hurling of labels from siblings and fellow school kids . . . and, yes, from adults (even brothers and sisters in Christ, albeit probably not face-on)?

A quote from Meister Eckhart approaches this issue from a refreshing perspective: "You may call God love, you may call God goodness. But the best name for God is compassion." When we consider the equation God *is* love, we recognize that love, and compassion in its wake, is much more than a name. It's an identity, a character blueprint, to borrow from Morris Mandel. It occurs to me that little people, and big people too—much as they hate to admit it—equate their identity with their name in much the same way. And not just their "given" name. Whatever names people see fit to "give" us have a way of seeping right through our outer dermal layer and making themselves at home in our psyche.

Post-ponderings: To what degree is name calling an issue in your home?

One-Sided Harmony?

"To love those who love us and are good to us is easy. To love those who are indifferent to us is workable, but to love those who have harmed us, intentionally or not, is true growth and realization."
—PATSIE SMITH

"'If you love those who love you, what credit is that to you? Even sinners love those who love them. And if you do good to those who are good to you, what credit is that to you? Even sinners do that.'" (Luke 6:32–33)

Read Luke 6:27–36.
I think back to the disconcerting reality years ago of being accepted into a friend's family but told in so many words by her mother that I was the exception: "We aren't nice people." While I appreciated the inclusion I felt the need to tread carefully. "Families aren't easy to join," observes Erma Bombeck. "They're like an exclusive country club where membership makes impossible demands and the dues for an outsider are exorbitant."

My hope is that this situation is the exception. I've never been welcomed into a second family through marriage, so I can't speak to that commonplace experience. But lack of acceptance by one's in-laws, for whatever reason and to whatever degree, can be tough on both spouses, not to mention their children.

Jesus had much more in mind with his words than melded families. But it occurs to me that this application touches the lives of many believing spouses. How do we respond when overtures in the direction of our "other" family are rebuffed? Jesus asks us to take the high road of continuing to love. "It's an act of our will," asserts Mary E. DeMuth, "to see people simply as wildly loved by God, to assume their beauty before guessing their depravity." Jesus' words signify God's approval when we do all *we can* to live in harmony.

Post-ponderance: How generous are you with gestures of caring that go beyond "your" people?

THE CENTURION:
HUMBLE AUDACITY

"A religious man is a person who holds God and man in one thought at one time, at all times, who suffers harm done to others, whose greatest passion is compassion, whose greatest strength is love and defiance of despair."
—ABRAHAM J. HESCHEL

"'Go! Let it be done just as you believed it would.'" (Matthew 8:13)

Read Matthew 8:5–13.
I'm uncomfortable with the connotations of the term "religious" (the Heschel quote)—that's a sensitivity many of us share. But beyond that the description seems to fit this Roman centurion remarkably well. He didn't inform Jesus that his valuable *servant* was incapacitated and thus unable to perform his duties. No, his concern was that *the man* was "suffering terribly." His stake in the situation was one human for another, not a master on behalf of his underling.

Nor did he, a Roman officer, approach this itinerant Jew with a superior attitude, expecting status-based service. Jesus, testing him, offered "Shall I come . . . ?" Still, he must have been caught off guard by the response: "Lord, I do not deserve to have you come under my roof. But just say the word, and my servant will be healed."

This Roman may have been a God-fearer. But the distinction between Jew and Gentile in terms of Jesus' ministry and message was understood by all. Despite his servile approach, the centurion—and everyone else within earshot—comprehended that the merest request on his part for healing was presumptuous. Beyond the officer's other commendable qualities—his compassion and humility—it was the very boldness of his faith that moved Jesus to action in this, his first remote healing.

Post-ponderings: When have you dared to lay before Jesus an audacious request? What was his response?

"DON'T CRY":
THE HEALER'S PAIN

"The day you stop being compassionate, your adjective of human drops!"
—MEHMET MURAT ILDAN

"As [Jesus] approached the town gate, a dead person was being carried out—the only son of his mother, and she was a widow. And a large crowd from the town was with her. When the Lord saw her, his heart went out to her and he said, 'Don't cry.'"
(Luke 7:12–13)

Read Luke 7:11–17.
We all know families or individuals who've had, from our perspective, more than their share of tragedy. In fact, I can look around my congregation on a Sunday morning and identify them, one by one. And that's one miniscule sampling of humanity. We hurt vicariously for this widow who has lost her only son. We don't know his age but can guess that he'd been her close companion and possibly even her sole means of support.

I'm touched by Jesus' words, but a little bewildered too; his full recorded conversation with her: "Don't cry." Two words—the same length as the shortest verse in Scripture, "Jesus wept" (John 11:35). It's as though Jesus was so pained by her tears that his heart couldn't bear them. James L. Halperin captures this dynamic with an observation: "Sometimes those who love most deeply can't get past the weight of their own feelings."

Jesus, the Healer, didn't frequently raise individuals from the dead; in fact, this was to be the first time. *How did he select these cases?* I wonder. In this situation it seems to have been the depths of his compassion. In the same way Christ hurts alongside and with us when we face devastation.

Post-ponderings: Who do you know who has been overwhelmed by circumstances? What can you do—even the smallest gesture can make a difference!—to help alleviate the pain?

JESUS' MOTHER AND BROTHERS: THE FAMILY PROBLEM

"When we put God first, all other things fall into their proper place or drop out of our lives. Our love of the Lord will govern the claims for our affection, the demands of our time, the interests we pursue, and the order of our priorities."
—EZRA TAFT BENSON

"'Here are my mother and my brothers! Whoever does God's will is my brother and sister and mother.'" (Mark 3:34–35)

Read Mark 3:20–35.

Despite Mary's partial grasp of Jesus' identity and purpose, his well-meaning mother and brothers were conflicted by what seemed to be his manic behavior. Fearing the situation was getting out of hand, they came to take charge, to extricate him from the madding crowds and escort him home to rest and safety.

Jesus' seeming rejection of his family of birth wasn't a matter of love; their lack of comprehension was undermining his work. It must have been with ambivalence that Jesus made the pronouncement above. From the human standpoint we can only imagine that he wanted nothing more than to relinquish himself to the care of a loving family. But his primary allegiance had to be elsewhere.

In a later discourse Jesus would make the same demand on his followers: "If anyone comes to me and does not hate father and mother, wife and children, brothers and sisters—yes, even their own life—such a person cannot be my disciple" (Luke 14:25). Everything in us wants to vehemently object to that statement, coming as it does from the God who *is* love. It helps to understand that Jesus wasn't talking about love versus hatred but about priorities in terms of our love and loyalty—an extreme exaggeration. Such sacrifices of family commitment do come into play in times and places where the Spirit is doing a new and radical work (as in the Middle East today). If fidelity has to be to one or the other—Christ's kingdom or family—there must be no contest.

Post-ponderings: Intercede for the millions around the world who find themselves obliged to relinquish loyalty to family in favor of Jesus Christ.

"Go Home to Your Own People"

"Having a place to go—is a home. Having someone to love—is a family. Having both—is a blessing."
—DONNA HEDGES

"'Go home to your own people and tell them how much the Lord has done for you, and how he has had mercy on you.'" (Mark 5:19)

Read Mark 5:1–20.
Unlike the disciples, at least some of whom left behind happy families and settled households, the man about whom Mark spoke had been estranged from his loved ones in the most tragic way for a very long time. Commendable as it would have been for him to want to follow Jesus, the Lord understood that this man had urgent, unfinished business right there at home. Not only were his family members in dire need of healing, but his countrymen in the area were so terrified over what had happened that they begged Jesus to vacate their territory. Jesus needed this revitalized man to evangelize the neighborhood as only he could.

Jesus values our service, but he wants us to customize and prioritize it in ways that fit our unique circumstances. In some cases he calls on us to focus on home, family, and close vicinity. If that seems to be the case for you, know that he doesn't appreciate your kingdom involvement any less.

Post-ponderings: Ask God for a fresh perspective on his calling for your life in its current season.

"Take Heart, Daughter":
Jesus' Heart for the Hemorrhaging

"'Good works is giving to the poor and the helpless, but divine works is showing them their worth to the One who matters.'"
—CRISS JAMI

"[The woman] said to herself, 'If I only touch his cloak, I will be healed.' Jesus
turned and saw her. 'Take heart, daughter,' he said, 'your faith has healed you.'"
(Matthew 9:21–22)

Read Luke 8:43–48.
In our day this suffering woman would have been a candidate for a DNC
or, that failing, a hysterectomy. Her relentless hemorrhaging was not only
physical, causing anemia and weakness, but emotional and spiritual. Cer-
emonially unclean, she had become a social pariah just as surely as if she'd
been a leper.

We know little about her beyond the fact that she appears to have been
utterly alone and desolate—untouchable by anyone else and disallowed
from reaching out and touching another. We can conjecture that it may
have been a very long time since anyone had pronounced her name, let
alone addressed her in an endearing tone. There are three instances in the
Gospels in which Jesus speaks a name—always a woman's—with a kind of
ringing pathos that makes us shiver: "*Martha, Martha*" (Luke 10:41), "*Mary*"
(to Mary Magdalene at the tomb, John 20:16), and here—"*Daughter*." It's
hard to imagine what his acknowledgment of her pressing need for a human, and above all a family, connection must have meant!

"Katerina Stoykova Klemer observes that "Everybody deserves love,
but nobody is entitled to it." Certainly not this outcast, especially not in
her own mind. And yet her faith triumphed, driving her beyond herself to
this tentative, tremulous gesture. In acknowledging and healing her, Jesus
did much more than stanch her physical flow. And we can be certain that
from this point on her gratitude flowed unabated.

Post-ponderings: What desperately lonely person do you suspect may be
long overdue for a touch?

Jesus' Counsel:
After Death or before Resurrection?

"I should not have loved my daughter as I did. Not in this world in which nothing lives for long. You children are flies. You are roses. You multiply and die."
—LAUREN DESTEFANO

"'Stop wailing,' Jesus said. 'She is not dead but asleep.' They laughed at him, knowing that she was dead. But he took her by the hand and said, 'My child, get up!' Her spirit returned, and at once she stood up." (Luke 8:52–55)

Read Luke 8:40–42, 49–56.
It's interesting that the woman in this double-miracle story had been hemorrhaging for twelve years—the same twelve years Jairus and his wife had been enjoying their vibrant only daughter. A few observations seem pertinent. Jairus, a synagogue leader with an urgent, acute health concern, finds himself superseded by an unclean outcast with a long-term, chronic disease. It may be that Jesus was allowing time for the girl to breathe her last (deliberately waiting, as he would prior to Lazarus's death in John 11). And that in the process he wanted to showcase the value of the woman everyone else looked down upon or beyond. It's also probable that Jesus wanted to display his transcendence not only over illness and death but over time.

Still, Jesus' words to this distraught father immediately *after* the death of his child ("Don't be afraid; just believe") seem counterintuitive and even callous. Of course Jairus would have been scared prior to his daughter's death. Encouragement to "just believe" would have made sense then too. What he didn't know is that the Healer's words were appropriate from Jesus' perspective. Jesus wasn't speaking prior to the girl's death; he was addressing her father just before her resurrection! No matter what you're facing, Jesus is telling you the same thing he told Jairus. He isn't being crass or clueless; he just has inside information. Don't be scared. Trust him!

Post-ponderings: When have you jumped to a negative conclusion, only to be surprised by God?

HERODIAS'S DAUGHTER: EXTENSION OF MOM

"Children are gifts. They are not ours for the breaking. They are ours for the making."
—DAN PEARCE

"At once the girl hurried in to the king with the request: 'I want you to give me right now the head of John the Baptist on a platter.'" (Mark 6:25)

Read Mark 6:14–29.
We think of women as natural nurturers, and many of the beloved women of the Bible fit this profile. Yet some of the most chilling and depraved characters in its pages—Jezebel, Athaliah, and now Herodias—are also women. They're frightening in a way the Bible's wicked men are not. These women seem to have been chiseled in stone; we see only one dimension of irredeemable evil. In contrast, Mark treats Herod sympathetically, explaining his conflicted feelings about John.

It's harder to get a handle on Herodias's appropriately unnamed daughter. A nymphet on the one hand, she seems remarkably unoriginal. Though her step-father was only a tetrarch—not a king as people dubbed him—we might have expected that wide-open "up to half my kingdom" to hang stars in her eyes. So we're surprised when she flits off to ask her conniving mother to prescribe the request. It seems clear that this young woman was Herodias's marionette, an extension of her mom. Still, her outlandish, mother-engineered request—as unforeseen by Herod as by anyone else—makes the story sizzle.

"He who is enamored of himself," notes C. C. Lichtenberg, "will at least have the advantage of being inconvenienced by few rivals." It's evident that neither husband nor daughter inconvenienced this narcissistic woman in that way. And John the Baptist, an inconvenience based on one incriminating observation, was in her mind easily dispensable. What a tragic and unnatural way for Jesus' forerunner to die!

Post-ponderings: Overheard from a narcissistic mother after learning that her daughter had been molested: "Oh my God! Do you think *I* was?" Are you acquainted with a parent with such tendencies? The good news (based on my reading) is that many of their children learn to adapt to normal thought and behavior patterns.

ELDER CARE, LOVE, AND HONOR

"Caring for our seniors is perhaps the greatest responsibility we have. Those who walked before us have given so much and made possible the life we all enjoy."
—JOHN HOEVEN

"'Why do you break the command of God for the sake of your tradition? For God said, "Honor your father and mother" and "Anyone who curses their father or mother is to be put to death." But you say that if anyone declares that what might have been used to help their father or mother is "devoted to God," they are not to honor their father or mother with it.'" (Matthew 15:3–6)

Read Matthew 15:3–9.
This particular mental workaround has no relevance to us, but the gymnastics behind it are familiar. The practice of slipping through loopholes is all too common in our society. My focus here, though, is on how easy it is for those whose love for parents is duty bound to rationalize behavior toward and decisions about eldercare their hearts might not have condoned.

The context of Jesus' words is that passage of life when the tables have turned from children relying on parents to an opposite dynamic. A decision about the care and well-being of dependent parents or in-laws can't be criticized, of course, without considering the complete set of circumstances. As long as the heart is engaged—and the homework done as thoroughly as possible—the decision made should represent a good and workable scenario.

Peggi Speers addresses the unanticipated direction from which eldercare, or the primary responsibility for it, can come: "By loving one another, we invest in each other and in ourselves. Perhaps someday, when we need someone to care for us, it may not come from the person we expect, but from the person we least expect. It may be our sons or daughter-in-laws, our neighbors, friends, cousins, stepchildren, or stepparents whose love for us has assigned them to the honorable, yet dangerous position of caregiver."

Post-ponderings: Whether or not you'll be primary decision makers for one or the other sets of parents, or the surviving parent on either side, are you giving thought to options? Is your heart in it?

THE SYROPHOENICIAN WOMAN:
THE FAITH OF A MOM

"The desperate usually succeed because they have nothing to lose."
—JODI PICOULT

"'Lord,' she replied, 'even the dogs under the table eat the children's crumbs.'"
(Mark 7:28)

Read Mark 7:24–30.
Was this woman's tenacity in character for her or the result of despairing mother love? What this foreigner lacked, reminiscent of the Roman centurion or the hemorrhaging outcast, was entitlement. She had no "right" to Jesus' help and knew it; yet she had a deeply felt—and very real—need that overrode this restriction. And in some sense overrode the strictures of common decency; clearly Jesus was tired and needed some breathing space.

None of that mattered at this moment; her daughter needed help—needed it now!—and no other consideration came close to mattering. Did she really consider herself, or her suffering child, a dog under the table salivating in its eagerness to scarf up the children's crumbs? From the little we see of her, my guess is not, though she rightly considered her argument difficult to circumvent. I sense in her an intensity of spirit, a self-esteem not easily daunted. Given her status as the mother of a terribly needy child, she couldn't afford to be intimidated.

In stark contrast to Herodias (see the reflection on Mark 6:14–29), this mother was living vicariously, not through her child but through that child's pressing need. Her love-based ferocity impressed and moved Jesus to another predictive action pointing to the way things were soon to be in terms of the inclusivity of the kingdom.

Post-ponderings: Have you ever found yourself in a situation in which your child's need was so paramount that you advocated with uncharacteristic intensity?

CHAPTER 19

Jesus—Ministry Years, Part 2

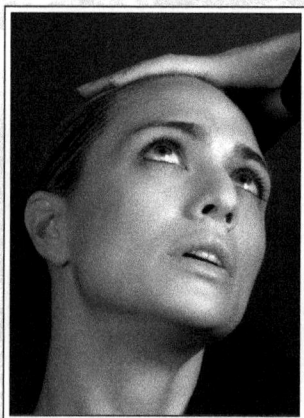

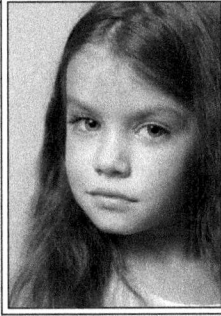

CHAPTER
INTRODUCTION

C hapters 18 and 19 divide chronological reflections from Jesus' ministry years into two equal groupings. All relate to Jesus' relationship with his own family members, to his interaction with other families or family members, or to his exhortations or parables on family themes.

"IF YOU CAN...":
THE CONDITIONAL PLEA

"What word or expression do you most overuse? Re-reading a collection of my stuff, I was rather startled to find that it was 'perhaps.'"
—CHRISTOPHER HITCHENS

"'I do believe; help me overcome my unbelief!'" (Mark 9:24)

Read Mark 9:14–29.
The contrast between this tentative Jewish father and the determined Syrophoenician mother in the last reflection is startling. Their situations are remarkably similar in terms of their need: father/son in a position much like that of mother/daughter. Yet their approaches couldn't have been more different. Contrast "But if you can do anything, have pity on us and help us" with "Lord, even the dogs under the table eat the children's crumbs."

How often don't we approach our all-powerful and all-good God mouthing disclaimers like "if it be your will" in an effort to limit our disappointment in the event he chooses not to come through for us! There's nothing wrong with recognizing the vital role of God's will in our planning, but we do well to remember that his will is always and only for our best. When we approach God believingly, without caveats or provisos in terms of our expectation, he will either meet our need or shower us with blessing far beyond that need.

Far from acknowledging God's will as a Catch 22 easing him off the hook from any obligation to answer our prayers, we need to anticipate his best and then accept its outworking in whatever form he opts to bless us. "I do believe; help me overcome my unbelief!" What a beautiful prayer for each of us as we with our loved ones face life's vicissitudes.

Post-ponderings: In what situations have your prayers incorporated "outs" for God? What, if you can recall, was your motivation? Was it for his sake or for yours?

LOVE FOR THE LAST,
THE LOST, AND THE LEAST

"I believe the best service to the child is the service closest to the child, and children who are victims of neglect, abuse, or abandonment must not also be victims of bureaucracy. They deserve our devoted attention, not our divided attention."
—KENNY GUINN

"'See that you do not despise one of these little ones. For I tell you that their angels in heaven always see the face of my Father in heaven.'" (Matthew 18:10)

Read Matthew 18:1–14.

At first glance it's easy to conclude that twenty-first-century America isn't about despising little ones. Parents and grandparents alike often live vicariously through them, intent on making sure they don't miss out on perks and do miss out on pain. As a society we protect our young fiercely and in unprecedented ways. That's the visible layer of reality—the level realized by vigilant parents and the institutions charged with filling in the gap for the rest of a morally lax society. The truth is that much of the legislated protection is necessary because a darker presence lurks beneath the surface. The private reality experienced by too many little ones is agonizingly harsh and lonely. We legislate and regulate because for much of society such precautions are no longer intuitive.

Jesus warns against systemic disregard for the needs of these afterthoughts and appendages pulled along in the wake of a self-oriented society exercising its adult freedom to indulge what feels good. The kinds of abuse and deprivation experienced by little ones in one society and time will look different from those of another. But children in a sinful world are always helpless—in too many instances the last, the lost, and the least. Which makes them precisely the kind of people Jesus came to seek and save! And he depends on us, his kingdom representatives permeating society, to look out for them on his behalf.

Post-ponderings: Identify some ways in which the society around you undervalues children even while indulging their whims and desires.

NOT FOR THE UNCOMMITTED:
A HEARTLESS COMMAND?

"He loves Thee too little who loves anything together with Thee, which he loves not for Thy sake."
—AUGUSTINE

"'Let the dead bury their own dead, but you go and proclaim the kingdom of God.' Still another said, 'I will follow you, Lord; but first let me go back and say goodbye to my family.' Jesus replied, 'No one who puts a hand to the plow and looks back is fit for service in the kingdom of God.'" (Luke 9:60–62)

Read Luke 9:57–62.

What are we to make of Jesus' troubling responses in this passage? In approaching any of his "hard sayings" it helps to bear in mind that our Lord was never inconsistent or untrue to his own character. If we're construing his words that way, we're reading something into them he didn't intend. Jesus wasn't advocating a dismissive attitude toward family or suggesting that his would-be followers steal away without a farewell or backward glance. While his responses were exaggerated, his point about the radical cost of discipleship needed to be clear. While family is and must be a high priority for Christians, it can't be the highest. The ironic reality—though this wasn't Jesus' point—is that we do a lifelong disservice to our family if we *don't* model putting Jesus first.

Jesus minced no words when it came to the issue of priority: "'Anyone who loves their father or mother more than me is not worthy of me; anyone who loves their son or daughter more than me is not worthy of me'" (Matthew 10:37). And "'Everyone who has left houses or brothers or sisters or father or mother or wife or children or fields for my sake will receive a hundred times as much and will inherit eternal life'" (19:29). The most obvious application of these verses is the sacrifice made by those loyal disciples, often in the company of their families, who devote themselves to mission work far from home. Whatever support the rest of Christ's body can offer—be it financial, prayer, moral, or practical—is appreciated as much by the Lord as by the recipient.

Post-ponderings: What would—or does—it look like for you to demonstrate, to your family first of all, your primary loyalty to Jesus Christ?

JESUS AND HIS BROTHERS: CHALLENGED BY THE SKEPTICAL

"What we know here is very little, but what we are ignorant of is immense."
—PIERRE LAPLACE

"When the Jewish Festival of Tabernacles was near, Jesus' brothers said to him, 'Leave Galilee and go to Judea, so that your disciples there may see the works you do. No one who wants to become a public figure acts in secret. Since you are doing these things, show yourself to the world.' For even his own brothers did not believe in him." (John 7:2–5)

Read John 7:1–13.

Jesus' response to his testing brothers sounds testy: "My time is not yet here; for you any time will do. The world cannot hate you, but it hates me because I testify that its works are evil. You go to the festival." In reality that reply was simply straightforward. The world had no reason to hate his brothers; they weren't challenging its cherished presuppositions and mores.

First-generation Christians and those with firsthand experience of families with divided loyalties know how it feels to be challenged in this way. Believers mystify the world because their values are counterintuitive. And precisely because they're enigmas they become the butts of jokes and the targets of ridicule. They're uncomfortable for the rest of the family to be around, not because they're judgmental but because their very presence, based on what they stand for, feels like an accusation.

I haven't faced this kind of opposition from family members, though I have experienced challenges from the "spiritually interested but not religious" boyfriend of one of my adult daughters. This thirties-something nonbeliever took advantage of every opportunity to engage me in conversation about my faith—primarily in an effort to provoke me to anger or back me into a corner. He enjoyed provocative statements about the "deficiencies" of the Bible, wielding his limited knowledge with a swagger. I can't help but believe, though, that he was testing the consistency of my character more than that of God's Word. Aware of that agenda, I tried to remain gracious. He is not to my knowledge a believer—at least wasn't when we lost track of him—but I can't help but believe our association piqued some interest.

Post-ponderings: Have you ever tried to argue someone into the faith? Did that technique work for you, or did you find modeling a lifestyle to be more effective?

Jesus Heals a Man Born Blind: Family Ramifications

"Guilt isn't always a rational thing . . . Guilt is a weight that will crush you whether you deserve it or not."
—MAUREEN JOHNSON

"'We know he is our son,' the parents answered, 'and we know he was born blind. But how he can see now, or who opened his eyes, we don't know. Ask him. He is of age; he will speak for himself.'" (John 9:20–21)

Read John 9:1–41.
The forty-one verses of John 9 cover a good deal of material; much of it is theological in nature, providing an extended metaphor between physical and spiritual blindness and their opposite, sight or insight. I'm opting to focus instead on the issue of guilt by association—a matter that can affect us in our family contexts. Since the Pharisees couldn't dispute the healing, they attempted to divert attention to the fact that it was done on the Sabbath. Getting nowhere with the man himself, they resorted to interrogating his parents.

Guilt by association—in this case no sin had been committed!—can sideswipe any of us if someone close to us is caught behaving badly. And the problem can involve humiliation rather than guilt. For example, the child following in the footsteps of an intellectually, physically, or emotionally impaired brother or sister can suffer mortification, perhaps felt more acutely by the nondisabled sibling than by the disabled, who may to some blessed degree be oblivious to the gestures and innuendos. Having done nothing wrong and in no way responsible for the sibling who is the primary object of ridicule, these children find something to feel guilty about, even if it's their well-concealed resentment of the other child. This kind of scenario calls for careful observation and intervention.

Post-ponderings: When have you felt guilty just because you suspected someone else suspected *you* of doing something wrong?

MARY AND MARTHA:
A STUDY IN OPPOSITES

"When someone loves you, the way they say your name is different. You know that your name is safe in their mouth."
—JESS C. SCOTT

"'Martha, Martha,' the Lord answered, 'you are worried and upset about many things, but few things are needed—or indeed only one. Mary has chosen what is better, and it will not be taken away from her.'" (Luke 10:41–42)

Read Luke 10:38–42.
What do you think of Jesus' response to Martha's demand? The answer depends on who you are. On whether you're spontaneous or structured, inclined toward improvising or impressing. Was Jesus playing favorites? That question has everything to do with how the Creator views intrinsic differences among the beings he has created to crown his work. Let's listen together to Jesus' opening words to this sister, using our best interpretive ability to infuse them with love and pathos: *"Martha, Martha."*

Notice that Jesus didn't say Mary was better. In fact, Jesus wasn't commenting on Mary at all, except parenthetically. Jesus appreciated the younger sister, but she wasn't the object of his immediate concern. Martha was. That frazzled, disheveled, perspiring, *wonderful* woman standing before him blurting out her pain. That sister with all those commendable qualities—who was hurting so profoundly at that moment when time stopped and two pairs of eyes locked.

Jesus had something to give, something Martha needed, and he wasn't willing to pass up the opportunity to state his offer. It's the same offer he makes to each of us. In the words of Joanna Weaver, "He's calling us to the Great Exchange—the one where we can never lose. As we trade the 'many things' that make us anxious, He gives us the 'one thing' that calms our hearts. Himself."

Post-ponderings: Why do you think God arranged to include this homespun account in his Word? If you're a woman, where do you stand on the Martha/Mary spectrum?

"The Kids and I Are in Bed": Inopportune Caller

> "The great thing, if one can, is to stop regarding all the unpleasant things as interruptions of one's 'own,' or 'real' life. The truth is of course that what one calls the interruptions are precisely one's real life—the life God is sending one day to day."
> —C. S. LEWIS

> "'Don't bother me. The door I already locked, and my children and I are in bed. I can't get up and give you anything.'" (Luke 11:7)

Read Luke 11:5–10.

Most of us wouldn't answer the door in the middle of the night—any more than we would frighten someone else by knocking on their door—unless we were certain of the caller's identity and purpose. Our reluctance wouldn't be a matter of not wanting to be roused but fear of violation of our hallowed security. Acutely alert rather than sleepy, we would surreptitiously investigate—cell phone in hand ready to call for backup. In our case the audacious disruption inducing frustration or anger would more likely come in the form of a thoughtless middle-of-the-night phone call or text.

Unlike you or me, who feel violated if the sanctity of our sleep is disturbed, God is never indisposed or negatively predisposed. And he doesn't mind late calls, including urgent pleas from us during the wee hours when our minds take advantage of the downtime to race in directions we don't particularly want to go. No request is beyond the ability or willingness of the sleepless One whose loving gaze encompasses his children while they sleep or thrash on the bed in pain or angst.

Jesus doesn't speak to the issue of our responding *with grace* to our neighbors' requests, but this extension seems natural—intrinsic to our identity as Christ-followers. This isn't to say we're obligated to let ourselves be exploited—at least not on a habitual basis. Still, we know that Christ approves of our opening, our giving, and our accepting inconvenience or interruption from others.

Post-ponderings: Where do you draw the line between allowing yourself to be disadvantaged and being chronically taken advantage of?

GOOD GIFTS

"'If you, then, though you are evil, know how to give good gifts to your children, how much more will your Father in heaven give the Holy Spirit to those who ask him!'" (Luke 11:13)

Read Luke 11:11–13.

"Mommy talks to herself and says yes to herself. Her always does that when she wants me to have something." My journal reminds me of this byte of wisdom from my granddaughter at the age of four. Who of us doesn't enjoy gifting a child—our own, if we're blessed with them, or others about whom we care? Occasion-al giving is fun, but perhaps especially delightful for both giver and recipient are those occasional "for no special reason" surprises.

God's gifts to us are anything but occasional—neither infrequent nor limited to specific occasions. Like the daily manna enjoyed by his people in the wilderness, they're continual, dependable, ample, and unfailingly good. Yet our Lord wants us to ask for them. As modeled in verse 3 ("Give us each day our daily bread"), Jesus wants us to acknowledge our dependency. And he asks us to express our gratitude (e.g., Colossians 3:16), even in advance of those regular blessings on which we've learned to rely. But another reason occurs to me. In Psalm 37:4 David urges us to "Take delight in the LORD," going on "and he will give you the desires of your heart." God delights in our delight, and we express it best when we tell him about it, acknowledging the connection to him.

Post-pondering: Make it a point both to articulate your needs and to thank God for his ongoing provision.

FATHER OF THE LOST SON:
HOPING AGAINST REASON

"The more you love, the more love you have to give. It's the only feeling we have which is infinite."

—CHRISTINA WESTOVER

"While he was still a long way off, his father saw him and was filled with compassion for him; he ran to his son, threw his arms around him and kissed him." (Luke 15:20)

Read Luke 15:11–32.

Have you ever found yourself, like this anguished father, waiting against reason, yearning against hope? I have, repeatedly during the middle teen years of one of my daughters. The earliest disappearances of this troubled adoptee—who joined the family at almost ten—were hardest. She would say a nonchalant good-bye, not to return for two or three days. I would search into the night—checking the creek and other known local haunts—only to learn that she'd been across town somewhere, her inhibitions negated due to drugs offered by an unhelpful acquaintance.

Poet John Ciardi commented that "every parent is at some time the father of the unreturned prodigal, with nothing to do but keep his house open to hope." That isn't literally true, but emotional and spiritual departures can be as devastating as physical. It may help to remember that, even as we keep our homes open to unreasonable hope, we're preparing for the awaited return, maximizing our welcome for when that time comes.

To view the parable from a different perspective, it helps to recall that, in Charles Stanley's words, we all at times play the prodigal. Sighting your plodding figure a long way off, the Father "throws His arms open, runs toward you, gathers you up, and welcomes you home." What better role model could we ask?

Post-ponderings: All three characters in this parable have something to say to us as family members. I've chosen to focus on the father for the parenting aspect, bypassing the older brother not because his role isn't critical but because it would have been impossible to do it justice in so brief a reflection. How does his role play out in your family context?

"IF YOU HAD BEEN HERE . . .":
THE SISTERS RESPOND

"There's a hurt that exists in the suspension between belief and healing.
A hurt, perhaps, that Martha and Mary experienced following the premature
death of their brother while Jesus walked the earth. The kind that exists in
the resignation, the heartbreak filling the space beyond when anyone would
even think to seek a miracle."
—LAURIE WALLIN

*"When Martha heard that Jesus was coming, she went out to meet him, but Mary
stayed at home. 'Lord,' Martha said to Jesus, 'if you had been here, my brother
would not have died. But I know that even now God will give you whatever you
ask.'" (John 11:20–22)*

*"When Mary reached the place where Jesus was and saw him, she fell at his
feet and said, 'Lord, if you had been here, my brother would not have died.'"
(John 11:32)*

Read John 11:1–45.
Despite only three Gospel appearances each, Martha and Mary are two of
the more fleshed out—and endearing—characters associated with Jesus.
Without coming off as one-dimensional, their respective words, actions,
and reactions remain remarkably in character. Martha's words, above, are
almost identical to Mary's, but I imagine their tones to have been in startling contrast. Matter-of-fact Martha moves beyond the reality of her brother's death—no point in second-guessing what *could* have happened—to a
willingness to talk theology. Mary, always her foil, responds in all the intensity of her emotion. How much reproach is implied in Mary's tone? It's hard
to interpret her statement without the cues of expression and inflection.

Unlike the situation in Bethany, the Christ who identifies so deeply
with our hurts and losses is ever present with us. And his plan encompasses
infinitely more than what we can discern from circumstances. The God
whose essence is love does nothing less than promote our well-being *and*
his glory. "Lord, if you had been here" has no place in our vocabulary, because the transcendent Christ was, is, and always will be with us.

Post-ponderings: What do you make of John's parenthetical mention in
verse 45 that many of the Jews who had come to visit *Mary* believed in Jesus
(see also verse 31)? Did Mary have a need for support her sister did not?

JESUS ON DIVORCE

"Marriage is what you make of it, and God has many versions of what that looks like based on what different souls need, in order to grow."
—SHANNON L. ALDER

"Some Pharisees came to [Jesus] to test him. They asked, 'Is it lawful for a man to divorce his wife for any and every reason?' 'Haven't you read,' he replied, 'that at the beginning the Creator "made them male and female," and said, "For this reason a man will leave his father and mother and be united to his wife, and the two will become one flesh"? So they are no longer two, but one flesh. Therefore what God has joined together, let no one separate.'" (Matthew 19:3–6)

Read Matthew 19:1–12.
It's easy for us to write off Jesus' words as no longer applicable in our different culture or more enlightened day. But a helpful background observation—suggested by Jesus' comment on Moses' permitting of divorce—is that the dissolution of a marriage, even on a whim, was common already in Old Testament times. Jesus' words were as radical and troubling in his day as in ours.

Paul—like Jesus a single man—weighs in on this issue in 1 Corinthians 7:10–11: "To the married I give this command (not I, but the Lord): A wife must not separate from her husband. But if she does, she must remain unmarried or else be reconciled to her husband. And a husband must not divorce his wife."

This is too broad an issue to "resolve" in a few paragraphs . . . or a few tomes! I'm opting instead to allow John Piper to speak to this issue: "Marriage is patterned after Christ's covenant relationship to the church. And therefore the highest meaning and the most ultimate purpose of marriage is to put the covenant relationship of Christ and his church on display. That is why marriage exists. If you are married, that is why you are married. *Staying married, therefore, is not about staying in love. It is about keeping covenant*" (emphasis added).

Post-ponderings: Divorce is an undeniable reality in our world, as it was in that of the Bible. What are your personal thoughts on this controversial issue for Christians?

Jesus and the MOPS Moms: "Bless My Child!"

"The soul is healed by being with children."
—ENGLISH PROVERB

"'Let the little children come to me, and do not hinder them, for the kingdom of God belongs to such as these. Truly I tell you, anyone who will not receive the kingdom of God like a little child will never enter it.'" (Luke 18:16–17)

Read Luke 18:15–17.

Always an advocate for the "little," Jesus had a keen and vested interest in children. From their side, what is there about the very young that makes them so open to God and faith? At heart is simply their disarmed and disarming simplicity. The path to a child—or childlike—heart is direct, and it's short. To introduce a new metaphor, exposing a child heart is altogether unlike peeling an onion. You don't have to unravel any smelly, tear-inducing layers to reach the center—which in this analogy can be hard to identity once you get there.

Yes, I'm going somewhere with this unlikely image. "A grownup," muses Woody Harrelson, "is a child with layers on." Layers of doubt, ambivalence, cynicism, resentment, pride, bias, anger, distrust, fear—the armor of wariness that comes with life's repeated disappointments and disillusionments. It can be tough for us to slough off that protective chain mail, but disarming is exactly what Jesus calls on us to be and do.

It was important for these mothers to receive confirmation of the nature of Jesus they had correctly intuited. Who of us as a parent doesn't relish Christ's blessing our little ones? But it was more critical at this juncture for him to demonstrate in yet another way to his at times dense disciples the true nature of his mission and priorities.

Post-ponderings: What can you do, today, to unkink the path to your own heart and soul?

JAMES AND JOHN
AND A MEDDLING MOM

"Mothers all want their sons to grow up to be President, but they don't want them to become politicians in the process."
—JOHN FITZGERALD KENNEDY

"'Grant that one of these two sons of mine may sit at your right and the other at your left in your kingdom.'" (Matthew 20:21)

Read Matthew 20:20–28.
We're slightly miffed by the audacity of this mom, but the nature of her request isn't all that different from the kinds of favors parents regularly ask on behalf of their kids. For many, requesting boosts and concessions, promotions and positions goes with the territory. The fact that this requested perk pertained to a heavenly plane makes sense, too, when we recognize the easy familiarity of the disciples, and evidently of their families, with the itinerant Jesus on Earth.

Jesus' extended response clues us, as Christ-followers, to the nature and implication of our following. The advantages of discipleship aren't to be the primary issue in our decision-making. We—and our children—at some point have to weigh the risks and tasks against our degree of willingness. It can be easy to get hung up on the inconveniences of any decision that will entail something less than immediate gratification—not that joy and peace in serving shouldn't be fulfillment enough; this hindsight discovery comes as a serendipity once the commitment is made. A lifestyle of voluntary servitude makes no sense to a wondering world, but its irony is one of the factors that piques people's interest, the first clue that there's something more to this equation.

Post-ponderings: How real a factor is the servant mindset in the living out of your faith commitment? Has your family gotten the message? Particularly if you have teens, does this mentality go beyond organized service projects to personal selflessness?

BEAUTIFUL THINGS: GRATEFUL SIBLINGS HONOR JESUS

"God created us for this: to live our lives in a way that makes him look more like the greatness and the beauty and the infinite worth that he really is."
—JOHN PIPER

"Six days before the Passover, Jesus came to Bethany, where Lazarus lived, whom Jesus had raised from the dead. Here a dinner was given in Jesus' honor. Martha served, while Lazarus was among those reclining at the table with him. Then Mary took about a pint of pure nard, an expensive perfume; she poured it on Jesus' feet and wiped his feet with her hair." (John 12:1–3)

Read John 12:1–11.

This third Gospel account featuring Mary and Martha flows naturally from the second. The banquet in Bethany is being hosted in Jesus' honor in gratitude for his having raised Lazarus from the dead. True to form, Mary serves, Lazarus reclines at table, and Mary . . . well, Mary kneels on the ground and pours a priceless jar of perfume on Jesus' feet.

For whatever reason the first Gospel writer's parallel account in Matthew 26:6–13 refers to Mary anonymously, but the story is the same. It's Jesus' well-loved words in this rendering that make it special to me: "She has done a beautiful thing to me. . . . Truly I tell you, wherever this gospel is preached throughout the world, what she has done will also be told, in memory of her" (verses 10, 13).

Yet it occurs to me that what Martha did was special too. Food preparation and service were Martha's art form, and I have no doubt she executed it beautifully. The truth is that whatever we do—and it matters more that we do it heartily than well—for Jesus is a thing of beauty and a source of delight for the recipients (very much including Christ). What's the nature of *your* beautiful offering? And who are the beneficiaries?

Post-ponderings: Jesus explains Mary's anointing as preparation for his burial. Do you believe that's what Mary had in mind? Do you suspect these siblings knew and understood—more than the disciples did—Jesus' purpose on Earth?

CHAPTER 20

JESUS' PASSION THROUGH ACTS

CHAPTER
INTRODUCTION

C hapter 20, rounding out the New Testament historical books, deals with the final week of Jesus' life through the end of Acts. More than the previous chapters that focus on Jesus, it treats some abstract or theological topics, based on Jesus' words during his final days on Earth, related to such family themes as God our Father, Jesus our Brother, and our brothers and sisters in Christ.

"Echoes of His Excellence": The Praise of Children

"The climax of God's happiness is the delight He takes in the echoes of His excellence in the praises of His people."
—JOHN PIPER

"When the chief priests and the teachers of the law saw the wonderful things [Jesus] did and the children shouting in the temple courts, 'Hosanna to the Son of David,' they were indignant. 'Do you hear what these children are saying?' they asked him. 'Yes,' replied Jesus, 'have you never read, "From the lips of children and infants you, Lord, have called forth your praise"?'" (Matthew 21:15–16)

Read Matthew 21:1–17.

The crowds surrounding Jesus during his entry into Jerusalem shouted Hosanna; after the cleansing of the temple and the healings in the courtyard the children were still at it. This was for them a novel event; not every day was an occasion for "Hosanna to the Son of David! Blessed is he who comes in the name of the Lord! Hosanna in the highest heaven!" The enthusiasm of the crowd had been contagious, and the contagion—for the little ones—lasted a while. The children may have been only minimally knowledgeable about what—or why—they were shouting, but God was orchestrating his own praise, to the indignation of the chief priests and teachers of the law.

Jesus referred to Psalm 8, with which all present were familiar, implying its fulfillment. Verse 2 reads, "Through the praise of children and infants you have established a stronghold against your enemies, to silence the foe and the avenger." His citation certainly did that. Their protest was squelched; we read only that Jesus left them.

It doesn't require deep theological comprehension for our little ones to render praise in which God can delight. The wonder of the gospel is that we don't need depth of understanding for meaningful praise—for echoes of his excellence!

Post-ponderings: Write out in a sentence or two a summation of the gospel message—as brief as you can without sacrificing the main points.

A TALE OF TWO SONS

"To procrastinate obedience is to disobey God."
—RANDY ALCORN

"'Which of the two did what his father wanted?'" (Matthew 21:31)

Read Matthew 21:28–32.
Our lip service to God—we all offer it—doesn't involve any large muscle groups. And intentions are remarkably forgettable, leaving us unaware when we've failed to translate feel-good thoughts into action. Our kids are adept at the same thing. "Okay" rolls off their tongues with ease, to be immediately forgotten through a few rounds of reminders or until the reminders stop coming. They learn soon enough that procrastination works much better than outright refusal.

What about us? When, if ever, have we dug in our heels with God and told him no, when stalling is so much more convenient? "Never put off till tomorrow," quips Mark Twain, "what may be done day after tomorrow just as well." *Good one!* I chuckle—until I come to the next quote, this one from Pablo Picasso. It starts similarly: "Only put off until tomorrow what you are willing to die having left undone." The frame of reference changes pretty abruptly, doesn't it?

If we knew we had a limited time in which to keep our promises—to obey—how different would our perspective be? I'm reminded of God's concession to Hezekiah to add fifteen more years to his life following his recovery from illness (2 Kings 20:1–11). I'm not sure I'd like that kind of arrangement at all; the upside is that my "to do" list would be specific and time-sensitive (I'd hope I wasn't putting off too much till year fourteen!). The obvious truth is that we do have a limited time here on Earth. No, our eternal destiny won't depend on our promise-keeping record, but our love and gratitude ought to propel us into action mode.

Post-ponderings: What is it you've been putting off in terms of your service for Christ?

THE GREAT UNKNOWN:
LIFE ON THE NEW EARTH

"Jesus's resurrection is the beginning of God's new project not to snatch people away from earth to heaven but to colonize earth with the life of heaven. That, after all, is what the Lord's Prayer is about."
—N. T. WRIGHT

"'The people of this age marry and are given in marriage. But those who are considered worthy of taking part in the age to come and in the resurrection from the dead will neither marry nor be given in marriage, and they can no longer die; for they are like the angels. They are God's children, since they are children of the resurrection.'" (Luke 20:34–36)

Read Luke 20:27–40.

"See, I will create new heavens and a new earth. The former things will not be remembered, nor will they come to mind." I recall a sinking feeling when I first encountered Isaiah 65:17 (see also the reflection on 2 Samuel 12:15–25 for this theme). How had I missed it before? My immediate association was with Jesus' comments, above, and my initial read of Isaiah suggested that my hopes of reunion with loved ones might not be valid after all.

I was relieved later on to encounter the explanation that Isaiah's words—and Jesus'—don't pertain to memory but to the passing of the old order (Revelation 21:4), which includes birth, marriage, and death. It's strange, isn't it, the way we cling to the familiar, certain deep down in our hearts that we'll be unhappy on the new earth, despite assurances to the contrary, without these constructs and passages? There's security in the known—for us that includes time, with its markings and passages.

It occurs to me that other pleasant associations, like eating and sleeping, might not be gone on the new earth as much as irrelevant or unnecessary; much as I cringe to admit it, references to banqueting and fruit trees can be more inviting to me than the prospect of being in the Lord's continual presence. Much of our lack of anticipation of the new earth lies in the absence of a frame of reference. When what we don't know is so far removed from our experience that we can find no intersection, our imaginations can't engage.

Post-ponderings: How do you picture life on the new earth? Marriage aside, do you anticipate being with those you've loved on earth? Engaging in activities you currently enjoy?

OUR SPIRITUAL HOME AND FAMILY: MUTUAL "IN-NESS" AND ONENESS

"Home wasn't a set house, or a single town on a map. It was wherever the people who loved you were, whenever you were together. Not a place, but a moment, and then another, building on each other like bricks to create a solid shelter that you take with you for your entire life, wherever you may go."
—SARAH DESSEN

"'On that day you will realize that I am in my Father, and you are in me, and I am in you. . . . Anyone who loves me will obey my teaching. My Father will love them, and we will come to them and make our home with them.'" (John 14:20, 23)

Read John 14:5–23; 15:1–17.
Home for the believer is a movable refuge, a carry-along security, and family members reside around the globe and in our hearts. While the unity theme finds limited traction in the Old Testament, it explodes on the scene with the coming of Jesus. The quality of "in-ness," if I may be permitted to coin a word, is intrinsic to the gospel message. Listen to Jesus' words to his Father in John 17:22–23: "I have given [all believers] the glory that you gave me, that they may be one as we are one—I in them and you in me—so that they may be brought to complete unity." Jesus in us and God in Jesus! And the picture is equally true moving in opposite directions.

The New Testament writers get a good deal of leverage from the unobtrusive preposition *in*. In terms of our personal relationship with Jesus Christ, the pervasive phrase "in Christ" affords us as much comfort as the knowledge of Christ in us. But the intimacy flows out from there to encompass our brothers and sisters in Christ. Unity, whether among God's Old Testament people, as in Psalm 133, or among the members of Christ's Church, is a rare and precious—not to mention a noticeable and noticed—commodity in a fractured world. Indeed, how good and pleasant it is when God's people live together—with him—in harmony.

Post-ponderings: On a practical level, what difference does the unity of believers make in your life?

OUR KEEPING LORD:
THE FATHER'S OWN, GIVEN TO JESUS

"[The] essential energy of the soul . . . is a fierce longing for God, an unyielding resolve to live in and out of our belovedness."
—BRENNAN MANNING

"'I have revealed you to those whom you gave me out of the world. They were yours; you gave them to me and they have obeyed your word. . . . I pray for them. I am not praying for the world, but for those you have given me, for they are yours. . . . Holy Father, protect them by the power of your name, the name you gave me, so that they may be one as we are one.'" (John 17:6, 9, 11)

Read John 17:6–19.

"Under his wings I am safely abiding; though the night deepens and tempests are wild, still I can trust him. I know he will keep me; he has redeemed me and I am his child." I awoke this morning to this song on the radio, and it has stayed with me. "I know he will keep me" has connotations for me personally.

It's been more than seven years since I "lost" my three oldest grandchildren, then four, five, and six years old—nearly eight years since their troubled custodial dad dragged them for the last time out of my reach, only to lose them permanently to an out-of-state child welfare agency. As the family had drifted in and out of homelessness, they had repeatedly found refuge with me for months at a time. And I had done all I could to love those little ones and provide for their spiritual nurture.

The last time the three spent a weekend in my home, four-year-old Tavis approached me with a solemn proposition: *"Gramma, please keep me!"* I told him I wanted to, that the decision wasn't mine. All the right stuff. But it wasn't enough. The fact is that we humans don't own one another. "Our" kids—these three seemed to be "mine" as much as anyone else's!— are placed with us in trust.

The last I heard, several years ago, my grandchildren were in the process of pre-adoptive visits with a Christian family. I trust that they'll remember me and that we'll one day reunite. In the meantime, I know that *God will keep them*—even though I can't—enfolded securely in his peace.

Post-ponderings: Who do you know and love who needs that keeping presence? God longs to respond to your plea.

MARY AND JOHN:
APPOINTMENT OF A SURROGATE SON

"The bond that links your true family is not one of blood, but of respect and joy in each other's life. Rarely do members of one family grow up under the same roof."

—RICHARD BACH

"When Jesus saw his mother there, and the disciple whom he loved standing nearby, he said to her, 'Woman, here is your son,' and to the disciple, 'Here is your mother.' From that time on, this disciple took her into his home." (John 19:26–27)

Read John 19:25–27.
We have no reason to suspect that Mary had a less than loving relationship with her own sons and daughters. But as far as we know none of them had to this point accepted their brother as the Christ. Despite their best intentions, without that commonality this soon-to-be-bereft mom would have felt alone in their presence. It's understandable that the bond between her and the "disciple whom [Jesus] loved" (John may have been her nephew, the son of Mary's sister Salome) would have been unique in strength and intimacy.

My two older "special-needs" daughters have over the years attracted friends, hangers-on—and husbands—with challenges similar to their own. I've had occasion to act as honorary mom to many of their friends and roommates, several of whom—some between homes and all misunderstood—were hungry for a relationship with an empathetic older adult. The same is true of more than a few children who've taken to calling me Gramma.

I've typically been chosen for this kind of relationship, as opposed to going after it. My openness has been perceived as an invitation—unattached individuals are adept at identifying approachable people. These hookups generally happen on their own—we never know what qualities or circumstances are going to recommend personalities to one another—but occasionally they're prearranged, as that between Mary and John. It's assuring to note that this living arrangement between two of the people Jesus loved best was lasting.

Post-ponderings: Paul must have experienced loneliness as a single man on the move. We see the other side of this picture in his letter to the Romans: "Greet Rufus, chosen in the Lord, and his mother, who has been a mother to me, too" (Romans 16:13). What single adult do you know who might welcome such a relationship?

"For You and for Your Children": Promise, or Hope and Opportunity?

"When children come to faith, it is due to the grace of God. But while parents are helpless, they are not hopeless, for God has promised in His Word to provide all needful things for His people and to bless them and their families. With faith in these grand promises, parents may raise their children in the nurture and admonition of the Lord with confidence that God will work savingly in their lives."

—JOEL R. BEEKE

"'Repent and be baptized, every one of you, in the name of Jesus Christ for the forgiveness of your sins. And you will receive the gift of the Holy Spirit. The promise is for you and your children and for all who are far off—for all whom the Lord our God will call.'" (Acts 2:38–39)

Read Acts 2:14–41.

What does it mean that God's covenant promise is to *us and our children* if their inclusion depends solely on God's call upon their lives? One thing this paradox *doesn't* call for is our angst. It does call for prayer—and God honors godly, persistent prayer. Waiting is no problem for him; at times he asks us to exercise patience as we rest in his grace. In our own dealings with our kids, "not yet" can be a write-off, but with God "not yet" and "no" are distinctly different answers. We aren't promised that our children will come to the Lord, but we are assured that he answers prayer, both for our good and for his glory.

A quote from Peter comes to mind: "You are a chosen people, a royal priesthood, a holy nation, God's special possession, that you may declare the praises of him who called you out of darkness into his wonderful light. Once you were not a people, but now you are the people of God; once you had not received mercy, but now you have received mercy" (1 Peter 2:9–10). The possibility exists that God in his wisdom has chosen not to include one or more of our children among his elect. But why would he not embrace them as a part of that special possession? I don't mean that question to be irreverent. We as godly parents have every reason for hope—and every opportunity to provide input into these young lives.

Post-ponderings: If you have children old enough to accept or reject God's promises, which trend are you seeing? Are you persisting in prayer and living in his grace and peace, relying on hope and trusting the Father's goodness?

ANANIAS AND SAPPHIRA: CONSPIRING TO DECEIVE

"It' discouraging to think how many people are shocked by honesty and how few by deceit."
—NOEL COWARD

"'How could you conspire to test the Spirit of the Lord?'" (Acts 5:9)

Read Acts 5:1–11.
This couple's "white lie" may seem understandable and even excusable—they weren't obligated, after all, to donate all of their proceeds. Yes, they lied outright (we can lie by implication, by the detail we conveniently leave out, and be just as guilty); it's possible they were hoping they wouldn't be asked. Ananias wasn't asked—the Spirit had already informed Peter of the truth—but Sapphira was . . . and she affirmed that the amount her husband had offered was the full purchase price. The donation may have been generous. It was a donation, after all. They weren't padding their pocketbooks; it was the desire to pad their reputation that led to the "innocent" fudging.

There's something in us that objects to the dire consequences of this oh-so-human yielding to temptation. I'm reminded of Uzzah's reflexive action in 2 Samuel 6:6 of reaching out his hand to steady the ark of God when the oxen stumbled—and its devastating consequence at the Lord's hand. How fortunate we are that this kind of situation is the exception in terms of God's modus operandi with his people. It isn't that we as sinners don't deserve death. Yet by God's grace we receive instead full redemption and life eternal on the merit of Christ's atonement.

Post-ponderings: What choice on your part, either as an individual or as a couple, might have been comparable to that of Ananias and Sapphira? Pause to ask God's forgiveness and to thank him for his grace.

The Widows' Dressmaker

"The purpose of life is not to be happy. It is to be useful, to be honorable, to be compassionate, to have it make some difference that you have lived and lived well."
—RALPH WALDO EMERSON

"In Joppa there was a disciple named Tabitha (in Greek her name is Dorcas); she was always doing good and helping the poor. About that time she became sick and died . . . When he arrived [Peter] was taken upstairs to the room. All the widows stood around him, crying and showing him the robes and other clothing that Dorcas had made while she was still with them." (Acts 9:36–37; 39)

Read Acts 9:36–43.

A widow isn't a family, but she may be the lonely vestige of one. A few years ago I attended the funeral of an aunt—twice a widow. On display at the funeral home were samples of her knitting projects—representing the work of a lifetime. Over decades Aunt Mina had been a Dorcas for the poor, donating what must have amounted to thousands of hand-knitted mittens, caps, and scarves to inner-city children. And the Spirit sees to it that the kingdom is equipped with countless quiet, faithful servants like her.

It can be easy to dismiss any felt responsibility for service (as opposed to financial donations) on the basis that we're lacking in skill, inclination, or time. But we all have abilities that, if not marketable, are useful for the kingdom. "I am only one," declared Edward Everett Hale, "but I am one. I cannot do everything, but I can do something. And I will not let what I cannot do interfere with what I can do." This same early American author, historian, and clergyman is also quoted as inviting God's people to "look up and not down. Look forward and not back. Look out and not in, and lend a hand."

Post-ponderings: A Swedish proverb has it that "the best place to find a helping hand is at the end of your own arm." How are your own hands—and heart—extensions of Christ's on behalf of others?

CORNELIUS:
HOUSEHOLDER OF FAITH

"The bonds we create in the household are the most important and lasting. Savor them; they're sacred."
—RAINN WILSON

Cornelius "told us how he had seen an angel appear in his house and say, "Send to Joppa for Simon who is called Peter. He will bring you a message through which you and all your household will be saved.""" (Acts 11:13–14)

Read Acts 10.
The term *household* in the New Testament implied more than immediate family. Slaves and other associates living under the same roof were included. These were cohesive units, with the non-relatives, depending on their status, enjoying dignity and even entitlement. A biblical household, explains Ken Collins, combined "the features of a modern family and a modern business. The family members, the employees, and the slaves all lived together in the same house, which functioned both as a home and as a place of business."

There are repeated instances in Acts of the wholesale conversions and baptisms of households, including those of Cornelius, this God-fearing householder of faith; Lydia in 16:15; and the Philippian jailor in 16:29–34. It would appear here that the Holy Spirit simultaneously "came on" the entire gathering of relatives and friends who had together been awaiting Peter's arrival, an event they understood would have momentous repercussions.

These new believers were coming to salvation in the same way we all do: as individuals (God hasn't changed his modus operandi in that regard); in these early days of the Church the Spirit called and convicted groups of persons, individually but en masse. It's difficult to imagine what this inclusivity must have meant for this, the first Gentile gathering chosen for salvation. The excitement was contagious—for Peter and the other Jews as well as for these newly minted Gentile believers.

Post-ponderings: Gentile Christians take for granted the change in God's dealings with people represented by this story, but it was at the time an earthshaking development. Based on your knowledge of biblical history, identify some hints that this change was coming.

BARNABAS AND JOHN MARK: A SECOND CHANCE

"It's foolish to believe that someone will be what you imagine them to be. And sometimes, when you give them a chance, they turn out to be better than you imagined. Different, but better."
—AUTHOR UNKNOWN

"Barnabas wanted to take John, also called Mark, with them, but Paul did not think it wise to take him, because he had deserted them in Pamphylia and had not continued with them in the work. They had such a sharp disagreement that they parted company." (Acts 15:37–39)

Read Acts 12:25; 13:13; 15:36–41.
The family of Barnabas and John Mark, his cousin, were well known to Peter and active in the early Jerusalem Church. It was to the home of Barnabas's aunt, John Mark's mother, that Peter retreated following his miraculous escape from prison. It appears that Mark was a younger man; in 1 Peter 5:13 Peter refers to him as "my son." Not only Peter but also Barnabas ("son of encouragement") took on Mark as a protégé. We don't know what spurred him to abandon Paul and Barnabas on that first missionary trip, but the abdication left a bad taste in Paul's mouth. Perhaps Mark's character needed some fine-tuning.

The disagreement between Paul and Barnabas over giving Mark a second chance served to double the effect of the missionary effort; not one but two teams were dispatched on this account to carry the gospel message. Alone with Barnabas, Mark evidently benefited from his cousin's one-on-one, patient discipling. Time was to prove Barnabas right about his cousin's potential, and Paul would more than come around. Listen to excerpts from two of his letters: "My fellow prisoner Aristarchus sends you his greetings, as does Mark, the cousin of Barnabas. (You have received instructions about him; if he comes to you, welcome him)" (Colossians 4:10). And "Get Mark and bring him with you, because he is helpful to me in my ministry" (2 Timothy 4:11).

Post-ponderings: When has your family, extended family, or congregation felt moved to offer a repeat opportunity to a younger member who has missed the mark in some way? What was the longer-term outcome?

Lydia:
A Gracious Invitation

"Hospitality means primarily the creation of free space where the stranger can enter and become a friend instead of an enemy. . . . It is not to bring men and women over to our side, but to offer freedom not disturbed by dividing lines."
—HENRI J. M. NOUWEN

"One of those listening was a woman from the city of Thyatira named Lydia, a dealer in purple cloth. She was a worshiper of God. The Lord opened her heart to respond to Paul's message. When she and the members of her household were baptized, she invited us to her home. 'If you consider me a believer in the Lord,' she said, 'come and stay at my house.' And she persuaded us." (Acts 16:14–15)

Read Acts 16:11–15.

Social responsibility for Christians dictated first the care of family. In Paul's words, "Anyone who does not provide for their relatives, and especially for their own household, has denied the faith and is worse than an unbeliever" (1 Timothy 5:8). But Paul took the mandate further, calling upon believing families and householders to throw open their doors to other Christians: "As we have opportunity, let us do good to all people, especially to those who belong to the family of believers" (Galatians 6:10).

Our Lord wants us to reflect his love and grace indiscriminately, yet Christ has a special, protective love for his own. At the very least, when it comes to extending hospitality, we aren't to overlook others in Christ's kingdom family. How slow we can be at times to set aside cultural and other differences to fully accept and trust one another. Lydia had nothing to fear, yet how sad that she felt the need to question whether or not the apostle considered her a believer! A fledgling Christian, she most definitely had it right: her intent was clearly to offer that freedom, undisturbed by dividing lines, of which Nouwen speaks.

Post-ponderings: What has the cordiality of fellow Christians meant to you during some particularly challenging time of your life?

PRISCILLA AND AQUILA: UNITED IN SERVICE

"The deepest level of communication is not communication, but communion.
It is wordless . . . beyond speech . . . beyond concept."
—THOMAS MERTON

"Greet Priscilla and Aquila, my co-workers in Christ Jesus. They risked their lives for
me. Not only I but all the churches of the Gentiles are grateful to them. Greet also
the church that meets at their house." (Romans 16:3–5)

Read Acts 18:1–6, 18–19, 24–28.

Priscilla and Aquila (her name is generally mentioned first) personify as no other biblical pair the single-mindedly devoted Christian couple. Whether it was in opening their home to Paul, providing him an opportunity to ply his trade in their company, accompanying him on a voyage, engaging in ministry together as a couple, or taking Apollos under their wing to update him on the whole truth about Jesus, this couple served tirelessly, evidently to the point of risking their lives for Paul's benefit.

Elsewhere Paul would tout the single life as the optimal situation for devoted service: "I am saying this for your own good, not to restrict you, but that you may live in a right way in undivided devotion to the Lord" (1 Corinthians 7:35). In this case, though, Paul would no doubt have conceded that "two are better than one," that "a cord of three strands [assuming Christ is interwoven into the mix!) is not quickly broken" (Ecclesiastes 4:9, 12). What "power" couples (powerful together in the Lord's strength) do you know—couples who accomplish much more in the Name than one or the other could ever manage alone?

Post-ponderings: Are you and your spouse engaged in joint ministry endeavors, or does your respective service tend to be more individual?

PAUL'S NEPHEW
STEPS FORWARD

"It is through our extended family that we first learn to compromise and come to an understanding that even if we don't always agree about things we can still love and look out for each other."

—SARA SHERIDAN

"When the son of Paul's sister heard of this plot, he went to the barracks and told Paul." (Acts 23:16)

Read Acts 23:12–22.

"The commander took the young man by the hand," Luke records, "drew him aside and asked, 'What is it you want to tell me?'" He said: 'Some Jews have agreed to ask you to bring Paul before the Sanhedrin tomorrow on the pretext of wanting more accurate information about him. Don't give in to them, because more than forty of them are waiting in ambush for him.'"

For the commander to take Paul's nephew by the hand implies that the young man was still a boy. And a plucky one at that. We learn nothing else about Paul's family after his conversion and wonder whether their support was motivated solely by family allegiance or stemmed from a mutual faith in Jesus Christ. For this young man to have learned of the plot suggests that he may not have been known as a Christ-follower—at any rate, he was evidently not viewed by the Jews as a security threat. If we knew this to have been the case, we would be doubly impressed by his courage in coming forward with his inside knowledge.

"There is no respect between the souls of two individuals if their minds can't trust each other," observes Anuj Somany, "and there is no trust between them if their hearts can't accept the truth of each other." Trust, not necessarily in conjunction with agreement, is necessary for respect to flourish—in this case in a family context.

Post-ponderings: When have you been able to respect someone even though you weren't of the same mind on an issue? On what did you base your trust?

FELIX AND DRUSILLA:
THE CONVENIENCE FACTOR

"I wasn't in the mood for a fight, but fights weren't always conveniently scheduled."
—SHANNON A. THOMPSON

"Felix, who was well acquainted with the Way, adjourned the proceedings. . . .
Several days later Felix came with his wife Drusilla, who was Jewish. He sent for
Paul and listened to him as he spoke about faith in Christ Jesus. As Paul talked
about righteousness, self-control and the judgment to come, Felix became afraid
and said, 'That's enough for now! You may leave. When I find it convenient,
I will send for you.'" (Acts 24:22, 24–25)

Read Acts 24.

It's interesting both that Felix was already acquainted with the Way and that his wife was Jewish. Given this background, it's possible the couple had discussed the pros and cons of the movement together. Typical of Roman officials throughout the New Testament, Felix was tolerant and fair-minded, his fault being his failure to make a timely decision about Paul's case; he was both stalling in the hope of receiving a bribe and anxious to appease the Jews by keeping Paul incarcerated. Felix's frequent audiences with Paul seem to hold out the hope of conviction; the apostle's references to righteousness, self-control, and judgment do in fact convict the governor—but of fear-induced guilt, not repentance. That convenient time, we're given to understand, isn't going to come around.

How often in our own lives doesn't that elusive convenience factor come into play? It may be that we're aware of a needed change—a healthier lifestyle, a more vibrant prayer life, curbing out-of-control spending, . . . any of a number of resolutions that seem at once decidedly inconvenient and not particularly time-sensitive. Avoidance. Procrastination. Promises. We know the pattern. What we don't necessarily recognize is that putting off the good, or the inevitable, may result in consequences far more dire than we might dream. In Felix's case, not only was the apostle to the Gentiles imprisoned unnecessarily for two years that could have been productive in terms of the spread of the gospel and the nurturance of the Church, but Felix himself—not to mention Drusilla—allowed an opportunity that could have transformed his eternal future to pass by.

Post-ponderings: In what areas are you procrastinating? Take the time to write down five of them, in descending order of importance. How many are of a spiritual nature?

UNDERSTANDING:
THE LANGUAGE OF FAMILY

"There is no hospitality like understanding."
—VANNA BONTA

"There was an estate nearby that belonged to Publius, the chief official of the island. He welcomed us to his home and showed us generous hospitality for three days. His father was sick in bed, suffering from fever and dysentery. Paul went in to see him and, after prayer, placed his hands on him and healed him." (Acts 28:7–8)

Read Acts 28:1–10.
Paul and Publius (indeed, the ship's crew and passengers and the Maltese strangers) had no prior knowledge of one another. But mutual understanding, a universal language, removed any barriers that might have gotten in their way. Paul refers in Romans 2:14–15 to the innate goodness often seen in nonbelievers, perhaps especially those who've never had an opportunity to hear the gospel message: "Indeed, when Gentiles, who do not have the law, do by nature things required by the law, they are a law for themselves . . . They show that the requirements of the law are written on their hearts."

Compassion and hospitality to needy strangers seem to be intrinsic values around the world—a result of the residual goodness God has permitted the human race after the fall—except when underlying ethnic or other hostilities get in the way. I'm moved by a reflection from Thomas G. Long: "The stranger at the door is the living symbol and memory that we are all strangers here. . . . [T]o show hospitality to the stranger is . . . to say, 'We are all beggars here together. Grace will surprise us both.'"

In this case the grace, from the human side, was presented by the unbeliever. The question comes to mind how well we as Christians stack up in the area of extending grace, hospitality, and healing to others, both to the stranger and to those closest to us (depending on our circumstances, either one can prove the more difficult). When we fall short in either area, a critical world is quick to take note.

Post-ponderings: Whom do you know who, despite a lack of religious faith, exemplifies in your mind a good person? How have you accounted for this?

THE EPISTLES, PART 1

CHAPTER
INTRODUCTION

Chapter 21, along with the first half of chapter 22, focuses on Paul's epistles. Its themes vary from practical material to "family" matters of the spiritual kind.

Pedigree: "Just Regular Human"?

Read Romans 8:1–17.

Several years ago my then preadolescent middle adopted daughter announced to dinner guests that she was "half Indian." "That's neat," was the polite response, "and what about the other half?" Angie had already expressed the one distinctive in which she took the most pride, but if the question gave her pause she quickly recovered, neatly packaging together every other aspect of her awakening self-image: "Just regular human, I guess."

We humans enter the world equipped with an uncanny compulsion to niche ourselves. Only one distinctive, though, divides us in an eternally meaningful way. We teach it to our children, too often as a novelty: "If anybody asks you who you are, tell them you're a child of God." In a sense we're all regular, and we're certainly all human, but we who are of the Spirit are infinitely more! We're so accustomed to the knowledge of having been chosen before the creation of the world that we accept the reality without wonder. We forget that we're adopted *to be* something—in Paul's words, to be holy and blameless in God's sight.

That doesn't mean we're holy in and of ourselves. But we've inherited this family characteristic on the basis of our relationship with our Brother, Jesus, and our Father, both of whom epitomize goodness and love. Our holiness is a reality in God's sight; it's a *legal* designation, though nonetheless real. The aura of this holiness, though, ought to be evident to those other regular humans around us. As Christ's brothers and sisters, we're here for a purpose—to represent our brother to a world in desperate need of relationship with him.

Post-ponderings: Express in a sentence or two what your adoption as God's own child means to you.

God's Inclusive Household

"[T]he household of God includes the family members (Father, Son, and Holy Spirit), the angels, the prophets and apostles, as well as the rank-and-file believers, who are being adopted as sons. We all live together in one house. We are empowered to carry out the business of our household, which is to redeem every human soul."

—KEN COLLINS

"See what great love the Father has lavished on us, that we should be called children of God! And that is what we are! The reason the world does not know us is that it did not know him. Dear friends, now we are children of God, and what we will be has not yet been made known." (1 John 3:1–2)

Read Romans 8:18–39.

The truth is that, despite the evident promise in the last sentence of the Ken Collins quote, we don't know how many, or which, human souls will be redeemed. Nor is that our concern—in terms not of our interest but of our business. We're to function as though every person is a potential new brother or sister in Christ, a prospective fellow member of his inclusive household. What a joy it will be on that day when the children of God are finally revealed. All creation waits with baited breath, and there will be surprises, not just in general but for each of us personally!

It's easy to write off seemingly disinterested people, or those we judge to be too far gone for redemption. How thankful we can be that this isn't our job. God's electing grace is a reality we believers see in our own lives in grateful hindsight, but the difficult truth that not all have been chosen ought never to dampen our enthusiasm for spreading—and living out—the news. God may be depending on you or me to be the catalyst for bringing some elect family member, neighbor, coworker, or acquaintance into his household. We'll never know what word, action, or gesture might be the deciding factor, or for whom. And how beautiful the knowledge that once those individuals know him they will also know us, their forever family.

Post-ponderings: If you're acquainted with a new Christian, have you shown an interest in their story? Approaching this from a different direction, in what ways have you been personally involved with bringing someone to Christ? (Your kids count!)

The Christian Parent as Role Model: "Do as I Intend"

"Every journey begins with the first step of articulating the intention, and then becoming the intention."
—BRYANT MCGILL

"Even if you had ten thousand guardians in Christ, you do not have many fathers, for in Christ Jesus I became your father through the gospel. Therefore I urge you to imitate me." (1 Corinthians 4:15–16)

Read 1 Corinthians 4:14–21.
How many of us as parents truly want our kids to imitate us? In general, yes, but we're painfully aware of our shortfalls. That's the impetus for the familiar "Do as I say, not as I do." That matter of *doing* is always the rub. As Paul laments, "I do not do the good I want to do, but the evil I do not want to do—this I keep on doing" (Romans 7:19). His conclusion provides a *phew!*: "It is no longer I who do it, but it is sin living in me."

A *phew!* yes—but as a reality check, not an excuse. The beauty for us as Christians is that our children from an early age discern motive. When we as moms and dads, with the help of the Spirit, seek wholeheartedly to do—both in our children's presence and out of their sight—what is right and true, they will perceive, and follow, those best intentions. When we in humility confess our slip-ups while striving to exemplify grace, truth, and peace, our kids pick up a dual message: intentionality matters and blunders are forgivable.

In this light we can confidently address the upcoming generation with Paul: "Whatever you have learned or received or heard from me, or seen in me—put it into practice" (Philippians 4:9). A second beautiful reality: through the process of sanctification our actions gradually come closer and closer to those best intentions.

Post-ponderings: How fortunate the young person who has additional guardians taking a special interest in his or her spiritual nurture. Who is playing that role for each of your children?

Paul on Marriage
to an Unbeliever

"If you are a believer married to an unbeliever I want to tell you that the greatest witness that you can be to them is to try to be the same all the time. Don't let the way they act control you."
—JOYCE MEYER

"Wives, . . . submit yourselves to your own husbands so that, if any of them do not believe the word, they may be won over without words by the behavior of their wives, when they see the purity and reverence of your lives." (1 Peter 3:1–2)

Read 1 Corinthians 7:12–16.
In the early days of the Church, as faith exploded on the scene, initial converts often represented one or the other spouse in an already established union. The apostle, articulating his own thoughts on the subject, though under Spirit inspiration, advocates against divorce in such cases, unless the unbelieving partner is unwilling to live with the other's faith. The possibility is real that the believing spouse may, based on lifestyle and consistency, influence the unbelieving in the direction of faith.

For an established Christian to join in matrimony with someone who doesn't share their faith is a more dicey situation (Paul minces no words on this issue in 2 Corinthians 6:14). Young people play with fire when they make the Christian faith a negotiable in terms of criteria for a future mate. Because influence, as many of us know from bitter experience, can go in either direction. An intractable, nonbelieving husband or wife can make the situation so difficult for the spouse trying to live out their conviction in isolation—and perhaps in a context of mockery, disgust, or deliberate temptation—that it becomes the path of least resistance (sadly, in an effort to maintain peace, 1 Corinthians 7:15) to let their faith go or to allow it to languish beneath the surface without living it out. The casualties in this case are multiple, very much including the children who grow up without the benefit of Christian modeling from either side. Which is not to mention that it's extraordinarily difficult to maintain, let alone nurture, a latent, hidden faith.

Post-ponderings: If you have unmarried, believing children, have you impressed upon them the priority of a Christian mate?

THE SINGLE LIFE:
GNAWING ON STYROFOAM?

"My most earnest of all pleas to singles is abandonment of the self, surrender to Christ of all unfulfilled longings, an unequivocal willingness to receive whatever God assigns, and a determination to practice the sacrificial principle of Isaiah 58:10–11. Life becomes not only far simpler, but surprisingly joyful and free."
—ELISABETH ELLIOT

"Now about virgins: I have no command from the Lord, but ... [b]ecause of the present crisis, I think that it is good for a man to remain as he is. Are you pledged to a woman? Do not seek to be released. Are you free from such a commitment? Do not look for a wife." (1 Corinthians 7:25–27)

Read 1 Corinthians 7:25–40.
Several years ago following a church service I handed my one-year-old grandson a Styrofoam cup filled with cheesy goldfish. Almost immediately he proceeded to pour out the crackers and gnaw contentedly on the cup. I *do* know how to give good gifts to my grandchildren (in Matthew 7:10 Jesus even uses *fish* as an example). But I couldn't force him to recognize this one as such.

How's your track record for identifying and utilizing God's good gifts? Take singleness—if this applies to you or to someone else you care about. If it's you, your energy level and zeal for the Lord may not match Paul's. But God didn't call *you* to be the apostle to the Gentiles. He may have called you to . . . bless your family (1 Chronicles 16:43)—whether that involves your family of birth, including nieces and nephews, or whether you, like me, find yourself in a solo parenting role. This calling seems to be the case for me. My adult children still present periodic crises, but I take comfort from the conviction that these adopted children constitute a significant part of my service opportunity.

Your situation may, of course, be entirely different, but there's some opportunity the Spirit holds out, specifically, to you. The single life may be exactly the last state you'd have opted for. If you feel this way, by all means continue to pray for a mate. But why not take some time to evaluate your role as objectively as you can. Is it just possible you've poured out God's good fish to gnaw on Styrofoam?

Post-ponderings: If you're married, who is there in your life who is struggling with the reality of singleness? How can you include this person and make them feel at home with you and your family?

THE APOSTLES:
TRAVELING PAIRS—AND/OR COUPLES

"Pastors: Put your wife second in your life. After your relationship with Jesus Christ, your bride is your highest priority. . . . Pastor, Jesus has a Bride, and you do, too."
—KEN WHITTEN

"Don't we have the right to take a believing wife along with us, as do the other apostles and the Lord's brothers and Cephas? Or is it only I and Barnabas who lack the right to not work for a living?" (1 Corinthians 9:5–6)

Read 1 Corinthians 9:1–18.
Paul's rhetorical questions, above, fall within a discussion of his status and rights as an apostle, which were being questioned by some in Corinth. The other apostles (Paul and Barnabas—not technically an apostle—evidently constituted the unmarried contingent) were accompanied by their wives on their mission travels and were relying on the churches for sustenance. While Paul was electing both to remain unmarried and to work for his living, it was his legitimate right—should he have chosen to exercise it—to opt in the other direction.

I'll have to admit that verse 5 took me by surprise. I had envisioned these itinerant pastors traveling alone or in male pairs—not as couples. While I'd known that Peter (Cephas) was married (Luke 4:38–39), the thought of the spouses traveling together hadn't occurred to me. Could wives and other family members (like James and John's mother, possibly Salome, Jesus' aunt; see the reflection on Matthew 4:18–22) have roamed the countryside with Jesus and the Twelve? The fact is that we don't know, but the possible new mental paradigm whets my interest.

The issue of self-supporting or bi-vocational pastors is real in our day, particularly in small, struggling congregations and recent church plants. If your pastor, whether married or single, is in this position, in what practical ways can you provide support and encouragement?

Post-ponderings: Pause to picture Jesus' original Twelve and/or the apostles (most are the same men) traveling in the company of their wives. Do you find yourself so familiar with the Bible's stories that you find a mental re-imaging refreshing?

Agreeable Disagreement:
A Healthful Nighttime Ritual

"Anger . . . it's a paralyzing emotion . . . you can't get anything done. People sort of think it's an interesting, passionate, and igniting feeling—I don't think it's any of that—it's helpless . . . it's absence of control—and I need all of my skills, all of the control, all of my powers."
—TONI MORRISON

"'In your anger do not sin': Do not let the sun go down while you are still angry, and do not give the devil a foothold." (Ephesians 4:26–27)

Read Ephesians 4:17–32.
My parents have lived their married lives by the credo of these two verses, making sure to resolve any lingering disagreements nightly before retiring. Not that they always agree, but they agree to disagree, agreeably. Paul was quoting Psalm 4:4: "Tremble and [some translations render this 'In your anger'] do not sin; when you are on your beds, search your hearts and be silent." Anger is an emotion, not a sin—a God-given release valve for pent-up tensions in danger of detonating. But if handled incorrectly, if nursed and cultivated for our private satisfaction, this potentially vindictive emotion leaves our heart vulnerable to sin and its most militant promoter.

How often have you lain in bed rehearsing the brilliant comeback you wish you had made, carefully strategizing a counterattack, or gleefully awaiting daylight to pounce on your unsuspecting opponent? The psalmist's injunction to "search your hearts" is a different proposition altogether. Heart (or soul) searching might result in unwanted complications—like misgivings, guilt, empathy, or a desire to forgive or make peace.

Post-ponderings: When is the last time you, or someone else in your family, went to bed mad? Was it worth the miserable night's sleep?

"As to the Lord": Headship and Submission

"The example the husband sets has eternal consequences. This means head-ship is more about controlling one's character than controlling one's wife. The man who is more concerned with how his wife should obey him than with how he should obey God fails the kindergarten of Biblical Headship."
—BRYAN CHAPELL

"Wives, submit yourselves to your own husbands as you do to the Lord. For the husband is the head of the wife as Christ is the head of the church, his body, of which he is the Savior. Now as the church submits to Christ, so also wives should submit to their husbands in everything." (Ephesians 5:22–24)

Read Ephesians 5:1–24.
"Submission is like a dance," reflects Angela Parsley. "If you have ever seen a partner dance then you know there can be only one leader. If they both try to lead they step all over each other and they do not flow. . . . Ephesians 5 tells us to respect our husbands. We need to respect them enough to al-low them to lead us in this dance of life."

Many women bristle at the idea of honoring their husband, to the point that some brides opt to scratch honor and submission from their vows. Not all men are hono*rable*, but God's will for us isn't thereby altered. There is, of course, a subtle difference between honor and submission. The first is an attitude of heart, a respect for the other's position, while the second is an action. We can respect the station of someone who is acting in defiance of God's law even as we, in good conscience, choose not to obey them.

A lot of words to cover the exception! What Paul had in mind was the norm for Christian marriage. He was advocating mutuality, mandating from the husband's side, "However, each one of you also must love his wife as he loves himself" (verse 33). Mutual submission is a natural outgrowth of mutual love. It's also the root of a beautiful marriage.

Peter O'Brien sheds light on these issues: "Subordination smacks of exploitation and oppression that are deeply resented. But authority does not mean tyranny, and the submission to which the apostle refers does not imply inferiority. Wives and husbands have different God-appointed roles, but all have equal dignity because they have been made in the divine image and in Christ have put on a the new person who is created to be like God."

Post-ponderings: If you're married, how do you interpret these vital issues? Do you and your spouse share an understanding? Is this something you've discussed?

MARRIAGE:
MYSTERY AND MYSTIQUE

"God created us in his image, male and female, with personhood and sexual passions, so that when he comes to us in this world there would be these powerful words and images to describe the promises and the pleasures of our covenant relationship with him through Christ."
—JOHN PIPER

"'For this reason a man will leave his father and mother and be united to his wife, and the two will become one flesh.' This is a profound mystery—but I am talking about Christ and the church." (Ephesians 5:31–32)

Read Ephesians 5:25–33.
I'll admit to being a little startled by Piper's exposition of this Ephesians quote. His "personhood" point makes sense, but "sexual passions" under the "so that" umbrella required for me a double take. We don't think of God as a sexual being, but he certainly epitomizes passion—much of it in our direction as unquenchable love.

Sheila Wray Gregoire comments, "Sex is not about genitalia. It's about relationship. When God said 'the two shall become one flesh,' he didn't mean it only physically." The sexual aspect of marriage is all about oneness, spiritual and emotional as well as physical. And so is God. (See the reflection on mutual "in-ness" and oneness at John 14:5–23; 15:1–17.)

The model of Christian marriage, including its sexual aspect—yes, both the "in-ness" and the oneness are appropriate metaphors—as an image of Christ's Church is appropriate and beautiful. This truth helps us recognize, perhaps in a new way, the sanctity of the marriage vows. It's the same commitment Christ has for his Bride, and the same consecrated devotion he rightfully expects from her.

Post-ponderings: Pause for a moment to reflect on the ramifications of both the Paul and the Piper quotes for your own marriage.

PARENTAL BOUNDARIES:
DISCIPLINED DISCIPLINE

"There is a big difference between hurt and harm. We all hurt sometimes in facing hard truths, but it makes us grow. It can be the source of huge growth. That is not harmful. Harm is when you damage someone. Facing reality is usually not a damaging experience, even though it can hurt."
—HENRY CLOUD

"Fathers, do not exasperate your children; instead, bring them up in the training and instruction of the Lord." (Ephesians 6:4)

Read Ephesians 6:1–4.
There can be a fine line in terms of a parent's wielding of authority between effective discipline and overkill. Paul makes the same point with a slightly different emphasis in Colossians 3:21: "Fathers, do not embitter your children, or they will become discouraged."

The missing component in abusive discipline is love—the main ingredient in God's chastening of us as his children. The goal for our discipline is to be the same. Far from being a feel-good flaunting of authority or the venting of pent-up anger, our aim must be the child's internalizing of the principles being taught—little by little taking over the role of the disciplined parent in relation to himself. How ironic that a lack of discipline on the part of the parent *in applying discipline* negates the whole point!

Once again according to Henry Cloud, "Training moments occur when both parents and children do their jobs. The parent's job is to make the rule. The child's job is to break the rule. The parent then corrects and disciplines. The child breaks the rule again, and the parent manages the consequences and empathy that then turn the rule into reality and internal structure for the child." I found it a useful exercise to reread that statement, substituting "God" for "the parent" and "the Christian" for "the child." While it isn't the "job" of the Christian to break God's rules, that is the natural tendency, especially of the unsanctified or as yet undisciplined child of God.

God isn't in the business of punishing his own—he reserves that approach for the recalcitrant ungodly in the judgment—though he does chastise for various reasons, all of them infinitely good and wise. We can do no better than to follow his lead in this vital area.

Post-ponderings: If you're raising children, what do you see as your primary motivation in discipline? Are you more likely to punish in anger or to chasten in love?

Preferring
One Another

"True strength lies in submission which permits one to dedicate his life, through devotion, to something beyond himself."
—HENRY MILLER

"Do nothing out of selfish ambition or vain conceit. Rather, in humility value others above yourselves, not looking to your own interests but each of you to the interests of others." (Philippians 2:3–4)

Read Philippians 2:1–11.
It's one thing—while not an easy one—to love our neighbors as we love ourselves (Luke 10:27). *So what's this now?* we might protest were we encountering the Philippians passage for the first time. Is Paul trumping Jesus' mandate by asking us to value others *more than* we do ourselves? Paul wasn't calling Christians to a false or neurotic self-abnegation. Nor was he attempting to squelch any vestiges of self-esteem. Far from it, Paul understood the tremendous worth God sees in each of us.

Again in Romans 12:10 Paul directs Christians to be devoted to one another in love, to *honor* each other above ourselves. He's talking about a decision to treat fellow believers preferentially, to mutually submit to one another on the basis of love and gratitude for the salvation and fellowship we share.

I'm drawn to an anonymous quote on a well-functioning marital relationship; I believe we can extend the premise to encompass relationships with other Christians, both individually and corporately: "You make me happier than I ever thought I could be and if you let me I will spend the rest of my life trying to make you feel the same way."

Post-ponderings: What does obeying Christ's mandate through Paul look like for you?

PAUL, SILAS, AND TIMOTHY: MATERNAL CARE ANALOGY

"I think we need the feminine qualities of leadership, which include attention to aesthetics and the environment, nurturing, affection, intuition and the qualities that make people feel safe and cared for."
—DEEPAK CHOPRA

"Just as a nursing mother cares for her children, so we cared for you. Because we loved you so much, we were delighted to share with you not only the gospel of God but our lives as well." (1 Thessalonians 2:7–8)

Read 1 Thessalonians 2:1–12.

Paul had a way of startling his readers with his analogies. His depicting himself as either a nursing mother or wracked by labor pains takes us aback; the use of these metaphors took courage for him, while clearly making his points for us. Listen again: "My dear children, for whom I am again in the pains of childbirth until Christ is formed in you, how I wish I could be with you now . . . " (Galatians 4:19–20). A single woman, I've never experienced either facet of motherhood, but I have no doubt what emotions this man was trying to convey.

An equal opportunity wordsmith, Paul also likens himself and his colleagues in this chapter to young children and spiritual fathers. Ironically, the single Paul had no personal experience with parenting from either side, but he employs every possible means to touch the hearts and minds of his audience. As he states elsewhere, "to the weak I became weak, to win the weak. I have become all things to all people so that by all possible means I might save some" (1 Corinthians 9:22).

Post-pondering: What lovely qualities that you traditionally equate with femininity are embodied by God the Father, God and Son, and God the Spirit? Why do you think so many men are uncomfortable exemplifying these traits?

"Walking Orderly"

"The virtue of the soul does not consist in flying high, but walking orderly; grandeur does not exercise itself in grandeur, but in mediocrity."
—MICHEL DE MONTAIGNE

"Make it your ambition to lead a quiet life: You should mind your own business and work with your hands, just as we told you, so that your daily life may win the respect of outsiders." (1 Thessalonians 4:11–12)

Read 1 Thessalonians 4:1–12.
I wouldn't expect to see "ambition" and "quiet" in the same short clause. But the lifestyle Christ expects of us, his followers, points others to his character, and the stakes are high: we Christians—as individuals and as families—are called to win the respect of outsiders on behalf of the One we represent.

I balk a little at the word "mediocrity" in the de Montaigne quote, having been taught to do my best. Perhaps "ordinariness" comes closer to the point for me. But semantics aside, it's your and my place to leave the grandeur to God while pointing others to him by a disciplined, ordered lifestyle.

We live in a frenetic, disorganized world. Heads spinning like tops, we spiral our way through the hours, dizzied by the day's demands and resonating with the protest "Stop the world; I want to get off!" What we may not recognize is that there are spiritual implications involved. "Life isn't logical or sensible or orderly," observes Charles Caleb Colton. "Life is a mess most of the time. And theology must be lived in the midst of that mess." The opposite of the reactive lifestyle is one that is responsive and responsible, deliberate and purposeful, all in the name of God. We serve a God of order, a God who calls upon his followers to walk orderly in the midst of flux.

Post-ponderings: If your family's lifestyle tends toward the chaotic or hectic, how do you—or can you—continue to walk orderly?

THE CHURCH COUNCIL:
EXEMPLARY FAMILY MANAGEMENT

"Never separate the life you live from the words you speak."
—SENATOR PAUL WELLSTONE

The overseer/elder "must manage his own family well and see that his children obey him, and he must do so in a manner worthy of full respect. (If anyone does not know how to manage his own family, how can he take care of God's church?)" (1 Timothy 3:4–5)

"A deacon must be faithful to his wife and must manage his children and his household well." (1 Timothy 3:12)

Read 1 Timothy 3:1–13.
Leadership by example—it applies to politics, to teaching, and to business. But most importantly to Christ's Church, because its leaders function in his Name. It can be easy for us to denigrate the importance of a volunteer position, and in some areas of life there is leeway there. Not so in the kingdom. Our Lord's reputation is at stake by the example we—and our spouses and children—set.

A part of the onus lies with the leader's family members, whether that leader is a minister of the Word, an elder or a deacon, or any other individual representing a congregation in some capacity. How seriously do we as church members take these criteria? In all likelihood those on the council responsible for accepting nominations or making appointments take them very seriously. The accountability may seem less significant to those being considered for offices or for other positions of authority within the body. If we ourselves are candidates, do we impress upon our family members the role *they* are called to accept in conjunction with our own?

Post-ponderings: Considering your local congregation, what importance do you place on the behavior of your leaders' families?

CHAPTER 22

THE EPISTLES, PART 2

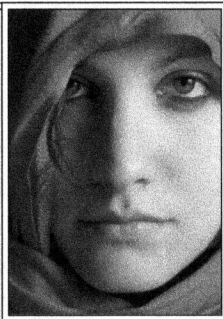

CHAPTER
INTRODUCTION

Covering the last of Paul's letters through the remainder of the New Testament, chapter 22 treats subjects that are as varied as the writings upon which they're based. As in chapter 21, metaphorical and theological material using the language of family is interspersed with reflections on the lives of individual Christian families and family members.

NEEDY WIDOWS
IN THE CHURCH

"To care for those who once cared for us is one of the highest honors."
—TIA WALKER

"Give proper recognition to those widows who are really in need. But if a widow has children or grandchildren, these should learn first of all to put their religion into practice by caring for their own family and so repaying their parents and grandparents, for this is pleasing to God." (1 Timothy 5:3–4)

Read 1 Timothy 5:1–16.
Paul's explicit guidelines in this passage are valuable for the diaconal ministry of the Church. I'm struck by the degree of accountability he places on widows themselves, as well as on their families and designated caregivers for their primary care. These principles allow a church to exercise effective, Christ-like compassion in conjunction with fiscal responsibility.

While *some* of these principles apply to the need assessment and giving of para-church organizations and other ministries focused on the general public, the references to personal responsibility apply specifically to church members. On first glance it seems confusing to speak of qualifications for particular widows. Jesus healed based on need, not merit, though the Gospels record several instances of his being moved by, and generous in response to, the unusual faith manifested by Gentiles.

It's important to differentiate a Christian lifestyle and values from good works mistakenly construed as meritorious for salvation. Paul's demands concerning the comportment of church members seem stringent; there's much at stake in the example we provide those outside Christ's Church. Considering the limited funding available to the local congregation, guidelines relative to members beyond the degree or nature of the need are appropriate for deacons.

Post-ponderings: How involved are you and your spouse in the well-being of your parents on both sides? Has your family reached the point at which the direction of care has begun to shift?

PAUL AND TIMOTHY:
TRUE SON IN THE FAITH

"It is not flesh and blood but the heart which makes us fathers and sons."
—JOHANN SCHILLER

"Paul, an apostle of Christ Jesus by the command of God our Savior and of Christ Jesus our hope, To Timothy my true son in the faith." (1 Timothy 1:1–2)

Read 1 Timothy 6:11–21.
"Paul came to Derbe and then to Lystra," writes Luke is Acts 16:1, "where a disciple named Timothy lived, whose mother was Jewish and a believer but whose father was a Greek." We don't know much about Timothy's father, including the degree to which he was involved with his son, but he was evidently uninterested in the things of God. It's probable that Timothy, still quite young, was an obvious candidate for a spiritual father figure—a need Paul intuited and filled, taking him under his wing as he and Silas moved on from Lystra.

We gather from Paul's remarks that Timothy was self-deprecating and frequently ill; Paul counseled him not to let others dismiss him on the basis of his youth and urged him to drink some wine for his digestive health. The apostle's final charge to his young protégé in the passage for this reflection has a tender tone, in keeping with that of a father with his cherished son.

Those actively engaged in ministry, and perhaps especially those unable to rely on a spouse for support, need the nurture of a mentoring relationship, especially in those lonely and overwhelming early years. What a blessing Paul, and the Lord through him, was providing for this developing evangelist.

Post-ponderings: Based on Peter's use of similar language—"She who is in Babylon . . . sends you her greetings, and so does *my son* Mark (1 Peter 5:13, emphasis added)—we can assume this is either idiomatic language or a common expression. Whom do you consider a spiritual son or daughter, or who has filled this role for you?

LOIS, EUNICE, AND TIMOTHY: MATRIARCHAL FAITH TRANSMISSION

"Only God Himself fully appreciates the influence of a Christian mother in the molding of character in her children."
—BILLY GRAHAM

"I am reminded of your sincere faith, which first lived in your grandmother Lois and in your mother Eunice and, I am persuaded, now lives in you also." (2 Timothy 1:5)

Read 2 Timothy 1:1–14.
Matriarchal faith transmission is a significant factor in many churches in which numerous faith-filled and faithful moms are carrying the bulk of responsibility for their children's nurture—in a spiritual sense as well as physically. You may be, as I am, a single Christian mother (my daughters are grown), or you may have found yourself in that position during some portion of your active parenting years. On the other hand, you may be a believer who carries a burden for the unique needs of the many moms in Christ's Church who are going it alone.

Authors Kimberly Morgan and Sally Steenland offer provocative thoughts on the role of the Church in helping to sustain mom-based families. A sampling: "As women (and men) increasingly grapple with shifting gender roles and responsibilities, as families face greater economic stress, and as women juggle multiple tasks in days that are too short, religious institutions can provide sustenance and support. . . . They need to provide for the spiritual and material needs of women and their families, while speaking out on behalf of a moral vision that values women and family in a way that is neither regressive nor nostalgic, but authentic and prophetic for today."

Post-ponderings: Are there struggling single mothers in your church who might appreciate a break or simply a word of encouragement?

"From Infancy":
A Scriptural Case for Gradual Conversion

"The world does not consist of 100 percent Christians and 100 percent non-Christians. There are people (a great many of them) who are slowly ceasing to be Christians but who still call themselves by that name: some of them are clergymen. There are other people who are slowly becoming Christians though they do not yet call themselves so."
—C. S. LEWIS

"But as for you, continue in what you have learned and have become convinced of, because you know those from whom you learned it, and how from infancy you have known the Holy Scriptures, which are able to make you wise for salvation through faith in Christ Jesus." (2 Timothy 3:14–15)

Read 2 Timothy 3:10–17.

Timothy was a member of the first generation raised in the Church from infancy. Different Christian churches stress—and expect—different kinds or conversion. My background tradition considers gradual conversion to be normative, though certainly not exclusive, for those born into the faith (that very phrase, I suppose, suggests this stance).

Churches espousing covenant theology baptize infants as recipients of God's promises made to Abram in Genesis 17:7: "I will establish my covenant as an everlasting covenant between me and you and your descendants after you for the generations to come, to be your God and the God of your descendants after you." It goes without saying that a profession of faith on the part of the young person be made at some point, indicating his or her acceptance of the terms of the covenant.

We all agree as Christ-followers that baptism signifies the washing away of our sins by the shed blood of Jesus Christ and the drowning of the "old man," our sin nature. And we all view the sacrament as a sign and seal of Christ's ownership. We also concur that conversion is never the end of the story. In fact, the process of growing more and more like our Brother goes on throughout our earthly lives, up to our final moments. "To say, 'I've been converted and that's that,'" points out Steve Goodier, "is to say you have decided to quit growing. If life is about anything, it is about growing. The day I quit changing and learning is the day I die."

Post-ponderings: What does your baptism mean to you? What comfort does it afford you?

THE RESPONSIBILITY
OF OLDER MEN

"If you would convince a man that he does wrong, do right. But do not care to convince him. Men will believe what they see. Let them see."
—HENRY DAVID THOREAU

"Teach the older men to be temperate, worthy of respect, self-controlled, and sound in faith, in love and in endurance." (Titus 2:2)

Read Titus 2:1–2.
I did a double take on my citation of the verse above. Should "teach older men," I wondered momentarily, have been quoted as "teach younger men"? No, the responsibilities of the younger men are addressed separately in verses 6–8. The same principle applies to "teach older women" in the next reflection. The older believers—all relatively new to the faith at the time Paul wrote, though a few decades had passed since the Church's inception—had to "get it right" before they could be of use in modeling for the younger.

It's easy for aging church members to view themselves as less vital to the body than they once were. But already in Old Testament times the writer of Psalm 71:18 lifted up this prayer: "Even when I am old and gray, do not forsake me, my God, till I declare your power to the next generation, your mighty acts to all who are to come." What a sacred trust and accountability! And this declaring is accomplished as much through habit and action as with words. "It is not about knowing, but about living," reminds Victor Manuel Rivera.

Post-ponderings: if you're a retired person—there's no such thing as a retired Christian!—what do you see as your opportunity for contribution in your congregation? If you're actively raising children, what role do you invite older believers to take in your family life?

THE RESPONSIBILITY
OF OLDER WOMEN

"We all know grandparents whose values transcend passing fads and pressures, and who possess the wisdom of distilled pain and joy."
—JIMMY CARTER

"Likewise, teach the older women to be reverent in the way they live, not to be slanderers or addicted to much wine, but to teach what is good. Then they can urge the younger women to love their husbands and children, to be self-controlled and pure, to be busy at home, to be kind, and to be subject to their husbands, so that no one will malign the word of God." (Titus 2:3–5)

Read Titus 2:3–5.
"Some people, no matter how old they get," reflects Martin Buxbaum, "never lose their beauty; they merely move it from their faces into their hearts." Paul points out in the above verses that God's very reputation depends upon that kind of inner beauty, reflected through *our* attitudes and actions. That's the kind of beauty that mellows with age, like a fine wine or a piece of driftwood sculpted by repeated exposure to the tides.

Marie Stopes captured something of this reality: "You can take no credit for beauty at sixteen. But if you are beautiful at sixty, it will be your soul's own doing." No, this author doesn't credit God for his sanctifying work, but she does, at least in my reading, catch something of Paul's point when he enjoins us to "continue to work out your salvation with fear and trembling, for it is God who works in you to will and to act in order to fulfill his good purpose" (Philippians 2:12–13).

I'm nearly sixty-three. Sure, I'm noticing a collagen breakdown, but hopefully my growth in grace is the more evident change. If you're a younger woman, are you modeling yourself after a mature Christian in the process of graceful aging? If you're in the role-modeling position, how seriously are you taking Paul's charge?

Post-pondering: Take a moment to consider Paul's remarks to Titus in the last two reflections. Are you struck here by the stakes of godly living?

THE HOUSEHOLD

"Command that in no way there be in your household any who make strife, discord or divisions in the hostel, but all shall be of one accord, of one will as of one heart and one soul."
—ROBERT GROSSETESTE, thirteenth-century English bishop

"Teach slaves to be subject to their masters in everything, to try to please them, not to talk back to them, and not to steal from them, but to show that they can be fully trusted, so that in every way they will make the teaching about God our Savior attractive." (Titus 2:9–10)

Read Titus 2:9–15.

It's difficult for us as twenty-first-century Christians to relate to Paul's messages to slaves. While our mindset immediately focuses on the injustices of slavery (and we don't want to downplay the inequalities in Paul's day), we may not recognize the different societal role played by this institution at that time than in recent centuries in the West.

Slavery was intrinsic to the culture of the Roman Empire, and it didn't necessarily connote all of the negatives we attribute to it. Paul made frequent reference to "households," a term that encompassed both family and other residents of the home, most often slaves (see the reflection on Acts 10). His brief letter to Philemon, owner of the runaway slave Onesimus, provides a telling picture of New Testament slavery, alluding to its upsides and downsides.

What catches my attention in the Titus quote is Paul's call to *slaves* to make the teaching of God attractive, primarily through their attitudes and behavior. We oversimplify this verse and others like it when we substitute "employees" for "slaves." No, we can't put ourselves in the sandals of a New Testament slave (assuming they wore them); that cultural gap is just too wide. But we can take note of God's expectation for his children, in whatever circumstances we find ourselves.

Post-ponderings: What presentation of the gospel do those around you glean from your outlook and conduct?

REFRESHING THEIR HEARTS

"The measure of a life, after all, is not its duration but its donation."
—CORRIE TEN BOOM

"Your love has given me great joy and encouragement, because you, brother, have refreshed the hearts of the Lord's people." (Philemon 7)

Read Philemon 1–7.
It wasn't that Philemon was doing anything so amazing. Sometimes it takes very little to refresh a heart. When have you heard "You've made my day!" in response to some simple kindness or affirmation? If someone makes that remark, he or she usually means it. And making someone's day is no small matter.

Each of us can look back on days that held little in the way of refreshment—perhaps many of them. No surprises, no serendipities, no encouragement, no "Way to go!" Too many people in our world plod through an endless round of days with no smiles, no eye contact, perhaps without even hearing the sound of their name. But it isn't only the destitute who benefit from an updraft! Our family members need it too, especially on those nondescript or preoccupied kinds of days—those monochromatic, "vanilla" Tuesdays that end, as they began, with nothing to set them off as special.

"Kindness begins in the heart of a willing mind," reflects D. A. McBride. The kind of mind that notices need, and the kind of heart that cares. Whom have you refreshed today, whether or not that individual shares your faith? It matters.

Post-ponderings: How do members of your family or congregation, or other fellow Christians, refresh one another's hearts? What kind of refreshment do you contribute?

DISTINCTIONS
IN THE CHURCH

"To maintain a joyful family requires much from both the parents and the children. Each member of the family has to become, in a special way, the servant of the others."
—POPE JOHN PAUL II

"Perhaps the reason he was separated from you for a little while was that you might have him back forever—no longer as a slave, but better than a slave, as a dear brother." (Philemon 15–16)

Read Philemon 8–21.

As we've discussed, slavery in Paul's day wasn't the same as its recent Western iteration: a slave, though owned, was a part of a household; less than family, he or she was never treated as chattel. One similarity, though, was the eagerness of slaves in both settings to join the Christian Church. The good news of the gospel, so far removed from their life experience, must have seemed good beyond belief! A reading of the short letter of Paul to Philemon suggests the unfortunate sense of awkwardness that a Christian Church welcoming all without distinction—as brothers and sisters and mutual servants—must have instilled within slave owners.

Besides the issue of slavery, the early Church squabbled over the treatment of Jewish versus Gentile widows, the rich versus the poor at communion feasts, and the list could no doubt go on. If there's one thing humans are good at—and Christians are hardly exempt—it's noting dissimilarity. Which can be an innocuous activity as long as the distinction isn't applied to the valuation of people.

Post-ponderings: Keeping in mind that the issue here is one of worth, not role, what potentially unhealthy distinctions do you see in your church? In your heart?

HOLY SEED:
SIBLINGS IN AND OF CHRIST

"I don't believe an accident of birth makes people sisters or brothers. It makes them siblings, gives them mutuality of parentage. Sisterhood and brotherhood is a condition people have to work at."
—MAYA ANGELOU

"Both the one who makes people holy and those who are made holy are of the same family. So Jesus is not ashamed to call them brothers and sisters." (Hebrews 2:11)

Read Hebrews 2.
"'Holy solitaries,' notes John Wesley, "is a phrase no more consistent with the Gospel than holy adulterers. The Gospel of Christ knows no religion but social; no holiness, but social holiness." This theologian wasn't touting what has become known as the "social gospel"; he was advocating the living out of Christian faith in community and shared communion.

Nor did Christ save us so we could bask in privilege, confident that our continued sinning, like our past sin nature, has been covered by his righteousness. "For those God foreknew," Paul reminds us in Romans 8:29, "he also predestined to be conformed to the image of his Son, that he might be the firstborn among many brothers and sisters." That's what being "Christ-ones" is all about. It's what it means to be Christ-like. It's living, not just as individuals but also corporately and communally, from the core of the sanctified holiness Christ has worked for us and his Spirit continues to work within us to achieve. It's the enhancement of Christ's reputation on Earth based on the comportment of his myriad brothers and sisters as they permeate society.

William Branks reminds us of our call to holiness (a call that's so much more than a suggestion): "Many Christians live as if salvation is the only reason Jesus died. Christ died so we would die to sin and live to righteousness (1 Peter 2:24) . . . His marvelous grace does not excuse us from His expectations of holy living."

Post-ponderings: Do you ever find yourself confusing holy living with works righteousness? What's the difference (hint: Is holiness a factor before or after salvation?)?

God's Discipline:
Painful to Pleasant

"We may feel God's hand as a Father upon us when He strikes us as well as when He strokes us."
—ABRAHAM WRIGHT

"My son, do not make light of the Lord's discipline, and do not lose heart when he rebukes you, because the Lord disciplines the one he loves, and he chastens everyone he accepts as his son." (Hebrews 12:5–6)

Read Hebrews 12:4–13.
The author of this beautiful passage goes on: "Endure hardship as discipline; God is treating you as his children. For what children are not disciplined by their father? If you are not disciplined—and everyone undergoes discipline—then you are not legitimate, not true sons and daughters at all. . . . No discipline seems pleasant at the time, but painful. Later on, however, it produces a harvest of righteousness and peace for those who have been trained by it."

I grew up in the fifties and sixties, back before spanking was frowned upon. A spanking from my dad's open palm, though unpleasant, was hardly painful, yet acknowledgment of its need certainly could be. But Dad's administering of discipline had a second phase. Once the sobs had subsided (for some reason I vividly recall my older sister and me lying on our shared double bed crying in synch), Dad would step into the room, sit down on the edge of the bed, and address his "captive"—but altogether willing and by now eager—audience about the infraction, the disciplinary measure, and his love for us. Those moments when strikes gave way to strokes were beautiful to me.

What caring parent would overlook consequence-ing a child, and why? Far from either extreme of making light of God's discipline or allowing it to crush our sensitive spirit, we do well to bask in the light of those heart-to-hearts that can follow.

Post-ponderings: What clues you in to the reality that God is chastening you? How have your early experiences affected your view of and response to God's discipline?

The Beautiful Christian Woman

"In our perfection-obsessed, air-brushed society, it can be tempting to measure our self-worth against its set of impossible standards. However, organic beauty is in the flaws that make us vulnerable, human and fallible.... We need to learn how to be unconditionally loving, accepting and forgiving of ourselves, first, if we wish to forge healthy and loving relationships with others."
—JAEDA DEWALT

"Your beauty should not come from outward adornment, such as elaborate hairstyles and the wearing of gold jewelry or fine clothes. Rather, it should be that of your inner self, the unfading beauty of a gentle and quiet spirit, which is of great worth in God's sight." (1 Peter 3:3–4)

Read 1 Peter 3:1–7.

I tend to be unfair to unusually attractive people—especially other women. They're suspect to me, guilty of snobbery until proven otherwise. Even when I see shining through them a gentle and quiet spirit, I'm wary, waiting for the biting remark, ungracious action, or evidence of superficiality I just know is coming. For someone like this to develop a lovely spirit may in fact require an extra measure of grace; beauty can be a hurdle to overcome.

On the personal side, how many of us aren't repulsed by the prospect of being average? We yearn to stand out—often in terms of our physical appearance—in some positive way. The apostle Peter spoke about a beauty that doesn't require preservation, an appeal so intrinsic that it becomes a permanent distinctive that others immediately associate with us.

Certainly it's good for us as Christian women—men too!—to keep ourselves up, to look and feel our reasonable best. But our core appeal has to do with our essence, our center. Real attractiveness is an "inside-out" proposition; it's the way God designed us. The physical Jesus may have lacked outward magnetism, but the Christ inside you wants to shine through you with all the splendor of eternity. You're at your most appealing when you allow yourself to reflect his loveliness.

Post-ponderings: What makes you attractive to others? What kinds of attractiveness do you seek—in yourself and in others?

FAMILIAL LOVE IN CHRIST

"No two people—no mere father and mother—as I have often said, are enough to provide emotional security for a child. He needs to feel himself one in a world of kinfolk, persons of variety in age and temperament, and yet allied to himself by an indissoluble bond which he cannot break if he could, for nature has welded him into it before he was born."
—PEARL S. BUCK

"Everyone who believes that Jesus is the Christ is born of God, and everyone who loves the father loves his child as well. This is how we know that we love the children of God: by loving God and carrying out his commands." (1 John 5:1–2)

Read 1 John 2:1–11; 3:1–24; 4:7—5:12

It seems fitting to close this book with an affirmation of the mutual, reciprocal love of the eternal family that enfolds and encompasses our own. How often over the course of years and varied experience haven't I paused to wonder how I would feel if I lacked the comfort afforded by that sense of belonging I carry within me. Truth is, I can't imagine the loneliness of the unattached individual who feels herself at complete loose ends, an isolated chunk of flotsam tossed about by the waves of chance.

I love the book of 1 John and hope you'll take the time to read the passages listed above. That said, I'm electing to close with inspiration from Paul and Peter, respectively, on that familiar, familial love in Christ:

"May the God who gives endurance and encouragement give you the same attitude of mind toward each other that Christ Jesus had, so that with one mind and one voice you may glorify the God and Father of our Lord Jesus Christ. Accept one another, then, just as Christ accepted you, in order to bring praise to God" (Romans 15:5–7).

"Therefore, as God's chosen people, holy and dearly loved, clothe yourselves with compassion, kindness, humility, gentleness and patience. Bear with each other and forgive one another if any of you has a grievance against someone. Forgive as the Lord forgave you. And over all these virtues put on love, which binds them all together in perfect unity" (Colossians 3:12–14).

"Love the family of believers" (1 Peter 2:17).

Post-ponderings: Describe in a sentence or two what the family of God means to you. Cite some practical examples if that feels more concrete.

INDEX OF
BIBLE NAMES
&
QUOTATIONS
ACKNOWLEDGEMENTS

INDEX OF BIBLE NAMES

(IN ORDER OF APPEARANCE IN REFLECTIONS)

Mahlon
Ruth 4:1–12   **123**

Manoah and his wife
Judges 13   **114**

Mark (see John Mark)

Martha
Luke 8:43–48   **284**
Luke 10:38–42   **297**
John 11:1–45   **301**
John 12:1–11   **303**

Mary (Jesus' mother)
Genesis 37:10–11   **59**
Luke 1:26–38   **263**
Luke 1:39–56   **264**
Luke 1:46–56; 2:1–19   **266**
Luke 4:14–30   **274**
Mark 3:20–35   **282**
John 19:25–27   **313**

Mary Magdalene
Luke 8:43–48   **284**

Mary, Martha's sister
Luke 10:38–42   **297**
John 11:1–45   **301**
John 12:1–11   **305**

Medad
Numbers 11:10–34   **89**

Mephibosheth
2 Samuel 9   **155**
2 Samuel 16:1–4; 19:24–30   **166**

Merah
1 Samuel 18:5—19:17   **141**

Michal
1 Samuel 18:5—19:17   **141**
1 Samuel 25   **144**
2 Samuel 2; 3:6–39   **149**
2 Samuel 3:1–16   **150**
2 Samuel 6   **151**

Milkah
Numbers 27:1–11; 36

Miriam
Numbers 12
Numbers 20:1–13, 22–29

Mordecai
Esther 2:1–15
Esther 4

Moses
Exodus 2:1–10 (1)   **74**
Exodus 2:1–10 (2)   **75**
Exodus 2:11–25   **76**
Exodus 4:1–17; 6:28—7:5   **77**
Exodus 11   **78**
Exodus 18:1–12   **79**
Exodus 18:13–27   **80**
Exodus 32   **83**
Leviticus 10   **85**
Numbers 10:29–34   **88**
Numbers 11:10–34   **89**
Numbers 12   **90**
Numbers 20:1–13, 22–29   **91**
Numbers 27:1–11; 36   **92**
Deuteronomy 6; Psalm 78:1–8   **94**
Deuteronomy 11   **96**
Judges 6–7   **110**
1 Samuel 16:7–13   **138**
Nehemiah 5   **203**
Psalm 8   **213**
Psalm 90   **224**
Ezekiel 24:15–27   **253**

Moses' Cushite wife (same as Zipporah?)
Numbers 12   **90**

Moses' father (possibly Amram)
Exodus 2:1–10 (1)   **74**

Moses' mother (possibly Jochebed)
Exodus 2:1–10 (1)   **74**
Exodus 4:1–17; 6:28—7:5   **77**

Moses' wife (Reuel's daughter Zipporah)
Exodus 18:1–12   **79**

Moses' wife and children
Exodus 18:13–27   **80**

Mother of James and John
Matthew 20:20–28   **304**

Mother of Rufus
John 19:25–27   **313**

**Mothers bringing children
to Jesus for blessing**
Luke 18:15–17   **303**

Naaman and his wife
2 Kings 5:1–6   **192**

Nabal
1 Samuel 25   **144**

Naboth
1 Kings 21   **190**

Nadab
Leviticus 10   **85**

Naomi
Ruth 1:1–13   **118**
Ruth 1:14–18   **119**
Ruth 1:19–22   **120**
Ruth 2   **121**
Ruth 4:1–12   **123**
Ruth 4:13–22   **124**
1 Samuel 1:1–8   **125**
2 Samuel 15:19–22 (unnamed)   **165**
Luke 7:11–17   **281**

Rachel
Genesis 29:1-30   **45**
Genesis 29:31—30:24   **46**
Genesis 31:1-18   **47**
Genesis 31:19-37   **48**
Genesis 35:16-20   **55**
Genesis 37:31-35   **61**
1 Samuel 1:1-8   **125**

Rahab
Exodus 34:1-28   **84**
Joshua 2; 6:15-25   **102**

Rebekah
Genesis 24:10-61   **36**
Genesis 24:62-67   **37**
Genesis 25:19-34   **38**
Genesis 27:1-40   **39**
Genesis 27:41—28:9   **40**
Genesis 33:12-20   **91**
Genesis 38   **62**

Reuben
Genesis 37:12-30   **60**
Genesis 42:25—43:14   **64**

Rehoboam
1 Kings 11:26—12:24; 2 Chronicles 10   **185**

Rekabites
Jeremiah 35   **253**

Reuel/Jethro
Exodus 2:11-25   **76**
Exodus 18:1-12   **79**
Exodus 18:13-27   **80**
Numbers 10:29-34   **88**

Reuel/Jethro's daughters
Exodus 2:11-25   **76**

Rizpah
2 Samuel 2; 3:6-39   **149**
2 Samuel 21:1-14   **170**

Roman centurion
Matthew 8:5-13   **280**

Roman official with dying son
John 4:43-54   **277**

Ruth
Exodus 34:1-28   **84**
Ruth 1:1-13   **118**
Ruth 1:14-18   **119**
Ruth 2   **121**
Ruth 3   **122**
Ruth 4:1-12   **123**
Ruth 4:13-22   **124**
2 Samuel 15:19-22   **165**

Salome
Matthew 4:18-22   **275**
1 Corinthians 9:1-18   **331**

Samson
Judges 13   **114**
1 Samuel 18:5—19:17   **141**

Samuel
Deuteronomy 21:10-14; 22:13-30; 24:1-5   **97**
1 Samuel 1:19-28   **127**
1 Samuel 2:12-17, 22-25, 27-36   **128**
1 Samuel 3   **130**
1 Samuel 15   **136**
1 Samuel 16:1-11   **137**

Samuel's sons
1 Samuel 2:12-17, 22-25, 27-36   **128**

Sarai/Sarah
Genesis 2:18-25   **4**
Genesis 12:1-9; Hebrews 11:8-12   **22**
Genesis 12:10-20   **23**
Genesis 16:1-6   **25**
Genesis 20   **30**
Genesis 17:15-22; 18:1-15; 21:1-7   **31**
Genesis 21:8-21   **32**
Genesis 24:62-67   **37**
Genesis 29:1-30   **45**
Genesis 29:31—30:24   **46**

Saul (Israel's first king)
1 Samuel 9-10   **134**
1 Samuel 14:24-48   **135**
1 Samuel 15   **136**
1 Samuel 18:1-4   **140**
1 Samuel 18:5—19:17   **141**
1 Samuel 20   **142**
1 Samuel 22:6-23   **143**
1 Samuel 30   **145**

Saul/Paul (see Paul)

Seth
Genesis 4:17-26   **10**

Shallum and daughters
Nehemiah 3   **202**

Shechem
Genesis 34:1-12   **52**
Genesis 34:13-31   **53**

Shelah
Genesis 38   **62**

Shem
Genesis 9:18-27   **12**

Shimei
2 Samuel 16:1-4; 19:24-30   **166**

Shunammite woman
Genesis 22:1-19   **33**

Shunammite woman's son
Genesis 22:1-19   **33**

Silas
1 Thessalonians 2:1-12   **337**
1 Timothy 6:11-21   **343**

QUOTATIONS ACKNOWLEDGMENTS

CHAPTER 6:
Moses and the Exodus, Part 2

Moses and Hobab: A Faithful Brother-in-Law (Numbers 10:29–34)   88

NOAH F.
http://www.reference.com/motif/arts/brother-in-law-poems

Moses' Caregiver Fatigue: Accepting All Available Help (Numbers 11:10–34)   89

TIA WALKER
http://theinspiredcaregiver.com/blog/?page_id=1651

Miriam, Aaron, and Moses: Rivalry Erupts (Numbers 12)   90

SUSAN SCARF MERRELL
http://www.publicdomainpictures.net/view-image.php?image=6306&picture=dune-fence&large=

Aaron: Death on the Mountain (Numbers 20:1–13, 22–29)   91

ERICA E. GOODE
http://www.searchquotes.com/search/Death_Of_Sibling/

Zelophehad's Daughters: Ambiguity Resolved (Numbers 27:1–11; 36)   92

MUSTAFA KEMAL ATATÜRK
https://www.goodreads.com/author/quotes/2793859.Mustafa_Kemal_Atat_rkand

Held and Upheld: In the Father's Arms (Deuteronomy 1:26–46)   93

HUDSON TAYLOR
https://www.goodreads.com/quotes/1053525-i-am-so-weak-that-i-can-hardly-write-i

The Divine Mandate: Pass the Word Along (Deuteronomy 6; Psalm 78:1–8)   94

CHARLES SWINDOLL
http://www.whatchristianswanttoknow.com/inspirational-christian-quotes-about-raising-children/

ROBERT FULGHUM
http://www.goodreads.com/work/quotes/2399046-all-i-really-need-to-know-i-learned-in
-kindergartenQuote

MARGARET THATCHER
http://www.brainyquote.com/quotes/quotes/m/margaretth114277.html

Durable Sandals: Four Maintenance-Free Decades (Deuteronomy 8)   95

CORALLIE BUCHANAN
http://www.goodreads.com/quotes/tag/provision

Historical Memory: From Generation to Generation (Deuteronomy 11)   96

ROSE CHERIN
http://www.freequotesomg.com/famous_quotes_topics/Family_Quotes/

Marriage Leave: Progressive Social Policy (Deuteronomy 21:10–14; 22:13–30; 24:1 5)   97

BRANDEN SANDERSON
http://www.goodreads.com/quotes/tag/priorities

The Secret Things and the Things Revealed (Deuteronomy 29)   98

JOSEPH HALL
http://www.winwisdom.com/quotes/author/joseph-hall.aspx

The God of Life (Deuteronomy 30)   99

AIDEN WILSON TOZER
http://www.goodreads.com/quotes/490952-you-can-see-god-from-anywhere-if-your-mind-is

QUOTATIONS ACKNOWLEDGMENTS   373

CHAPTER 7:
The Conquest and the Early Judges Era 100

Rahab: Debatable Credentials? (Joshua 2; 6:15–25)   102

C. J. MAHONEY
http://www.goodreads.com/quotes/tag/sin?page=3

God's Storytellers (Joshua 4)   103

PHILIP PULLMAN
http://www.goodreads.com/quotes/152657-thou-shalt-not-is-soon-forgotten-but-once-upon-a

PETER HANDKE
http://www.goodreads.com/quotes/448826-if-a-nation-loses-its-storytellers-it-loses-its-childhood

ANNE WATSON
http://www.aaronshep.com/storytelling/quotes.html

Caleb and Aksah: Another Daughter's Request (Joshua 14:6–15; Judges 1:12–15)   104

UNSPECIFIED AUTHOR
http://www.christianbiblereference.org/faq_womensrights.htm

Memorial Altar East of the Jordan (Joshua 22:10–34)   105

TAVIS SMILEY
http://www.goodreads.com/quotes/tag/legacy

"As for Me and My Household": Legislating Faith? (Joshua 24:1–28)   106

MICHAEL NICHOLS
http://www.michaelnichols.org/non-negotiable-family/

Othniel, Israel's First Judge: Familial Faithfulness (Judges 3:7–11)   107

UNKNOWN AUTHOR
http://www.raisinggodlychildren.org/2013/08/family-worship-why.html

Deborah: Societal Mom (Judges 4–5)   108

GLORIA STEINEM
http://www.goodreads.com/quotes/72290-we-ve-begun-to-raise-daughters-more-like-sons-but-few

Sisera: A Mother's Angst (Judges 5:28–30)   109

NISHAN PANWAR
http://www.searchquotes.com/search/Parenting_Adult_Children/4/

Gideon: Least of the Weakest? (Judges 6–7)   110

JONI EARECKSON TADA
http://hopeforthebrokenhearted.com/chronic-illness-quotes/

"As Is the Man . . .": Jether's Reluctance (Judges 8:1–21)   111

G. K. CHESTERTON
http://www.great-inspirational-quotes.com/boy-quotes.html

Jephthah and His Brothers: Illegitimate Son / Mighty Warrior (Judges 11:1–28)   112

JACK BOWMAN
http://www.searchquotes.com/search/Gangs/2/

Jephthah and His Daughter: A Rash Impulse (Judges 11:29–40)   113

ROBERT BRAULT
http://www.quotegarden.com/parents.html

Manoah and His Wife: A Plea for Guidance (Judges 13)   114

ROSE KENNEDY
http://www.parents.com/baby/new-parent/emotions/motherhood-fatherhood-quotations/

When Parents Won't Let Go (Judges 19:1–10)   115

CHUCK PALAHNIUK
http://www.searchquotes.com/search/Overprotective_Parents/3/

CHAPTER 10:
Early Kingship—David, Part 1 146

MARIANNE MOORE
http://www.brainyquote.com/quotes/quotes/m/mariannemo379085.html

MARY WOLLSTONECRAFT
http://www.goodreads.com/quotes/444181-it-appears-to-me-impossible-that-i-should-cease-to

Heritage and Reward (Psalm 127) 226

AMOS BRONSON ALCOTT
http://www.lotsofkids.com/LOK-Parent/general/largefamilyquotes.php

JOHN W. WHITEHEAD
http://www.goodreads.com/quotes/22675-children-are-the-living-messages-we-send-to-a-time

HENRY WARD BEECHER
http://www.scrapbook.com/quotes/doc/17903.html

CARL SANDBURG
http://www.goodreads.com/quotes/18066-a-baby-is-god-s-opinion-that-the-world-should-go

The Father's Love: Conception and Beyond (Psalm 139:13–18) 227

MARTIN H. FISCHER
http://www.finestquotes.com/select_quote-category-Pregnancy-page-0.htm

JOAN RAPHAEL
http://www.finestquotes.com/select_quote-category-Pregnancy-page-0.htm

CHAPTER 15:
Wisdom Literature 228

Incidental Learning (Proverbs 1:1–9; 4:1–27) 230

UMBERTO ECO
http://www.goodreads.com/quotes/tag/parenting

The Discipline/Delight Connection (Proverbs 3) 231

ARTHUR MILLER
http://www.etni.org.il/quotes/children.htm

Marital Fidelity: One's Own Cistern (Proverbs 5) 232

JEANETTE WINTERSON
http://www.goodreads.com/quotes/tag/fidelity

The "Lived in" House (Proverbs 14:1–11) 233

PROVERB
http://thinkexist.com/quotation/marrying_is_easy-it_s_housework_that-s_hard/149178.html

LETTY COTTIN POGREBIN
http://www.winwisdom.com/quotes/author/letty-cottin-pogrebin.aspx

The Family That Dines Together (Proverbs 15:1–17) 234

FRANCINE DU PLESSIX GRAY
http://www.freequotesomg.com/famous_quotes_topics/Family_Quotes/

MARGARET LAURENCE
http://www.searchquotes.com/quotation/
In_some_families,_please_is_described_as_the_magic_word._In_our_house,_however,_it_was_sorry/5434/

Generational Appreciation (Proverbs 17:1–6) 235

SAMUEL TAYLOR COLERIDGE
http://www.searchquotes.com/quotation/I_have_often_thought_what_a_melancholy_world
_this_would_be_without_children,_and_what_an_inhuman_wor/232219/

"Disregarded Entities" (Proverbs 19:1–8) 236

MOTHER TERESA
http://www.goodreads.com/quotes/tag/poverty

CHARLES L. ALLEN
http://thinkexist.com/quotation/when_you_say_a_situation_or_a_person_is_hopeless/201140.html

The Rekabites: Unquestioned Obedience (Jeremiah 35) 251

ELISABETH ELLIOT
http://www.goodreads.com/quotes/tag/obedience

Deprivation of the Very Young (Lamentations 2:8–13) 252

NEIL GAIMAN
http://www.goodreads.com/quotes/tag/hunger

A Private Sorrow (Ezekiel 24:15–27) 253

MEGHAN O'ROURKE
http://www.brainyquote.com/quotes/quotes/m/meghanoro498179.html

MILAN KUNDERA
http://www.goodreads.com/quotes/tag/death-of-a-loved-one

HENRY WADSWORTH LONGFELLOW
http://www.wisdomquotes.com/topics/griefsorrow/index2.html

Hosea and Gomer: The Longsuffering Spouse (Hosea 1:1—3:5) 254

JENNIFER EGAN
http://www.goodreads.com/quotes/tag/adultery

Led, Not Pushed (Hosea 11) 255

SHANNON L. ALDER
http://www.goodreads.com/quotes/tag/god-s-will

SIMONE SIGNORET
http://www.goodreads.com/quotes/301024-chains-do-not-hold-a-marriage
-together-it-is-threads

Historical Memory: Passing along the Hard Stuff (Joel 1:1–12) 256

LOIS LOWRY
http://www.goodreads.com/quotes/200442-the-worst-part-of-holding-the-memories-is-not-the

Cows of Bashan: Complacent in Zion (Amos 4:1–5; 6:1–7) 257

BENJAMIN WHICHCOTE
http://www.searchquotes.com/search/Overbearing_People/3/

The Time of Confusion: Family Disintegration (Micah 7:1–7) 258

WINSTON CHURCHILL
http://www.goodreads.com/quotes/tag/division

The Inscription (Zechariah 14) 259

ABRAHAM MASLOW
http://www.goodreads.com/quotes/679395-the-great-lesson-is-that-the-sacred-is-in-the

EVELYN UNDERHILL
http://www.brianniece.com/2008/09/24/quotes-for-the-incarnational-journey/

CHAPTER 17:
Jesus—The Early Years 260

Zechariah and Elizabeth: The Delight Factor (Luke 1:5–25) 262

UNKNOWN AUTHOR
https://www.google.com/search?q=quotes+on+unexpected+blessings

The "Right" Question? (Luke 1:26–38) 263

MADELEINE L'ENGLE
http://www.goodreads.com/quotes/tag/faith?page=2

ELIZABETH GILBERT
http://www.goodreads.com/quotes/tag/faith?page=4

MARTIN LUTHER KING JR.
http://www.goodreads.com/quotes/tag/service

Co-Incidence (John 4:43–54) 277

MEHMET MURAT ILDAN
http://www.goodreads.com/quotes/tag/coincidence

"Raca!": What's in a Name? (Matthew 5:21–26) 278

MORRIS MANDEL
http://thinkexist.com/quotes/with/keyword/name_calling/

MEISTER ECKHART
http://thinkexist.com/quotes/with/keyword/name_calling/

One-Sided Harmony? (Luke 6:27–36) 279

PATSIE SMITH
https://www.goodreads.com/quotes/tag/acceptance?page=14

ERMA BOMBECK
http://www.searchquotes.com/search/Family_Loyalty/

MARY E. DEMUTH
https://www.goodreads.com/quotes/tag/acceptance?page=11

The Centurion: Humble Audacity (Matthew 8:5–13) 280

ABRAHAM J. HESCHEL
http://www.searchquotes.com/search/Showing_Concern_To_Others/3/

"Don't Cry": The Healer's Pain (Luke 7:11–17) 281

MEHMET MURAT ILDAN
http://www.goodreads.com/quotes/tag/compassionate

JAMES L. HALPERIN
http://www.goodreads.com/quotes/tag/compassionate

Jesus' Mother and Brothers: The Family Problem (Mark 3:20–35) 282

EZRA TAFT BENSON
http://www.goodreads.com/quotes/363779-when-we-put-god-first-all-other-things-fall-into

"Go Home to Your Own People" (Mark 5:1–20) 283

DONNA HEDGES
http://www.quotegarden.com/family.html

"Take Heart, Daughter": Jesus' Heart for the Hemorrhaging (Luke 8:43–48) 284

CRISS JAMI
http://www.goodreads.com/quotes/tag/compassionate

KATERINA STOYKOVA KLEMER
http://www.goodreads.com/quotes/tag/entitlement

Jesus' Counsel: After Death or before Resurrection (Luke 8:40–42, 49–56) 285

LAUREN DESTEFANO
http://www.goodreads.com/quotes/tag/fever

Herodias's Daughter: Extension of Mom (Mark 6:14–29) 286

DAN PEARCE
https://www.goodreads.com/quotes/tag/parenting?page=5

C. C. LICHTENBERG
http://izquotes.com/quote/247449

UNKNOWN AUTHOR
http://postcardstoanarcissist.wordpress.com/writings-thoughts-quotations-and
-sayings-about-narcissists/

Elder Care, Love, and Honor (Matthew 15:3–9) 287

JOHN HOEVEN
http://www.searchquotes.com/search/Caring_For_Elderly/3/

PEGGI SPEERS
http://www.goodreads.com/quotes/tag/aging-parents

www.ingramcontent.com/pod-product-compliance
Lightning Source LLC
Chambersburg PA
CBHW062357090426
42740CB00010B/1314